PAINE: How We Dismantled the FBI in Our Pajamas

Mike Moore

ISBN-13: 978-0692190470
ISBN-10: 0692190473

DEDICATION

For my incredible wife who stood by me and never
flinched when the FBI tried to take us down.

To my sons: Never back down from a good fight and
never give up on yourself, even when others count you
out.

CONTENTS

PREFACE

Perhaps the sentiments contained in the following pages, are not yet sufficiently fashionable to procure them general favor; a long habit of not thinking a thing wrong, gives it a superficial appearance of being right, and raises at first a formidable outcry in defence of custom. But the tumult soon subsides. Time makes more converts than reason.

As a long and violent abuse of power, is generally the Means of calling the right of it in question (and in matters too which might never have been thought of, had not the Sufferers been aggravated into the inquiry) and as the King of England had undertaken in his own Right, to support the Parliament in what he calls Theirs, and as the good people of this country are grievously oppressed by the combination, they have an undoubted privilege to inquire into the pretensions of both, and equally to reject the usurpation of either.

In the following sheets, the author hath studiously avoided every thing which is personal among ourselves. Compliments as well as censure to individuals make no part thereof. The wise, and the worthy, need not the triumph of a pamphlet; and those whose sentiments are injudicious, or unfriendly, will cease of themselves unless too much pains are bestowed upon their conversion.

The cause of America is in a great measure the cause of all mankind. Many circumstances hath, and will arise, which are not local, but universal, and through which the principles of all Lovers of Mankind are affected, and in the Event of which, their Affections are interested. The laying of a Country desolate with Fire and Sword, declaring War against the natural rights of all Mankind, and extirpating the Defenders thereof from the Face of the Earth, is the Concern of every Man to whom Nature hath given the Power of feeling; of which Class, regardless of Party Censures.

SOME writers have so confounded society with government, as to leave little or no distinction between them; whereas they are not only different, but have different origins. Society is produced by our wants, and government by our wickedness; the former promotes our happiness Positively by uniting our affections, the latter negatively by restraining our vices. The one encourages intercourse, the other creates distinctions. The first is a patron, the last a punisher.

Society in every state is a blessing, but government even in its best state is but a necessary evil in its worst state an in tolerable one; for when we suffer, or are exposed to the same miseries by a government, which we might expect in a country without government, our calamities is heightened by reflecting that we furnish the means by which we suffer! Government, like dress, is the badge of lost innocence; the palaces of kings are built on the ruins of the bowers of paradise. For were the impulses of conscience Wear, uniform, and irresistibly obeyed, man would need no other lawgiver; but that not being the case, he finds it necessary to surrender up a part of his property to furnish means for the protection of the rest; and this he is induced to do by the same prudence which in every other case advises him out of two evils to choose the least. Wherefore, security being the true design and end of government, it unanswerably follows that whatever form thereof appears most likely to ensure it to us, with the least expense and greatest benefit, is preferable to all others.

And as a man, who is attached to a prostitute, is unfitted to choose or judge of a wife, so any prepossession in favor of a rotten constitution of government will disable us from discerning a good one.

Mankind being originally equals in the order of creation, the equality could only be destroyed by some subsequent circumstance; the distinctions of rich, and poor, may in a great measure be accounted for, and that without having recourse to the harsh, ill-sounding names of oppression and avarice. Oppression is often the consequence, but seldom or never the means of riches; and though avarice will preserve a man from being necessitously poor, it generally makes him too timorous to be wealthy.

A government of our own is our natural right, and when a man seriously reflects on the precariousness of human affairs, he will become convinced that it is infinitely wiser and safer to form a constitution of our own in a cool deliberate manner, while we have it in our power, than to trust such an interesting event to time and chance.

O ye that love mankind! Ye that dare oppose not only the tyranny but the tyrant, stand forth! Every spot of the old world is overrun with oppression. Freedom hath been hunted round the globe. Asia and Africa have long expelled her.

It is the good fortune of many to live distant from the scene of sorrow; the evil is not sufficiently brought to their doors to make them feel the precariousness with which all American property is possessed. But let our imaginations transport us for a few moments to Boston, that seat of wretchedness will teach us wisdom, and instruct us for ever to renounce a power in whom we can have no trust. The inhabitants of that unfortunate city, who but a few months ago were in ease and affluence, have now no other alternative than to stay and starve, or turn out to beg. Endangered by the fire of their friends if they continue within the city, and plundered by the soldiery if they leave it. In their present condition they are prisoners without the hope of redemption, and in a general attack for their relief, they would be exposed to the fury of both armies.

Men of passive tempers look somewhat lightly over the offenses of Britain, and, still hoping for the best, are apt to call out, 'Come we shall be friends again for all this.' But examine the passions and feelings of mankind. Bring the doctrine of reconciliation to the touchstone of nature, and then tell me, whether you can hereafter love, honor, and faithfully serve the power that hath carried fire and sword into your land? If you cannot do all these, then are you only deceiving yourselves, and by your delay bringing ruin upon posterity. Your future connection with Britain, whom you can neither love nor honor, will be forced and unnatural, and being formed only on the plan of present convenience, will in a little time fall into a relapse more wretched than the first. But if you say, you can still pass the violations over, then I ask, Hath your house been burnt? Hath you property been destroyed before your face? Are your wife and children destitute of a bed to lie on, or bread to live on? Have you lost a parent or a child by their hands, and yourself the ruined and wretched survivor? If you have not, then are you not a judge of those who have. But if you have, and can still shake hands with the murderers, then are you unworthy the name of husband, father, friend, or lover, and whatever may be your rank or title in life, you have the heart of a coward, and the spirit of a sycophant.

-- Thomas Paine, 1776, Philadelphia

Mike Moore

FOREWORD

After years of trying to keep a lid on it, the news of Osama bin Laden living in Iran, in a series of clandestine safe houses did leak. It was CBS News' 60 Minutes that started conducting interviews about an incredible story – in fact, one almost too insane to believe: The U.S. had knew bin Laden was tucked away in Iran yet sent U.S. military soldiers into Afghanistan to search for the terror mastermind and al-Qaeda front man. America was fighting the war on terror, but the biggest trophy was 900 miles away from Afghan strongholds and caves. And America's boys were getting mowed down, killed in a war that was shaping up to look like a politically-generated mirage.

CBS killed the story which was scheduled to run two months before Obama's 2012 presidential election. For obvious reasons: If the story ran, Mitt Romney would have been elected president and not Obama.

When I watch the DC insiders and elites lose control and make outlandish anti-Trump statements on social media before and since Trump's election, it has rung a familiar bell. You quickly learn patterns during criminal investigations and through the travels of a Certified Fraud Examiner. Whether it was my time working for Fortune 100 companies or as an attaché to the federal government, or an award-winning career in journalism, people with something to hide act in certain identifiable ways. If you are astute and experienced you understand who to start probing based merely on their rhetoric. Posts on social media. Comments on TV news or news sites.

So it comes as little surprise that many of the loudest Trump critics are implicated in one of the greatest cover-ups in American history. In fact, to a seasoned investigator, it comes as no surprise. Their words and actions exposed their plot long ago. It was merely a matter of finding the evidence to expose them. A game of cat and mouse where the suspects are outwardly daring seasoned investigators to find the evidence to expose their illegal actions. Hiding in plain sight. A brazen lot. Many do this because they do not have the fortitude and morals or mores to confess what they did. So they are asking for others to help absolve them. Evil people, yes. But massive weaklings too.

Understand these folks do have political labels and known affiliations but broken down they are not Democrats or Republicans. Not conservatives or liberals. Strip away that veneer, and you only have people who made a string of bad choices. And then worked to keep those choices hidden. But deep down inside most, they understood these choices – to participate in a conspiracy to protect America's Most Wanted terrorist – would one day become public. Ying and yang. The lessons of history seldom change, just the players and scandals.

So here we are.

America's clandestine operation to shroud Osama bin Laden (OBL) got out of hand. U.S.

soldiers began to die in Afghanistan searching for OBL and his lieutenants, disciples. Other veterans returned home maimed. For folks like Brennan and Bush and Obama, there was no turning back. The Deep State had passed its point of no return. The only mission was to continue the cover-up. And crush anyone who may have known about it.

Operators like me. Congressmen too.

And pay off entities – like Iran – it couldn't overtly and covertly crush. Who needs to upend a regime when you cal shower it with pallets of cash worth $1.8 Billion on top of the $150 Billion to buy the regime's silence — at least until Obama and Kerry were out of office. And Hillary's legacy was safe for another possible presidential run in 2020, if required. Have you wondered why Joe Biden hasn't committed to a presidential run? Wonder no further.

The foundations of such a monstrosity of a scandal – spanning two different presidents in two different parties – are not much different from any significant political scandal. There are differences here, however, that are stark. To any observer outside the beltway at least. The scheme to hide OBL spanned both Republican and Democratic White Houses. What began under George Bush was continued through Barack Obama, and all the inside players remained silent. If you are one of the Americans who believe there is a vast difference between the Republicans and Democrats in Washington D.C.'s national politics, think again. If there were, in fact, two separate and distinct political parties at play in the nation's capital, ask yourself why Obama did not blow the whistle on Bush's scheme to hide OBL while war raged on in Afghanistan. Ask yourself. Why did Hillary, as Secretary of State, remain silent just as Condi Rice had? You've seen the photos and video of the Bush clan embracing the Obamas and the Clintons embracing the George W Bush after the Clintons themselves were embraced by George Bush Sr. after their ascension to the White House.

Yet none of the aforementioned players and Deep State sentinels embraced Donald Trump's clan. Coincidence? Hardly.

After working in the beltway and for D.C. elites j for over 30 years – as well as covering them as a journalist - I can attest Washington does not host a two-party government. There is one party. And they protect each other at any cost. When a major player goes off the reservation – like Anthony Weiner – and begins stockpiling evidence against the Elected plutocracy – he or she ends up in prison. Or sometimes worse. Dead. The D.C. elites use such intelligence – that a player helped sneak OBL out of the country – as leverage against other insiders. Likely to get reelected. They put America's dirty secrets in their back pockets and save them for a rainy political day to sell or trade while the fabric of the Constitution slowly erodes.

Therefore mammoth scandals cross-pollinate to different White House administrations and even 'different' political parties because again, they all share the same goal – staying in power at any cost -- and belong to the same unnamed 'party.' The Bush family are the same as the Obama family and both are the same as the Clinton family. There are slight differences, absolutely. But they share more in common, especially the fact that they care very little for you or what you want. The media performs its tasks to make Americans believe there is a continental divide between the parties. But it's merely a well-honed mirage.

Until an outsider is elected against all the odds.

The same exact comparison can be made between Saudi Arabia and Iran. The ancient stronghold is that these two countries despise each other. But now, that is proven a modern fable. Seasoned Intel pros who were in the Middle East theater verify this, as do White House documents of conversations with Saudi royalty.

And everyone in D.C. – the gatekeepers of the lies – lash out like terrified rats fleeing a burning ship. The fact that the United States failed to act on intelligence time and time again to hunt and kill bin Laden is another dirty secret insiders had tucked away so nicely in their back pocket. Exposing such a mess would threaten their livelihood and possibly their freedom. Standard operating procedure in Washington – a predictable staple for decades – has suddenly been flipped. Right onto the heads of the perpetrators. And chaos should ensue. In truth, we the public get to see the true side of these beltway cronies the deeper they become entrenched in the scandal. It indeed is a predictable process to the cerebral observer. And amid the meltdowns, the hate-infused rhetoric and panicked social media posts there is a certain classical opus to the outsider. If telling state lies was its own opera, players like Brennan, Obama, and Hillary certainly could rival Luciano Pavarotti. The Bush clan too.

The storylines here and the troubled story pieces

likewise dovetail better than any William Shakespeare tragedy or Hemmingway novel. This is because true stories are the most compelling and the details surrounding a cover-up of this proportion require little editorializing or creative license. Americans were sold out and lied to. Other Americans died as part of the scheme. My life and others were turned upside down by the people we elected to office. We're now legally molested by government employees in the airport in the name of OBL and al-Qaeda. The TSA is keeping you safe. Let them fondle your breasts, grab your junk, humiliate you in front of your fellow citizens who nonchalantly breeze past you like they are watching a street mime performance on a busy city sidewalk -- while fellow Americans are being felt up and shuffled like cattle through airport security lines.

We're keeping you safe from OBL, folks. Don't you get it? Sure you have to surrender your freedoms – and even remove your belt preflight like you do during processing at any county jail. The cost of keeping you safe. Remember the FBI and TSA's incessant boasting about how they kept America safe from further OBL and al-Qaeda terror attacks after 9/11?

They left out the part where they harbored OBL and lied about his ability to run his worldwide terror network. Or was the Deep State running if for him? Brennan's CIA is implicated as well as Mueller's FBI. No wonder they each want Trump's head on a stake.

Why should Americans believe one fucking word from the mouths of these traitors? Whether Republicans, Democrats, Independents or unattached from politics.

You thought the Deep State cover-up, the illegal surveillance of Trump and his associates, orchestrated by the FBI, DOJ, and other intelligence agencies here and in the United Kingdom was an elaborate scheme to keep Trump from getting elected merely because of dislike and disdain for his politics and at times seemingly outlandish platforms.

You, like myself, thought wrong.

The end game was to ensure that even bigger secrets stayed a secret. Billions were paid in blackmail cash to keep Iran quiet, AND A RIGGED 'NUCLEAR DEAL' WAS STRUCK where the U.S received nothing of value in exchange for untold riches and favors given and earmarked for a terror regime. Meanwhile, common sense Americans shook their heads in disbelief wondering what in God's name was compelling Obama and his cohorts to happily sell America down the river. Blackmail works that way. Textbook.

Meanwhile, illegal scheming to keep Trump away from the keys of the D.C. vault warehousing such D.C. secrets was launched The mainstream media gladly complied. The Deep State would ensure Trump wouldn't reach the White House and unveil a dirty secret that would likely put the major players behind bars. Treason has no statute of limitations.

You see, they never cared about getting caught wiretapping Trump and concocting a sham investigation into his presidency and White House. In fact, they wanted to get caught in order to orchestrate, via their loyal media partners, a sideshow. A distraction. Away from Iran and OBL and God only knows what else. And it has worked for the most part. Look over here at the outrageous antics of the

Deep State ... look over here at what Brett Kavanaugh did in high school ... so you wouldn't look at the reasons why they all collaborated to manufacture a scandal. Employing the U.S. intelligence apparatus and the Executive Branch of the United States government is the real bombshell. The illegal wiretapping of Trump and the assorted spying is problematic. But the former makes the latter look like a church picnic. It's a betrayal that when it finally goes mainstream will shock Patriots to their cores. And if this doesn't prompt Americans to get off their couches and do something to effect a change in this country, nothing ever will. This level of betrayal should never stand in this country, especially understanding the colonists revolted for far fewer grievances against the English Crown.

King George – and his redcoats didn't fly jet airliners into the World Trade Centers and the Pentagon. And George Washington would not have given safe harbor to the mastermind behind such terror while pretending to hunt him down to the four corners of the earth. Losing good soldiers along the way. Good men who sacrificed their lives because they genuinely believed they were hunting a killer. Not a ghost, like bin Laden who was 900+ miles away.

Our founding fathers could have never envisioned such nefarious public servants who would plot such evil. It was unfathomable in the 1700s, and it remains identically unbelievable today.

Then when Trump was elected, a new even-more elaborate scheme was launched. And the man running the investigation of Trump – who knew OBL was tucked away in Iran – is now in charge of trying to lock up the president of the United states.

Mueller is into this up to his neck. But if he can eliminate Trump for his Deep State puppet masters he gets to keep his legacy free from the OBL Iran disaster. And line his pockets in the process. Brennan is the same. He shares parallel interests and conflicts. And guilt.

Meanwhile, Gold Star mothers and fathers, families and friends all mourn the loss of loved heroes who lost their lives in the Afghan theater. Chasing a ghost who was protected by the very country they swore to protect. And thousands of miles away from danger. Like you, these soldiers were also betrayed. But it cost them their lives. A dark chapter in our country's history, crafted by even darker people.

Perhaps Trump has the capacity – as an outsider and outlier – to bring those responsible for such a deadly conspiracy to justice.

~ Mike Moore

Mike Moore

1 DOMESTIC TERROR; FBI

Vengeance is Mine; I will repay.
In due time their foot will slip;
for their day of disaster is near,
and their doom is coming quickly. -- Deuteronomy 32

I can say with certainty, my decision to journey back into journalism was made after the FBI pointed guns at the heads of my wife and children. I knew that first morning (the FBI actually raided my home twice and terrorized my family both times at gunpoint) when federal agents raided our home three definitive things were going to unfold:

1. If my kids or wife were shot by the FBI, it was going to get very bloody in my house that day. And I might be included in the casualties. But not before I did some significant damage too.

2. If no one in my family was injured, the goal was to get these assholes out of my house ASAP.

3. These bastards -- and their bosses -- were going to pay for violating my family. My kids. My home. One way or the other, I would have the last word. As I have throughout my life and career.

I always win. You'll learn that about me in the

coming days and weeks. In fact, I already have won. The FBI learned it too. And I have much more to teach the Bureau if it decides it hasn't been educated enough.

Let's start now with some of those supplemental lessons for my former Intel client, the FBI.

My name is Michael Moore. No, not the Lib movie guy Michael Moore (Now you understand why I use a pseudonym). I have won numerous awards in journalism, including the Gerald Loeb Award. None of that much matters in the scope of things but being nominated for Pulitzer Prizes while in your 20s is something I can tell my grandkids about. And the Loeb speaks for itself.

But it is time for Thomas Paine to go public. The good guys don't hide, as a Congressman recently told me. Especially after being terrorized by the FBI.

These are the times that try men's souls, the real Thomas Paine penned. Especially when a dozen FBI agents are pointing high-powered rifles at my children during an early-morning search warrant raid. My boys. Then eight and twelve. With M-4 carbine rifles pointed at their wet heads just before getting on the school bus. One slip of a finger and poof, they're dead. Courtesy of cowboys from the FBI. And when the FBI raids your house it sounds like someone just drove a truck through the front door, the loud banging and the boisterous shouting from keyed up agents:

"FBI! FBI! OPEN THE DOOR.
FBI, COME OUT MICHAEL MOORE!"

Like I had just robbed a bank. For some reason,

Feds always knock seven times.

The first raid was the first time in about twenty years I seriously thought about going back into journalism. And do things my way this time around. To unmask mother fuckers like these FBI agents who were terrorizing my kids and wife. That was the seed that created True Pundit. But it wouldn't fully sprout until later when the FBI and its concocted charges prevented me from attending my mother's funeral. Or visiting her when she was on hospice with a day to live. She was a three-hour drive from my house.

But back to the first FBI raid. They're trying to goad me into making a mistake, maybe take a run at one of them – or draw down with my Sig -- so they could blow a hole in my pajamas. And be done with me, like their bosses hoped.

BECAUSE as an FBI contractor I knew too much. And I still know too much. And it is NOW time to tell the world all about it -- why the FBI turned on me. And hoped I'd eat my gun after the Bureau savaged my life and career. My so-called friends too. The reasons are hard to stomach, but I am safer now that all know the truth.

While the FBI was tossing my house and asking me dumb questions the wheels in my head were already years ahead of those chaotic moments. My wife and boys were in tears, but I was already thinking about how this could play out.

Taking violent retaliation off the table, getting back into journalism could be the play.

If I could stay out of prison. And stay alive.

For a good stretch that morning I was convinced they were going to stuff me in a van and drive away. But these cowboys were driving Toyota Prius' and

Ford Escapes. Not the black SUVs. I suppose they were all on loan for the FBI-themed TV shows and movies, you know the ones where agents swoop in to save the city from a nuclear bomb blast with time left to spare to go out on the town. They never show the episode where the little kids and their mother get terrorized with weapons. At my home this day, this was not the FBI's varsity. I worked for the varsity. That last conversation I had with the FBI before that encounter was with the Bureau's third man in charge of the entire FBI at HQ in Washington D.C. He had asked my Intel group to investigate members of the Justice Department, including Eric Holder, among other tasks I keep in a safe deposit box – tucked away for a rainy day if the Feds want to play. That is what was on my mind during the raid – the work we did against Holder. This was payback, I thought. Sure. I could understand that. But why would someone like Holder or any of his high-ranking goons in Justice send these FBI flunkies to my door?

On a bad day – at a different place – they were potential sitting ducks. But they knew the kids were home and well … things worked out this time for all involved. Luckily.

The FBI agents interrogating me were young, inexperienced and pumped up on adrenaline from their 'big' raid. But they weren't the brass I was used to. With all due respect, these guys were lightweights. I was a mile ahead of the interrogation and leading it after 30 minutes, getting more from them than they were getting from me. These were not seasoned agents. Some Feds – experienced or not – simply have "it" and you'd be wise to tread lightly with gifted Intel guys. These folks didn't have it. So what the fuck were they doing in my house?

I am thinking Holder, who was the attorney general in waiting, employed his DOJ network to harass me. Or perhaps it was President George W. Bush's DOJ" Barack Obama was poised to win the White House at the time and Holder was largely expected to follow. It did cross my mind that I could be in hot water because I had gone off the reservation as a federal Intel contractor and started to investigate disturbing information I gleaned from a respected Democratic Congressman. But that would be insane. All I did was ask some questions and make some phone calls to well-placed folks in the State Dept. and beyond seeking to clarify the wild rumors. Why would the FBI raid and toss my house for that?

My wife is beside herself. It is 7 am or so and she is taking the boys to a remote part of the house where they can collect themselves, but she pulls me aside for a quick huddle in the kitchen. I notice several FBI agents have draped their ballistic vests on the back of our kitchen chairs and leaned their M-4 rifles against the table. They don't see me as any type of threat, I quickly surmise. But why would you let your guns dangle against my kitchen table. My kids are in the damn house. And I could be a complete wild man. Not the brightest group I'm dealing with.

"The two female agents said they love our kitchen," my wife says in disbelief. "They said: 'You have a lovely home.' "

My wife is bewildered. She thinks I arranged some type of strange training Op or something but this is no training Op.

Meanwhile, a team of Feds are rifling through every room, every drawer looking for anything they can use as leverage against me. Ripping our home to shreds and the sun isn't even up all the way.

Rousted out of bed, I'm in my pajama bottoms and T-shirt and groggy. And I'm struggling to formulate a strategy to handle this massive, invasive morning. But some instincts kick in finally. The lead FBI agent is a fucking prick. I've already deciphered that, so I can use that against him. Hubris kills. It is an advantage to be able to mark an adversary. I direct these clowns to our living room. My wife is from western Pennsylvania and if you know anything about Pittsburgh you know that the living room or "front" room is the part of the house no one is allowed to trek into unless you're "company" or someone in the family died. Or the FBI shows up. My wife actually asks these mutts – who are trashing her homes -- if they want coffee. That's who and how she is.

So I take these agents into that forbidden room. It's a special occasion after all. How many times does the FBI raid your house? I sit on the couch; two FBI agents sit on an adjacent couch and start peppering me with sophomoric questions. The prick is 'leading' the interrogation, and he's fumbling like Steeler running back Rashad Mendenhall in the Super Bowl against the Packers.

The sun is up now and rising above the trees in our front yard. I quickly realize these are junior varsity agents from the Philadelphia field office taking orders from Washington D.C. to basically harass me. They are spilling the beans and don't recognize it. My mind starts to wander a bit because they are not engaging me and I think who trained these guys? They let me pick the room for the interview; they allowed me to choose my seat, and they sat down after I sat down.

They are sitting in a spot with the morning sun directly in their eyes, there is no way they can have an unobstructed view of the room and of me. That sun is a problem in the morning in the Front room. And it gets really hot. And I'm enjoying watching them flinch and fight it.

You've seen cop-movie interrogations with the bright, white-hot light in the suspect's face? Well, you get the setting.

When thinking of this now, I recall Hemingway's verse in Old Man and the Sea. His character battled a giant Marlin, and I too was engaged with a significant foe – the massive apparatus of the Justice Department.

Hemingway wrote:

"But he seems calm, he thought, and following his plan. But what is his plan, he thought. And what is mine? Mine I must improvise to his because of his great size. If he will jump I can kill him. But he stays down forever. Then I will stay down with him forever."

So I played it just like the Old Man played the fish. Rousted out of bed, I would keep my cool if they kept theirs. I just want these fucks out of the house and far away from my young boys and bride. But like the Old Man in the story, I can get nasty too with these fish if required. But restraint is the catch of the day on this day.

Plus, tucked beside my right arm inside the couch is a Sig Saur P-245 pistol. I got six rounds. And there's two of them peppering me with questions. Neither swept the room or the couch for weapons before they sat down. The lead agent is talking but I'm calculating: they are carrying two Glocks and a third in a thigh holster. That gives me 48 rounds if these agents' weapons are running hot (15 in the clip, 1 in the chamber) to pave my way to the kitchen where I have their rifles and vests. But my kids are still in the house, upstairs. And I'm wearing pajama pants. But if my kids get hurt ... or I hear any blood-curdling screams from my wife ...

The mind can play tricks on you when you're rousted out of bed, and your adrenaline is spiking. I have no intention of killing or harming these folks – or anyone unless my family is hurt. But I could. Easily. That gives me the upper hand in an interrogation because they are on my turf and I am comfortable knowing I am not at risk as long as I stay cool. So I try to keep cool. You learn working with and for the Feds that their primary weapon is fear. They are fear brokers: they peddle it at every turn. If you can get beyond that, it's like the first time you fly in an airplane and break through the clouds and understand there is a whole world above the cloud cover. And it's beautiful. Even during a morning storm.

I am convinced at this point that some job I did for the Feds went sideways and I've been compromised. Or my rogue research could have triggered bells and whistles with high-placed D.C. elites – possibly all the way to the White House. Or someone in my group got leaned on and gave me up, divulged some of the sensitive things we worked on for these guys. We pulled many jobs, mostly for the federal government and top brass in the FBI and many other agencies. If you are familiar with Fusion

GPS in 2016-2018, I was the grandfather of that type of amphibious Intel operation where we combined Feds with retired journalists and rained holy hell on private targets. That was in the mid-1990s, long before Fusion GPS. Name a government agency, and we worked for it, along with Fortune 100 companies. We could glean corporate Intel from under-used databases, nab public records, or get our hands dirty. We quickly gained a reputation as being among the best at what we did, but we stuck to Intel and digging for Intel and did not cross over into setting up targets like Donald Trump as Fusion GPS did.

But we worked also against Trump many years before his political life. We ran an Intel arm for Steve Wynn's Mirage out of Las Vegas. Wynn and Trump were embroiled in an epic legal battle. It was personal, and it was nasty. The stakes were sky high, and the money was flowing as these two billionaires went toe to toe with each other. Wynn wanted to come back to Atlantic City, and Trump wanted a gaming license in Las Vegas. These two magnates had a team of Intel and ex FBI, CIA on their payrolls digging dirt on one another. We were up to our necks in anti-Trump dirt, working for Wynn's security Chief Tom Sheer, former FBI SAC of the New York FBI. My crew was on Team Wynn, and we were battling Team Trump. And Sheer was a ball buster and detail-oriented taskmaster, having spent decades working his way up the FBI ladder. This was his first job post-Bureau. But I respected him. And that is important in Intel.

Once at breakfast at the Four Seasons in Philadelphia, Sheer complimented me on the group's performance for gathering Trump Intel for Wynn.

"I don't understand how you find this stuff," he

said. "We couldn't find this kind of intelligence in the FBI. However you do it, keep on doing it. Mr. Wynn is happy."

For the time being at least. Guys like Wynn were rarely happy. He had all the money he could ever want and privately on conference calls he questioned how Trump's Intel operation was always a step ahead of Mirage's group. Whatever Wynn threw at Trump, Trump had something better to counter with. And it drove Wynn mad. That wasn't a reflection on my group, however. We were only a part of Wynn's machine, and we had little say about formulating a strategy to take on Trump.

That is when I first grew respect for Trump. He was a bright adversary and always a step ahead. Just ask Steve Wynn. It was interesting to watch the two men embrace during Trump's presidential campaign in 2016. I had a front-row seat years earlier where these two billionaires tried to destroy each other, throwing untold millions at dirt digging. Politics is a funny thing.

But I am way ahead of the story.

The seeds of True Pundit were sewn shortly after Barack Obama's election in 2008 when Holder started to grab the reigns of the Justice Department. And the FBI pointed guns at my sons. Twice.

During the interrogation by FBI agents, I referred back to some "federal" training I had after I left journalism in 1996 at The Record in Hackensack, N.J. My Intel godfather was Dick Callaghan a north Jersey and New York Intel legend who literally wrote the fugitive apprehension manual for the U.S. Marshals before he took on different, more complicated assignments for the Agency and other clandestine folks. Callaghan lured me out of journalism because he thought I was wasting my talents toiling away at a large daily newspaper and fighting editors to get investigative stories published. He was right.

In two years at The Record, I had gone from writing obituaries to running the newspaper's investigative reporting department. That is quite the climb. But it was making long-time journalists at the paper uneasy and spiteful. Unless they require your help with a story, of course. There were many talented reporters at The Record. Editors also. I was winning awards, national awards but it was getting much harder to get investigative stories printed. Nearly impossible. My stories had jolted roughly everyone at the paper out of their comfort zones. But the job had become too political, worrying about the ruffled feathers and injured egos of reporters. When you're 27 years old, and 28 and have to apologize for being exceptional – and working hard -- you know it's time to exit such a work environment. And perhaps the industry.

Dick Callaghan was more like a father to me than a mentor. My old man split when I was 12. He was a junkie and a lousy Dad. Sounder Callaghan's tutelage I mimicked his old school way of intelligence gathering based on the primary tenet: Never Rat on Your Friends, Colleagues. Always have their six.

But Callaghan had an even more critical mantra, one I failed to yield: Never Trust the FBI. And he was right about that too. More than anything else. I mean he was right in 1994. "One day," he used to say, "people will realize the truth about those rat bastards."

Dick's standing joke was something he picked up while working undercover to infiltrate organized crime in New York City.

"It was a running joke for decades with the Gambino crime family as well as NYPD," Dick would retell time and times again. "One of the only things both sides could agree on."

Dick: "What are the three most overrated things in the world?"

Whomever Dick Was Asking: "I give up. What are they?"

Dick: "Home cooking. Home fucking. And the FBI."

Fast forward to 2018. Dick was right. But it was not easy getting here. The road was a brutal one. In fact, I almost didn't make it here – courtesy of the Justice Department.

It was the FBI who recruited my crew to work for them in 1996. Right after my journalism career, I took my first FBI job. I was winding down at the newspaper, and the money was too good to pass up. I had a newborn son, and as one of the top investigative reporters in the country but I was rifling through the couch and car seats to roust up loose change to buy diapers. I was working, but we were a new family. Happy, but struggling. Callaghan always coached me up about working for the FBI once he knew we were doing contract work for the Bureau. Take their money, he said, but watch your back.

Callaghan was like the Justice Department's version of Yoda. He never seemed to be wrong. And he always had the jump on things months before anyone else. It was my privilege to have him looking out for me early in my Intel career and to learn from a legend who worked undercover in New York City for years gathering Intel on La Cosa Nostra.

Fast forward. As I sat in my front room being questioned by these mutts from the FBI, Dick's wisdom echoed in my head. I should have kept a better eye on the FBI. Because they were definitely keeping an eye on me. The lead agent reminded me of some of the guys I used to work with the night crew at Shoprite, re-stocking canned goods before the store opened. Callaghan, along with my DEA friends had poked fun at FBI agents for decades. This guy was the poster boy for such ridicule. He's trying to play me like a discount target at Hogan's Alley at the National Academy in Quantico. And he keeps beating around the only questions I care about: What the fuck are you doing in my house? Why are you here? Where's the warrant? How can I get these assholes and their guns away from my home? My family?

The agent is boasting how he sifted through our garbage the last month looking for evidence. At that point, I begin to realize they don't have much but – they do have a warrant.

I am convinced, at this point, someone with real chops is going to show up and take over the interview. I'm thinking the real lead agent got jammed up on I-95 and he or she is running late. I am also convinced whatever national security job I messed up, or we messed up, for whatever agency we did it for – it must be pretty bad for the FBI to be sitting in my house. If it is nasty, I will just walk away from the interview. There is no arrest warrant, and I am only talking to these guys to extract Intel from them. I can march at any time. I can even go down the road for breakfast. And they have to allow me to walk away. Those are the rules. But I'll play stupid for as long as I can get away with it. With this crew, I'm not worried about playing a little Lt. Columbo.

We worked many cases for Marshals, FBI, DEA, White House and many others including the Secret Service and some involved truly sinister suspects and defendants. These were bad guys. But I can think of few, if any, of those cases where federal agents rolled into those people's homes and pointed guns in the faces of their children. That's only asking for trouble. Even when NY DEA arrested Peter Gatien in the 1990s – a story I scooped New York's Post, Daily News and Times on – federal agents allowed the famous nightclub magnate – who owned the Limelight, Palladium, and Tunnel -- to put his glass eye in and change out of his pajamas before he was stuffed into a G-ride (government car). You won't read that anywhere else. I might have sat in on the federal wiretaps of Gatien too, but don't tell anyone. And also conducted surveillance with the Feds at the clubs, but again, don't tell anyone.

On many fronts, the FBI's behavior at my house baffles me to this day. If the FBI had waited another hour and my kids were off to school, things could have been much different. But the lead agent didn't have the brains or experience to comprehend he had put his crew into a potentially dangerous situation. He was too busy sifting through our garbage. He did no recon on when my sons went to school. And unwittingly -- years later -- he ultimately unleashed a clandestine collection of current and former law enforcement officials onto his employer in the form of True Pundit. That was a mistake.

You should never underestimate a target. Or treat one like a dog either. DEA treated Gatien like a human being. Respect goes a long way.

But the FBI did not make that mistake just once. The same crew of federal cowboys returned to my home years later with their guns, terrorized my youngest son who has special needs and bloodied my head. I was unarmed, did not resist, and was making my son breakfast before school.

A moment later I was dragged from the house at gunpoint, tackled by multiple agents and I hit the cement steps outside my door face first because they were holding my hands behind my back. My youngest son, then 11, looked on while screaming with tears rolling down his face. Frozen. Terrified. Armed federal agents ripping your father from the house and beating him down before breakfast – years after storming your home with guns – is not the best recipe for a kid already suffering from anxiety and depression.

What was my alleged crime? You would think espionage or perhaps another capital crime like losing 33,000 classified and top-secret government emails.

No. All my worries about past jobs for the Feds going sideways were unwarranted. Or so I thought. The FBI was at my house to harass me for copyright infringement. I had a side business and hobby of selling and trading vintage hockey games and old hockey highlights. Some were on VHS; some on DVD. The FBI terrorized my kids twice at gunpoint – and my wife -- and harassed my family for an intellectual property "crime." Usually a civil law issue at best.

The FBI and Justice Department sanctioned pointing automatic weapons at the heads of my young children and wife and beating me down over hockey tapes. Not the dozens of illegal jobs I spearheaded for the Deep State and FBI. These were vintage hockey videos and games, with much of the footage 40 to 50 years old. And none of it was copy written. But that is a story for another day.

The Deep State made sure I lost my job at Citi too. As a Certified Fraud Examiner, I ran Citi and its affiliates' anti-money laundering division in Delaware, Chicago and Los Angeles for nearly a decade. The FBI went out of its way to ruin my career.

The Deep State had struck. But Why?

I knew too much. And I still do. And now you get to know also. Funny how that works. If you're trying to silence an Irishman, you better just shoot him. Otherwise, he might only rise up from the ashes of his life and come looking for you and your bosses. A rising Phoenix. They're always the most dangerous folks because they had to stare into the abyss, a daunting gauntlet that can strip a man of most fears.

I am at peace with myself and how I arrived here, at this point in my life. I believe I had to weather this journey to uncover the corruption in the FBI and DOJ and I have, along with True Pundit. But we are NOT done. I have been on a well-oiled mission since the FBI tried to ruin my life. And they almost took my life too. I nearly cashed it all in because I was at rock bottom. My life was in tatters. I allowed these bastards to terrorize my family at gunpoint and I stood and watched as they did it. Twice. I had to keep cool then, so I didn't get gunned down or locked up. But I had to respond. I had to punch back, albeit late and in a non-violent manner.

"Are you going to let the FBI get away with all this?" my quiet, normally reserved wife asked me one Sunday morning.

She and others now know the answer.

The FBI tried to ruin me – or get me to kill myself so I would not reveal the truth about the Deep State. But I was raised in a broken home and lived in the projects, so I had the strength to rise from the ashes and haunt those who tried to ruin me. Without having to weather personal turmoil at home beginning in grade school – I doubt I would have survived this battle. But in the end, the FBI didn't kill me, they made me stronger. When they came into my home and threatened my family, they fucked up. It is my firm belief that the facts in this book will change the landscape of the Deep State. It may take some time because we -- as a rule at True Pundit -- are way out in front of other news media. The disturbing revelations herein are the beginning of the end of the Deep State. Hopefully, all the collaborators too will be fully exposed and punished accordingly.

I have the goods and always deliver what I promise. In journalism or Intel. Now it's time for payback. Although we have had fun dismantling the FBI for two years now, we graduate to exposing a vast underbelly plaguing America.

The Deep State's tale is one of sheer hubris and skullduggery employed against the best interests of the United States and the safeguards of the Constitution. May God have mercy on their souls (part of me doesn't honestly mean that) but may they also pay a hefty price here on earth for their treason and deceit. And the lives of soldiers killed and maimed by the proceeds of this brazen political treachery. A lawless, Godless lot. Taking them head-on is no easy feat, and I understand I am in uncharted waters here, but I do feel these are waters I was meant to be in. Even though the fish I have on this line is a huge fish. Or is it I who is on their line? If so, I'm hardly a big fish.

But I have weathered the crucible to get here, to deliver this message. And I hearken back to Hemingway's big fish story where he wrote in part, about the deathly battle:

"I must save all my strength now.
Christ, I did not know he was so big.
I'll kill him though. In all his greatness and his glory.
But I will show him what a man can do and what a man endures."

What a man can endure, indeed...
I've survived the Feds' treacherous gauntlet.
Now it was their turn to run mine.

2 FINAL NAIL IN COFFIN

When you sit down and put your thoughts on paper, you never anticipate the emotions and even some skeletons such a process will churn.

My Mom comes to mind. During my case against the government and FBI – or really their case against me (The United States of America vs. Michael Moore – sounds daunting), my mother got sick. Very sick and very quick. She had multiple health challenges through the years, and if you ask her, she would say many stemmed from standing on her feet all day working as a cashier at Shop Rite for nearly 20 years. Much of that tenure was long before barcode scanners and heated check-out aisles.

But it was the cigarettes that did her in, destroyed her lungs. And while I was fighting the DOJ and FBI she was fighting COPD – (chronic obstructive pulmonary disease.) And she was losing worse than I was.

Mom did the best she could for my brother, sister and myself. I still don't understand how we all survived on her $13,000 a year salary. We lived in government housing for a time, but it wasn't like it's portrayed on television and the movies. Neither were the people. In fact, these were some of the most helpful folks I have ever met. We were low-income, but my Mom never made us feel like we were. Nobody did. We still had enough money for a set of Mylec goalie pads for street hockey a game which helped pass the time all year long.

Now I bring up the topic of my Mom because, without the events that unfolded at this time of her decline, I am confident you would never have even heard of me. There would be no Thomas Paine of True Pundit.

My father was a junkie and one of the largest drug dealers in Philadelphia – a fact I learned after his death when the former president of the Pagan's Motorcycle Club offered his condolences. The Pagan's are one of the most dangerous biker gangs in America. They also traffic and manufacture methamphetamines. A whole shit ton of meth.

Given that backdrop of my childhood, you may understand why my mother was such a critical role model. If my Dad ever knew I would one day be working Intel for the DEA – and helping the agency establish a stealth technology for its wireless phones – he would have gotten a kick out of the irony. I am sure. And my FBI affiliation? The old man would have passed out after learning that. He was not a fan of the police. But it was thanks to my Mom that I did not follow my father's footsteps. Don't get me wrong, having a bankroll of cash -- $10,000 or more -- in your pocket is attractive when you're a broke teen, but trekking to dialysis in your late 40s to stay alive because you blew your kidneys out using "crank" is a big downside.

My Mom. God love her. I want to tell folks about this incredible woman who raised us Roman

Catholic and saved me from that kind of life, that type of fate. Because I was headed there. It's a potent lure even though my Dad never seemed to have money for us growing up. That still is a head scratcher because he HAD cash on him all the time.

My Mom's name was Rose, and her life began much like a Norman Rockwell painting. A hard-working girl from Altoona, PA who fell in love as a 1960s teenager with Elvis Presley, rock n roll music, dancing, and the Jersey Shore.

Ultimately, my Mom didn't live that promise-filled life that youth's new canvass offers, or anything even close to picture perfect. But she lived life just the same, trumping its abstract disappointments and a chronic chain of illnesses with a trademarked quiet, poetic-like courage of a poised yet battered prizefighter.

Her fight to survive in her final weeks of life was as inspiring as it was often brutal. But entwined in her suffering, a prophetic lesson was woven: when all the medicines and treatments no longer work, your spirit and true character will carry you farther than a failed body ever could. And a life-long Christian faith, tempered like steel through trial after trial, provides grace and dignity amid the physical chaos of one's uncharted final hours.

This was all unfolding while I was fighting the federal government. So I derived much of my strength from watching how my Mom handled what proved to be her final waltz with illness.

Rose lived by the unwavering belief that people, in general, were good at heart. She treated others as she wanted to be treated and expected the same.

Rose's one romance that never disappointed was

21

her love affair with the Jersey Shore. Her affection for Cape May and its surroundings was forged as a teenager when she first stepped off the sand and into Tony Mart dance hall in Somers Point. She relished the music that made the 1960s and the Shore famous and learned how to 'Do the Twist' on the dance floor by the back bar at Tony Mart to Bill Haley and the Comets, Del Shannon's chart-topping Runaway and The Fall Guys house band.

When she was 'Down the Shore,' life's tribulations melted into the ocean, and just like the ocean, that proved a constant. Rose grew to adore many of the Shore's flavors as well, such as: saltwater taffy, Tastykakes, ginger ale, cheese steaks, and candy.

She took the dance moves honed at Tony Mart to the national stage; American Bandstand. Along with Dick Clark, Rose and her friends thought they were merely making a road trip from Altoona to Philadelphia, but they all ended up making history.

The youngest of four children from German-American parents, her first job at 16 was at Cross' Ice Cream in Altoona. She then worked at SKF Industries in Altoona, after attending business school and later as a longtime grocery store cashier in Broomall, PA and finally at QVC in West Chester, PA. Many years she worked two simultaneous full-time jobs.

She truly cherished her years at Cross'-- serving up hand-dipped ice cream and chocolate malts to many of her Catholic school peers and 'Greasers' at the popular gathering spot during an era that she often described as a 'front-porch' time in society.

"No one locked their homes," she often reflected. "People were more considerate. Life was simple. People were happier with what they already had."

Rose was a generous woman, always gifting more than she could afford and apologizing that it wasn't more. She was a giddy child around the holidays, with Elvis on in the background or singing Silent Night in German like her mother taught her. Christmas Vacation was her favorite movie, and it fed her infectious laugh. A huge heart wouldn't even allow her to wait for Christmas morning, converting the celebration for her children to Christmas Eve instead. Giving made her as happy as scoring a bargain from QVC. Her feet were two different sizes from childhood Polio, so she was always looking for a deal on shoes, even after she was bedridden. A good deal was a good deal.

The daughter of a fireman, Rose admired her father for running into fully involved buildings with just a wet rag for lung protection to help and save strangers. She likewise marveled at how her mother always had fresh clothes, and a hot meal and bath ready when he returned from long hours of battling western Pennsylvania fires throughout the 1930s-1960s. That selfless blue-collar mentality became an essential part of her fabric and helped forge the metal required as a single-parent. This was a role she embraced, enduring long work hours for low wages amid declining health for decades. Her plight wasn't anything out of the ordinary, she often lamented. Plenty of folks walked a harder road.

Nonetheless, Rose was a fighter, fierce advocate and provider for her daughter and two sons, all who -- she often boasted -- graduated college; got married; had families of their own.

Loved ones, by nature, are often memorialized in their prime. Young. Attractive. Healthy. But Rose's final life phase proved that often an actual window into the soul is found amid the simple, not so storybook-like moments of adversity. She knew she was dying but battled to dictate just when. Squelching pain and ignoring decline, she fought to extend each extra moment; another day to Skype and connect with her eight grandchildren; another rerun of the Golden Girls; just a few more laughs; another rosary.

Mom had fallen so many times in life, only to get right back up again. It was her final, often cruel battle which proved a metaphor for her a turbulent 68 years:

Life is hard.

Don't complain.

Find happiness wherever you can.

Laugh. Work.

Love your family.

Pray and forgive.

Don't worry about me. It's alright to be scared but have faith in God who promised a quieter, simpler place on the other side.

I am confident she is there now. If she is not, then no one is.

When my kids today look at some of the pictures from my childhood they ask why I was always wearing a coat or a hat inside our apartment. They thought I was some kind of strange guy who never changed clothes. Then I tell them we often had no heat. Or the thermostat was set at 58 degrees to save money that my Mom didn't have anyway. But I guess I didn't really understand it all either, at the time.

These are the memories that haunt me from time to time, remembering Mom and all she did for us.

And years later, she was proud of me, my wife, and her grandchildren. But all the while I was fighting the Feds, and my life was spiraling out of control. I never told her about it, and I told her brothers and sister not to tell her either. With COPD, she was fighting for her life – and every breath – and my legal concerns were not something she needed on her plate. Plus no matter how good you think your chances of prevailing against the federal government are, when you are indicted and arrested it sends a shockwave through your entire family. You are labeled. Scorned.

I didn't want that from my Mom or for her. I think it is a natural thing though, to think someone is guilty before any trial or before you hear their back-story. But Mom knew something was wrong. Even when I used to pull pranks at Temple University Hospital to get her to laugh or make fun of her doctors or mess with her "roommate" in the next bed, she would blurt out:

"You don't seem yourself," She said. "Is something going on with you, with the work you've done for the government?"

I'd get back home after visiting her in Philly and tell my wife late at night.

"Mom knows."

And the whole time I thought I was keeping things together. But a Mom just knows these things.

Writing all these words about my Mom has been the toughest part of the book. I knew it would be and I put it off for as long as I could. Also, that is the challenging thing about a book like this. I had to relive all the emotions and the lows – and the disdain – in order to capture it here. Often, I have not been fun to be around lately and I apologize to my family for being on edge. When this is over, I want to put it down and move on. Here's 400 pages or so on my life and in many ways it is for my sons and grandkids to look back on it if they want and see that you can't quit. And getting even is OK, as long as you do it legally. I try to write the hard pieces -- like about my Mom -- after everyone has gone to bed so if I break down and start sobbing I don't look like a basket case. But letting Mom down is something that haunts me. And not being able to share the toughest fight of my life – during the toughest fight of hers – is equally disappointing. I wish I could have been a better person and risen above all the shame that comes with getting arrested and paraded in the media as an arch criminal. But I wasn't at that stage yet. It does take time to bounce back.

But I got to that stage after the Justice Department would not allow me to attend my Mom's funeral. Or visit her during the final hours she was still alive. Those were the last straws for me. They were pushing it too far. Too fucking far. My Mom was a three-hour drive away in the same state. But I couldn't get a green light from the fed to pay my respects. Then on the day of her funeral, a federal probation agent visited my house to make sure I hadn't attended the funeral. Then, later, his supervisor showed up too to harass me.

Soon after, my Uncle died. My mother's brother. A Franciscan priest and Friar who probably saved my life. I was expelled from Cardinal O'Hara High School, outside Philadelphia, my freshman year of high school. Actually, they told me just not to come back. So my uncle arranged my schooling at St.

Francis Preparatory School in Pennsylvania, a boarding school run by the Franciscan brothers and priests. We had no money, and we were living in Section 8 housing. He arranged a scholarship.

Three years later, I graduated at the top of my class, versed in literature, humanities, and some of the best pranks and hijinks imaginable. And that is where I decided I wanted to be a journalist. My younger brother followed in my footsteps, also on scholarship. Where else could a couple Irish, German and Polish Catholic boys from Delco with no money interact with the sons of Mexican bankers and Venezuelan oil barons? My uncle had given us both the opportunity of a lifetime, one that no money could ever repay. He passed away soon after my Mom. The Justice Department would not allow me to attend his funeral either – again three hours away in Pennsylvania.

Like with my Mom, I never got the chance to say goodbye and thank you to her or her brother -- two of the most influential people in my life. Without them, I would likely not be here – have an incredible family -- and I certainly wouldn't have been a writer.

These government fucks kept kicking me in the teeth. And this was the final straw.

To me, at that point, I had been radicalized. That is when I decided to get back into the game. For the first time since my arrest, I no longer cared who knew that I was a felon – a dangerous hockey tape felon. I understood I would take more lumps and criticism by getting back into the game and I embraced it. Because I could counter punch and knock people – or an entire beloved institution like the FBI -- the fuck out. And I made a list, and I didn't check it twice like Santa Claus. I checked it ten times. And when all the smoke cleared, that list was narrowed down to one entity: The FBI.

It would be war with the FBI, I decided. And I was content and excited because in my heart I knew what I could do to the Bureau to expose it for the corrupt circus it had become. Because I have done the same thing my entire life – starting with the day my Dad walked out on us. I win. I always win. You beat me; I come back and one-up you. You may win some battles, I win the war. If you outsmart me, I study and work harder, and I come back for a rematch. And I win.

And for the first time in a long time, I got my fire back, that fire these fuckers took from me. My swagger was back. In my mind now, this was a war, and I would win. I was convinced of it. But we're going to outsmart these assholes and expose them at the same time. There is no need for any violence or threats because that is what they want. They want you to dig the hole they tossed you in even deeper. No, we'd beat their asses with our brains. We would outthink them, outmaneuver them, and outsmart them. This was the genesis of my comeback. This was the birth of True Pundit.

Then it hit me: Perhaps I was supposed to be in this place. Right here. Right now. It sounded crazy, but perhaps I was meant to be seeking redemption. Whatever the reasons – or the alignment of the cosmic tumblers – it sure felt right and for the first time in a long time, felt good. Now all I had to do was infiltrate the FBI and Justice Department.

But first, I had to cut the grass. My wife was riding my ass about cutting the lawn. Lawn first, then begin to dismantle FBI. All on a Saturday at the Moore house.

Now the first step in the natural Intel selection process was to round up a crew, get the band back together. Solid Intel guys and gals. I made a list of some of the top folks I once employed and started narrowing down their backgrounds to hone in on cracking the Bureau. Keep in mind, the Justice Department is monitoring – at the time – every dime coming in and out of our bank accounts. And there wasn't much cash coming in after the lead FBI agent went out of his way to ensure I was fired from Citigroup on the day of my sentencing.

Moreover, I could not take any new work – including Intel work – without the Justice Department's approval. Yes, you are correct: At every turn, these people have you under their thumb. And they let you know it because many of these players on the DOJ roster are the kind of fucked up people who enjoy this type of power.

The Feds want to make sure you fail. They want you to bankrupt out and be tossed from your house via foreclosure. When you have an opportunity to make money, the Feds get to dictate whether that happens. If you have a problem finding a job – even though the DOJ went out of its way to ruin your career – they dictate they will find you a job. Sure it pays $8 an hour and is 90 minutes each way from your house. But you're going to work a job, even if we find you a job. This is a recipe for psychological and financial disaster.

But how am I supposed to put a crew together when the electricity has been cut by the power company twice in the last three months because we couldn't make payments? I told my wife I was putting a crew back together and she quickly reminded me we couldn't even buy a loaf of bread. Instead of paying the mortgage I had come up with a relatively brilliant strategy of paying lawyers to fight the mortgage company for a reduction, and I had that matter nicely tied up in court. So the cash we usually would fork over to the bank was going to lawyers and anything extra we were putting toward monthly bills. But they were piling up. And they just continued to pile up. Big piles. The Justice Department had us in a severe cash squeeze. And that is how they break you. They put you in their vice and crush you, grind you down day by day. Mentally. Financially. Emotionally.

Many crack under such pressures. Many times, the spouse walks away from it too – leaves the marriage. In the back of my mind, I wondered how far God was going to punish me – I was convinced he was teaching me a lesson for my indiscretions committed while working Intel. Would my wife leave me? Was that the next life disaster? And did I have enough in the tank to weather it? Instead, God had blessed me with a loyal and strong wife who was also an incredible mother to our kids. Even when the FBI barged into the house wielding guns, she was a beacon of calm – shuffling the kids away from these fucking assholes and consoling them. It ripped my heart out watching her at my sentencing hearing tearing up to Judge Schiller. She gave an emotional and impassioned plea to spare me from federal prison. All the while, I was thinking these fucks were going to remember the day they tortured my family.

But I didn't start the day thinking that. I was fairly mellow in the morning. Even in the courtroom, I was reasonably relaxed because we had hammered out a solid plea deal and we negotiated the hell of that plea so it was solid. Or so I thought. This was my mistake, my error: trusting the word and promises of the DOJ. Hollow words from hollow people. Originally, these crime fighters wanted to put me away in federal prison for 35 years on what amounted to a $40,000 civil beef with the NHL. So tell me again how this had anything to do with hockey videos.

It was a pure intimidation play. And I wasn't game. My attorney Kathy Henry struck a plea deal. I would plead out to one count of copyright infringement instead of seven. In return, the DOJ represented they would not seek prison time. The FBI also guaranteed they would stop issuing their ridiculous press releases which made me look like I was some video pirate kingpin running a Chinese sweatshop. It was a masterstroke on Henry's part, striking this plea deal. But much of it had to do with a strategy I urged her to employ. Delay, delay, delay. I had seen that tactic work wonders through the years for criminal defendants, and now I would employ it. And it was working.

The FBI and Justice Department are fear brokers. And real professionals at the fear game. They use fear to try and make a defendant make quick decisions absent careful consideration. Would you buy a house from a broker who demanded you had to purchase the property or else? No. Then why would you dance because some lawyer pulls the same antics? Many people do panic and surrender themselves to brutal plea deals. Not me. I'm worried but the fear factor -- the Feds' bread and butter -- is at a minimum, so I feel like I hold at least a couple cards.

We would wait and delay because that is just

about the only currency we have against a mammoth like this, a machine that is geared to destroy your life. So we delayed, several times, and it worked. It got to the point where the U.S. Attorney was merely looking to clear this case because it had dragged on for so long. And that is a good position for a defendant. So the deal was in place, and the Feds were somewhat disgusted this case hadn't been cleared.

I had heard from sources in the FBI that the lead agent's colleagues were routinely poking fun at him for not even being able to get a plea out of the hockey tape guy and clear the case. Hell, I can only imagine the fun they must have had making fun of him for not knowing how to break a door down, properly handcuff me or how he fumbled like a dork with a bra clasp on prom night trying to fingerprint me. There was plenty of material there to keep his FBI pals busy. (Where do they find these guys?)

The point here is about the delay strategy. It had worked, and because of it, we had struck a very favorable plea deal.

But during sentencing, both U.S. Attorneys – one from Philly and another who came up from D.C. – changed gears on the fly. They asked Judge Schiller for prison time, a complete violation of the plea deal. They wanted to put me away for four years. But that wasn't part of the agreement. They didn't care. This was their entire strategy, to fuck me during sentencing.

This is how gutless liars work.

This is a window into today's Justice Department too. It is run by weasels and worms. And I had a front row seat, watching my life come tumbling down in a courtroom in Philadelphia. And I had to sit there quietly and pretend I didn't want to lash out and exact my own revenge.

I remember it vividly like it happened 15 minutes ago.

I leaned over to my lawyer, covered the court mic on the table and said:

"This wasn't the deal, and they're trying to railroad me, this is fucking bullshit."

"You need to relax," Kathy said. "This isn't going to go their way. The judge is watching how you react, just stay cool and let me handle it."

"I'm going to fucking drop this guy (the U.S. Attorney) at the podium," I said.

"I know they're fucking the worst people," Kathy said. " But I am watching the judge, and it is not playing well. Trust me on this."

All of the dozens of horror stories about the FBI shared and swapped by federal agents over beers were rifling through my head. I should have known better. Jesus, I should have known. I'm better than that. Normally, without the stress.

When I watched Brett Kavanaugh snap at his final Senate hearing last week, I said BOOM: They got him too. They sent him over the edge. He had reached the end of his rope. And I remembered my sentencing hearing.

I usually don't want to punch a U.S. Attorney in the back of the head. And I had done a masterful job of staying calm the entire day. Until they pulled that bullshit where the DOJ tossed the plea deal on the fly and tried to lock me away. I have jumped out of airplanes before, skydiving, and after you are so ramped up on adrenaline – it's a fantastic feeling. Yet it doesn't come close to my adrenaline level when these fucks were pleading with the judge to put me away. So yes, I may sound out of line. Understood. But these bastards take you to the edge, and they don't care if you jump off. They want you to snap so they can say:

"See, your honor. He's unhinged. This is what we were talking about. This is why he needs 48 months in federal prison. You can see, your honor, He's a hockey video pirate and a thug. This is why he needs to be incarcerated."

They are trying to goad me again just like they did at my house, see if I slip. Maybe they can add a charge of assault, a new indictment, and a new judge since Schiller would be a fact witness. A judge who can't smell their bullshit they're selling in his court. These are evil fucking people who have convinced themselves that they represent truth and justice.

The two U.S. Attorneys in the court, the FBI agents – all fucking liars. They broker in lies, intimidation and peddle fear for a living. But I had previously been warned.

"Keep our eye on the U.S. Attorney," Callaghan warned me before he died."Philly is a liberal shit hole. He's probably a fucking worm."

He was.

And now the country has a front-row seat to what I learned. The Rosenstein's, the Ohr's of the DOJ. The Comey's and McCabe's and Strzok's of the FBI.

They are all fucking liars who do whatever they need to do to further their careers. And you wonder why I decided to expose these people and their ilk? These are not honorable people. They are not. They believe they are saints – but so did most of the ruthless dictators in world history. Ideologues. And like those tyrants, these mutts too are on the wrong side of history.

I sat in court – calmed down somewhat – and trusted in my attorney. My oldest son was in the courtroom. So I did not want to do anything stupid to embarrass myself but honestly, these people push you over the edge. They really do. My attorney and my wife agreed that my younger son should not attend the sentencing hearing because of his anxiety, depression and special needs. He had seen these assholes point guns at him twice and bloody me. So the court room was not the place for him that day. Judge Schiller was beyond cordial with my wife and older son. He asked him how his hockey season was going and wished him luck with NCAA recruiting. That put me at ease. When you get sentenced the Feds put together a presentencing report detailing your family history, work history and social life. If you smoked marijuana in high school, it's in the report. If your son is being recruited by Michigan State for ice hockey, it's in the report. If your son is in therapy twice a week and on medication because the FBI stormed his home twice with guns pointed at him and he's terrified every time there is a loud noise or knock on the door, it's in the report.

And Judge Schiller's comments about NCAA hockey was a tell to me that he read the report. Perhaps more than once.

You know, I was never worried about handling a stretch in federal prison, but I was worried how it would harm my kids, especially my younger son who was struggling already with what we had been through. I grew up without a father in the house so it had me concerned. And I wanted to walk out of that courtroom and in a way, say fuck you to the FBI and Justice Department that you had your shot at me and you fell short. Believe me, probation without jail time is a failure to these mopes. They love boosting their incarceration statistics. A probation-only sentence is a defeat for these guys and obviously a win for me.

So the judge put me at ease and then he ripped the Justice Department and its case to shreds. I felt things start to sway in our favor and my attorney nudged me and gave me a head nod. Regardless, the Justice Department was still pushing for four years of prison time.

These dysfunctional mopes, I thought, tossing my freedom and my family's future around like the Roman soldiers rolling craps for Christ's tunic. Carpetbaggers. We would eat them for lunch at Citi. They wouldn't make it past their probation employment period in corporate America. They would fit right in though in any liberal newsroom and thrive. And perhaps one day they might end up employed in one, who knows?

I fumbled to silently pray, "The Lord is my shepherd; I shall not want ..." But I struggled to remember the second verse and the rest of it so I just kept repeating that part in my head like Dustin Hoffman's Raymond Babbitt character in Rain Man repeating that K-mart is on 400 Oak Street in Cincinnati. Stress is a funny thing. You lose all track of time and dimension under super stressful situations. Some things seemingly move in slow motion, sometimes words are hard to hear, like someone turned your ears down and the mind can wander.

These institutionalized prosecutors are trying to sell me down the river by sending me up the river but I am thinking back to when I was arraigned in this same federal court room, after sitting in prison with some hard core dudes on the day these cowboys tackled me on the front step of my house. That was three years prior. In Philly after my arrest, you get put into a general population in federal holding with six to eight guys in one cell, a fact I was warned about by the lead agent in my case who always reminded me of a guy who should have been working at BestBuy and helping old ladies pick out laptops.

"Very shortly, you might be in a prison cell with murderers and rapists," the FBI case agent said to me on the drive to the federal building in Philadelphia. "You never know, some real dangerous guys. Nasty stuff."

I hold back a couple one liners that fire into my brain and pause. He's looking at me in his rear view mirror -- of his Ford Focus I think it was or a Prius -- to see how I react. His partner is in the back seat with a rifle on his lap, barrel pointed in my direction. Nice guy, actually. From Pittsburgh. But the guy driving, Agent Best Buy, just did a geek's rendition of Scared Straight, to try and spook me about getting rolled in federal holding.

"You know what?" I retorted. "The McRib is back. I know you guys love a couple McRibs, especially on your salary but it's only back for a limited time."

Agent Best Buy is steamed. Agent Pittsburgh is laughing and admits they do in fact like the McRib. I just nod my head and look out the window. We're driving past the Philly Navy Yard and that means I'll be meeting my new cell mates very soon. I guess I'm supposed to be scared straight.

Again, I have trekked back to the day of my arrest, while these prosecutors are still rambling on about locking me up, almost pleading with the judge now to teach me a lesson and incarcerate me. But for some strange reason – amid all the chaos -- I'm in another place and I remember a black guy I was arraigned with on the day of my arrest. We have seven or eight guys in our cell and there were other cells filled too. The Marshals take you upstairs to court in groups of four and you wait while everyone in the group is arraigned. Then it's back down to holding. But this guy said the funniest thing to me and for some reason, in the middle of my sentencing hearing, I'm thinking about this guy who was in for a gun charge. On the way back to holding he spoke up.

"Man, when the FBI brought you in here today that agent was acting like you were some motherfucking serial killer. We were all talking who the fuck is this white boy? He's some kind of bad ass. Now I just heard you're in for intellectual property and hockey tapes? Man, I don't even know how you got in here for whatever intellectual property means but you better come up with a better fucking back story before we get back downstairs cause intellectual property ain't going to cut it, my man. You better say you killed some motherfucker with a hockey stick. That will work. Go with that."

I laughed. You can't give a high five when you're hands are cuffed behind your back. And these cats cuff them tight. But I would have. That was some classic ball busting. And even the Marshals laughed.

I am quickly brought back to reality by the news

unfolding in the courtroom. Judge Schiller agreed with my cell mate. No federal prison for me. Probation only. Three years and the first year would be house arrest. A long probation but a minor setback really, versus the alternative. My wife is emotional and who can blame her. I look at the other table — the U.S. Attorneys -- in disgust. I still shook their hands. That's just me. They each had that dead-fish handshake. You just knew they would.

And the Feds were not happy. Fuck them.

It's over, I thought. It's over. Their secret little game — to renege on the plea deal like a pack of rats — exploded. in their faces.

A hard-fought victory against one of the most ruthless machines you could ever face. An unfair fight in every way and at every turn. A truly rigged process. I had survived but was battered, broke (money) and nearly broken. At one point during this nightmare I had contemplated suicide. I envisioned different scenarios and I'll be honest, it is damn frightening and lonely at rock bottom. Psalm 144 — the first couple verses -- and my kids. That is what saved me.

1. *Praise be to the LORD my Rock,*
    who trains my hands for war,
    my fingers for battle.
2. *He is my loving God and my fortress,*
    my stronghold and my deliverer,
 my shield, in whom I take refuge,
    who subdues peoples under me.

I had never walked away from a fight. Down but not out. And they would never expect me to come back and then go right at them. So, I would wait and plan on how to dissect the FBI, one brick at a time – like I had done to so many other criminal enterprises in my career as a journalist and gathering Intel.

"The LORD my Rock who has trained my hands for war, my fingers for battle." I pondered that and what it could mean applied to these circumstances. How was I going to pull that off – a war and battle with the same people who just turned my life upside down? Especially when I'm on federal probation.

I'd do from it behind a computer and keyboard.

3 BACK IN THE GAME

As I sit writing this book, I hear seven loud bangs on the door. I know that knock very well. It's a cop knock. The day is Oct. 9, 2018 — just days before this book was published. It's after 9 am and I'm wearing pajama shorts and a ratty shirt because it's 9 am and because I can wear those. These dudes always catch me in my pajamas. So much has changed for me yet at the same time I have circled back to federal agents at my front door. At the same time, I'm inside writing about federal agents at my door years earlier. The neighbors by now think I'm Al Capone. That's good. Keeps them in line.

This round the agents are not pointing guns at me or my family so we're off to a great start. And I immediately like these guys because they're young and respectful. That goes a long way with me and others. I checked the one agent's creds, look legit. I check their shoes. Look legit. Both are carrying concealed, and they are right handed. But the one agent crosses over when showing me his creds and shield and handles them with his right hand. So I know right away these guys do not see me as any threat whatsoever — or he slipped. Typically, you wouldn't handle your creds with the same hand you shoot with. If something goes bad, you need to have your shooting hand free. So I am relaxed now. I can talk to these guys. It appears they are not here for me. And why would they be? I've been a fucking boy scout for years now, steered clear of any trouble. You learn that on federal probation. I didn't even have a beer in three years. I walked the line because I wasn't going to allow these people to toss me in prison for drinking or anything else. I damn near vanished. I was the invisible man.

But these Feds are at my doorstep to talk about a story in True Pundit about a member of Congress.

"Are you guys looking at me," I say.

"Not at all," the lead agent replies. "No."

"Cause if you're looking at me, I have to talk to my lawyer, that's just the way it is," I say.

They assure me that I am not a target. Now, why do I think I'm a target at all? What did I do wrong? Did you read the first chapter? I mean, seriously.

I called the lead agent back a couple hours later and asked him straight up if he was sincere about getting Intel or if he was sent as an intimidation play to spook me on behalf of a U.S. Senator. He seemed floored that I would openly air that possibility. If they did come to harass me, I'd burn them in a True Pundit article. But my street sense tells me they are legitimately working a criminal inquiry involving a high-profile member of Congress. That's what they say – and even knowing they use deceit as a tool during interrogations – their narrative fits.

"A corrupt guy," one of the agents chimed in during our chat.

So this is getting really interesting. The things we know about this poser in Congress. If he ever runs for president, well, it will be fun. I decided to give these guys some Intel that wasn't in the True Pundit stories and we start chatting, and they give some Intel back. This is turning out to be a good morning. If these guys keep talking, I might invite them in for coffee. I drop a couple fed haunts near where they work, and that puts them at ease. One eatery in particular and we all get a chuckle at how great the place is. These guys are in their mid to late 30s, and I'm thinking, these guys were me 15 to 20 years ago. We worked the same beat and chased the same type of folks. When I was learning under Bruce Locklin at The Record, he was chasing Sharpe James, the late and convicted felon who was the long-time and celebrated mayor of Newark, N.J. At that time the Feds were chasing James too. Locklin was obsessed with investigating James, and for good reason. But he wasn't supported by management at the newspaper and they hung him out to dry before he could really nail James. It was a shame to watch, really. I liked Bruce and learned much from him. We won the Loeb award together. He was a reluctant mentor though at times, but I wasn't easy to work with. And little has changed. But Bruce did teach me to ease into difficult and tense interviews with targets of investigations. That has paid off massive dividends. Treat folks with respect – until you get a green light to drop the hammer. But don't start with the sledgehammer. Respect goes a long way. If the FBI respected my family and me no one would even know who in the hell I am. But they didn't, and this is life.

"Sharpe James is a fucking criminal, dude, why are you treating his office and staff with such courtesy?" I once asked Bruce.

"He's an interesting guy, and I want HIS story," Bruce replied. "He's not ashamed of being corrupt. It's expected of him; it's fascinating."

It never occurred to me that bad guys – criminals – they have stories too; until I became a felon and sat down to tell mine. Life is funny. Bruce was a smart guy. A pain in the ass at times, but who could blame him with a twenty-something outlier full of piss and vinegar as an understudy. He introduced me to Dick Callaghan too. That changed my life.

But these guys at my door today get it – they understand the respect. And we're off to the races, exchanging Intel in yet another city and Democrat bastion of lawlessness and graft. Speaking on Newark and Sharpe James – and Democratic circus'-- I rode many nights with the Union & Essex Counties Auto Theft Task Force – the "Wolf Pack," who scoured Newark at night for carjackers and fugitives. These guys were legit. Real tight crew. Newark was a battlefield. During one car heist gone bad a perp's mother bum rushed me in a bathrobe and hair rollers at 2 am – after her son tossed a gun on the roof of the house after stealing a car. And that was a tame bust. And we're not even talking about the infamous Newark Police crime-scene chicken incident where auto theft responded to a shooting at a chicken takeout joint. While cops were marking off a perimeter outside the restaurant -- a guy slid inside past detectives, stepped over the pool of blood and the dead body sprawled in front of the counter – and announced he was there to pick up his takeout order of two buckets.

Newark is no joke.

But back to the Feds on my doorstep – standing

in the same place where three or four FBI agents rode my back and pounded my face into the cement. And I gladly replay the play-by-play of that to these two gentlemen, and they look at me like I'm from another planet. But these Feds are asking questions about a national politician – he must be a serious target, I thought. Or someone else linked to him is in trouble. Feds don't drive two hours from HQ on a whim to talk to a journalist. In his pajamas.

We may have started something again. I just can't stay out of trouble with members of Congress. I ripped North Jersey to shreds in my twenties working for The Record. But I outgrew the place mostly because it didn't want to print the truth unless it didn't offend friends of the multi-millionaire publisher. Friends like Sen. Robert Torricelli. But that's another story for another time.

Man, I thought the Torch (Torricelli) was slick. But felon Sharpe James was right when he warned insiders in North Jersey that Cory Booker – a youngster at the time in the 1990s – would eclipse all other charlatans who came out of New Jersey politics.

I bring up Booker here to illustrate New Jersey politics and the culture of corruption. Callaghan said New Jersey was the second most corrupt state in the country, a close second to Rhode Island. Both Democrat utopias. Purely coincidental I am sure. These New Jersey politico players always seem to burn out like a quasar before they reach the big stage – presidential contention. With a little pressure and a national spotlight, a guy like Spartacus would fold faster than a Fort Lee dry cleaner. Booker may have to fake rescue himself from a burning building this time if he throws his hat into the presidential ring.

(Google it, kids.)

How do the details of the most recent fed visit fit into this book? I mean if you can't write about the Feds banging on your door when you're literally writing a book about other Feds banging on your door – you just can't make this stuff up.

The October 2018 incident with Feds proves once again, in my life, what's old is what's new still. And I live this daily. I spent years working for weekly newspapers in my late teens through my mid-twenties, literally toiling in the minor league of journalism and torching anyone in my way. I caught a break at The Record in Hackensack, but they brought me in as a news clerk, even though I had already won numerous awards by that time. So I was responsible for taking phone calls and messages for other reporters, taking shit from them as well, and writing obituaries. I knew I was better than most of the newsroom even at that time and it was a quiet, respectful confidence but I often wondered how many of these reporters got to where they were. Most of the reporters.

Here I was writing obits and taking messages for these people, but I actually enjoyed the folks I was working with. News clerks worked hard, and they were spat on for the most part. If someone needed coffee, we literally had to get them coffee. Not many asked, but there are always those people who defy human decency and abuse any power they have, no matter how small it may be. Two years later, I was running the investigative division at the newspaper. And I got my own fucking coffee and bought the news clerks donuts. And I was both liked and despised by my colleagues. "How in the hell did this guy go from writing obits to running the investigative division in two years?" That was the question that tortured many spiteful reporters. Jealousy. Envy. The newsroom is often anything but a balanced, harmonious workplace. My rise had knocked folks even further off their axis.

Of course, the answer to that question, about rising to the top, is rather simple. Hard work. And I had some talent. Not really as a writer. I've never considered myself a gifted writer because I've worked with gifted writers. But mostly hard work. And God had blessed me with a gift for finding things quickly that few could duplicate. I could earn people's trust too and that's when they tell you the good stuff. I could also spot patterns in criminal behavior and understand complex schemes rather easily. That helps when you're investigating because if you can think like a criminal, you can unravel a criminal enterprise. And I have helped unravel many a criminal enterprise. And now – thanks to my battle with the federal government -- I am a criminal, a felon. And I embrace it because being labeled that by an organization that is beyond corrupt – the definition of corruption – is undoubtedly no scarlet letter. I do, however, wear my battle scars with the FBI and DOJ with pride. I graduated from shame and stigma that comes with the process of them tearing you down as a human being – an American -- and treating you like an arch criminal. But the experience made me who I am today, and I like who I am today. And where I am. A tough journey but my family is tight, and we all survived, and now we get to punch back. Daily.

Again, little has changed. Our work at True Pundit – our breaking stories and high-profile scoops

— are rarely credited to us. Instead, right-wing media often swipe our scoops and repackage them as their own. Breitbart, Daily Caller, Fox News – the list goes on and on. And our readers know this. It is not news to them. When the MSM picks up our stories, they cite True Pundit. What does the right-wing media do? Rewrite the story to make it look like their scoop – or wait weeks and months and put it out as "breaking news." Imagine Julius Caesar gets assassinated and six months later a Roman scribe calls it "breaking news?" You just have to laugh at how insecure these folks are. THESE ARE THE SAME kind of people who hated me in the newsroom. Small people. Nothing in journalism has changed. I have to sit back and laugh.

In two years True Pundit has embarrassed the right-wing media – scooping them on too many stories to count and even beating them on breaking news. I am reliving my days in The Record's newsroom. I chalk it up to what I learned in my twenties in the newsroom and later in Intel. Some people are assholes, and some people are insecure assholes. And journalism is a magnet for both.

Regardless of the downsides, I have met some great people in journalism. Worked with some too like my old partner Jim Consoli who was like a brother to me in North Jersey. Unfortunately, some relationships go up in smoke when the FBI kicks in your door. Losing close friends is part of running this unfortunate gauntlet. There are casualties, and this is life. Some people stand beside you and others run away. There is no reason to resent those who flee. I think it's human nature in a way. For me, such personal losses motivated me more to seek justice in my own manner; legally and absent violence. This is the power the FBI and Justice Department wields over us all. If they paint you like a criminal – even a hockey tape "kingpin" as one prosecutor incredibly said – your reputation is tainted. And folks walk away from you. But I would be lying if I said there weren't friends that I do miss. There are. And this has been a cross I carried, personal guilt that I let other people down somehow. But I am laying that cross down now, stepping away from that baggage. I am who I am and if that's not good enough for friends and family – take a fucking walk. Please know that either way, I no longer care. I am free of that nonsense. Plus, my kids got a kick out of the "kingpin" label. They said KingPin is a beefy, bald-headed Marvel or D.C. comic villain, so they thought it was kind of cool at the time when they were in their early teens: Dad is a KingPin, according to the U.S. government.

I knew in high school that I wanted to be an investigative reporter and worked hard at it. I was – and I still am – a purebred bloodhound journalist. This is an ugly business, a terrible industry and a profession of guttersnipes and vagabonds who would stab you in the back for a day-old ham sandwich. I mourn real journalism and its roots daily. I came up reading the greats in New York: Breslin, Hammill, Dwyer, Deford on the sports page. I was raised in that gilded age, and now I watch people's personal brands elevated as the spokespeople and ambassadors for this profession. I watched the same thing happen at The Record when I was their coffee bitch. And I want nothing to do with the ego game, really. Nor do I need to join the media echo chamber on the Right, which is turning out to be almost as bad as the one on the Left. know I am not as good as I think I am, and I work hard every day trying to get better. I am confident and at times cocky, but I am humble enough to get up every day and work harder at this journalism thing. And now, we tackle a massive scandal because we can. We have earned that via hard work and tradecraft over 30 years. God has blessed me with this opportunity, there is no doubt.

The parallels between 'then' and 'now' are uncanny. And the irony indeed is thick. In two years I went from fetching coffee and writing obits to taking down politicians, prosecutors and running the investigative division for one of the top newspapers in the country. And winning a Loeb award and Pulitzer nominations, while many of my colleagues sat around scratching their heads and backbiting.

In two years we took a $100 investment, launched True Pundit and became a player in the media – while working in our pajamas and sweatpants. And now we unravel one of the biggest scandals in U.S history -- while many of my colleagues sit around scratching their heads and backbiting.

Very little has changed.

I still get my own coffee too.

And I'm writing another obit too -- the Deep State's.

In two years we dismantled the FBI and are now unraveling the biggest Deep State fraud in U.S. history. To my detractors in the media: What have you done to rival that? Look in the mirror, ask yourself that question. For me, there is nothing particularly notable about grinding out a career of playing it safe. Journalism and journalists have spiraled so far down in the last twenty years that politicians and entrepreneurs no longer fear them. Or respect them. So these entities – drunk on power -- run wild, and unchecked. Do you think Barack Obama feared the media? He and the members of his cartel laughed at the press. Daily.

We'll try to change that fact in the coming chapters of this book.

The checks and balances of the fourth estate -- the press -- have eroded. What's left is a self-appointed media Sanhedrin, governing both the Left and the Right, who celebrate industry-wide mediocrity and treat the outliers – independent thinkers who work hard to uncover corruption – like the hired help. But times are changing. Fast.

During my first year at a daily newspaper, one of the veterans pulled me aside and lectured me.

"Hey you need to stop walking around the newsroom like you own the place and slow down on the page-one scoops," he said. "Are you trying to make us all look bad?"

Like I said, nothing has changed in journalism, despite a 25-year hiatus. The makers make, and the takers take, even when the takers are raking in millions in print and television journalism. At least in Intel, there is some degree of honor. No wonder folks despise the media. During my career, history has proven critics of my work chronically incorrect time and time again and after 9/11 -- I no longer listen to them much. In fact, I don't even read our 'bad' press. Or negative stories about me. I know who I am so why should I read some dope's story about who he or she thinks I am. If you're writing about me in the first place – you already lost. Because it makes my group strong. I would never write about me or someone comparable when Washington D.C. is a virtual candy store of corruption with no shortage of targets. I always punch up. And I rarely punch down when focusing on an investigative target.

I learned that lesson the hard way on Sept. 11, 2001 and it still makes me uneasy just thinking about it, like a riddle inside of another riddle, it is hard to wrap my head around it.

I also learned that when you have the goods – as a journalist – and you have nailed a story, you do not have to worry about critics. The truth always has a way of rearing its head no matter how ugly it is. Nail it. Write it. Publish it. And fuck the haters. Let them dig themselves a deeper hole so that when the Intel you printed is proven true, they're in too deep to get out.

The day was Sept. 11, 1996 – exactly five years before the 9/11 attacks on the United States. I was still toiling away at The Record and in fact, I was wrapping it up – getting ready to transition into a full-time intelligence career. But during the summer of 96' I spent a large amount of time undercover at Newark International Airport working on a blowout story. Massive scoop as a follow up to the TWA Flight 800 breaking story I worked on. Through contacts and undercover work, I was able to breach any and all security protocols at the airport and its terminals. I was in baggage areas, jet cockpits, tarmac. You name it, I was there. I was so entrenched at Newark International – now called Liberty International – that the top editors of the newspaper thought I had quit the paper. But my editor knew what I was doing and we didn't really want to tip off the brass because we feared they might shut down the Op. And we had a good thing going so why ruin it by sharing the premise and progress with news bureaucrats? Like mushrooms, it is often best to keep top editors -- and top Intel bosses -- in the dark and feed them shit.

We published the story on these breaches at Newark on Sept. 11, 1996 in a story that quickly went viral nationally by 1996 standards. The FAA quickly launched an investigation. But the Port Authority of New York and New Jersey – who manages all the international airports in the New York City metro area, including Newark, took an opposite tact. They threatened to prove I had fabricated the entire story, a 1996 version of fake news. Now anyone who has to pay through the teeth to use a tunnel or bridge in North Jersey and New York City understands that Port Authority is a corrupt cartel and has been for a long time. So Port Authority brass called a sit down at their Manhattan offices the day after the story and we trekked across the George Washington Bridge to attend it to hear them out.

Their original tactic was to paint me as the problem – a rogue reporter "trying to make a name for himself" and deflect the glaring security holes at Newark, at the time the thirteenth busiest airport in the United States. They were posturing to see if I would buckle during the tense standoff at their offices and they lined up all these important executives to pepper me with questions. My editor and a newspaper lawyer were present as well. But we stood behind the story. Didn't flinch.

Port Authority officials threatened to hold a news conference in response to the article and accuse the newspaper of fabricating the story. They were going to sue as well absent a retraction and a story walking back the blowout scoop. So they said we better come clean now. Or else. And for me? My career was finished. I'll never work in New York metro again. They would see to that. Of course, this fits a pattern many guilty parties follow and Port Authority – a Democratically-run bastion of graft – was no exception. Have you seen this pattern in D.C. lately? Try the Brett Kavanaugh circus that unfolded in Senate hearings. Same tact, different spin.

Someone I was supposed to be impressed by was pontificating about my impending doom and I just blurted out:

"You should check your security camera footage. I'm sure it matched up with the video I took inside the airport and planes. So feel free to hold your press conference and I will take a copy of the video to ABC here in New York or CBS and see what they have to say about who is telling the truth."

That quickly ended their charade.

We jump ahead to the days after 9/11 – five years later in 2001 and I am working Intel, retired from journalism. I am talking to my old editor at the time and I tell him that the Newark Airport story we did was published on 9/11 -- five years before the 2001 attack. Very spooky fact, but it gets more macabre.

United Airlines Flight 93 was a passenger flight hijacked by four al-Qaeda terrorists. Supposedly targeting the White House, the plane crashed into a field in Somerset County, Pennsylvania, while passengers and crew members tried to wrestle control from the terrorists. By flight time, the plane was about 11 minutes away from Washington, D.C. Everyone on board was killed, including the four hijackers. The Boeing 757 was flying United Airlines' scheduled morning flight from Newark International Airport in New Jersey to San Francisco International Airport in California.

The plane originated in Newark, the same airport Port Authority said was safe despite my breaches of security. Hard to think about.

"Do you remember those Port Authority executives who tried to muscle us up in their offices after the story ran?" my old editor reminisced. "I wonder how many of them are dead now."

I was stunned by the comment.

I had forgotten Port Authority's headquarters-- the office we met in five years earlier -- was on the 68th floor of 1 World Trade Center. That tower was the first tower to be struck by a hijacked airplane. And the first tower to collapse. Port Authority was also the landlord for the World Trade Center.

Forty seven Port Authority employees died on Sept. 11, 2001 – including its executive director.

And 44 people died in the hijacked 757 that originated from Newark airport.

Five years to the day after my undercover Newark Airport security breach story was published.

Below is a reprint of that story:

DANGER AT THE GATE?
SECURITY GAPS WIDESPREAD AT NEWARK
The Record
By MICHAEL MOORE and DEBRA LYNN VIAL
Staff Writers
Published: September 11, 1996
Seven weeks after the crash of TWA Flight 800 first prompted President Clinton to order tighter airport security,

gaps still exist at Newark International Airport that could leave millions of passengers a year vulnerable to terrorism.

Most international airlines at the nation's 13th-busiest airport rarely X-ray or hand-search checked luggage, despite the fact that both Clinton and the Federal Aviation Administration strongly suggest that these measures could help prevent explosives from being smuggled on board.

In addition, security is so lax at the hectic international terminal that a Record reporter was easily able to wander restricted areas. Without carrying the required identification, the reporter bypassed security three times, gaining access to such sensitive areas as baggage rooms and the tarmac.

On one occasion, a security guard posted outside a restricted area was sleeping in a chair. On another, the reporter stood with his foot on the wheel of a plane, but was never questioned or told to leave by the half-dozen employees near him. Most employees just said "hello."

The reporter's easy access to the restricted areas underscores what security experts say is the most troublesome problem at Newark and elsewhere: Baggage handlers and security officers are poorly trained.

Many who have access to planes undergo rudimentary background checks rather than criminal, character, and financial screening. Low pay leads to such high turnover that some supervisors at Newark say they rarely have employees last longer than a year. And the firm hired to supply security and to X-ray carry-on baggage at the international terminal has a history of lapses at other airports, including one recent instance in which workers failed to spot a .25-caliber handgun in a woman's purse.

These loopholes raise the risk that the international hub and its 3.8 million yearly passengers can fall victim to a terrorist act.

"You can put anything you want in a suitcase and nobody

checks it out," said a baggage handler, who spoke under the condition of anonymity.

"The first day I started working here, I went home and told my parents, `You're not going to believe this, but the airlines don't check for bombs or weapons,'"

said the worker, who handles luggage for about six airlines. "I couldn't believe the bags basically go straight to the aircraft. It has always been that way here."

Little effect from Clinton plan

The lapses in security were uncovered by The Record during numerous firsthand inspections of the airport and interviews with dozens of security experts, airline and airport employees, and officials.

They include some of the same concerns that Clinton addressed Monday when he released a $429 million plan to improve air safety. But most of the problems found at Newark would not be corrected under Clinton's plan.

Officials at the Port Authority of New York and New Jersey, which manages the airport, declined to comment on security in general, and refused to address such specific issues as The Record's ability to enter restricted areas.

"We defer comments to the airlines on this," said Port Authority spokeswoman Gwen Williams. The FAA mandates that airlines handle security directly related to passengers, including luggage screening.

Citing security concerns, most airline officials also declined to comment in detail. "It's very secure, and we do have tight security measures there," said Barbara Vente, coordinator of marketing services for Swissair. "I can assure you it's safe."

Newark has made some improvements in security since 230 people perished in July's fiery explosion of TWA Flight 800 off Long Island just minutes after taking off from John F. Kennedy International Airport. Following Clinton's orders for all airports, Newark no longer allows curb-side baggage check-

in on international flights, and has airline employees inspecting cabins and cargo holds of planes before takeoff.

In the first frightening days after the crash, Newark Airport also closed the underground parking garage and increased scrutiny of the 10,500 international passengers and their bags that leave on some 90 flights each day. But these heightened actions were temporary and recently have been relaxed to pre-crash standards. The garage has reopened, and scrutiny has lessened.

Although federal investigators have not determined what brought down Flight 800, they say the most likely theory is a bomb smuggled onto the 747.

But only a handful of the 28 airlines that fly to international destinations from Newark X-ray all check-in luggage, said airline officials, baggage handlers, and officials of the three subcontractors hired to handle baggage for most of the airlines.

Among the airlines that routinely X-ray all check-in baggage are British Airways, Virgin Atlantic, El Al Israel Airlines, United, and Korean Air.

Those that don't according to the subcontractors and the airlines themselves range from smaller lines such as Alitalia and Air Jamaica to Continental, Newark's largest international carrier, which flies approximately 100,000 passengers abroad a month.

Although many passengers may believe their check-in luggage undergoes inspection when it leaves their hands, the FAA only recommends that airlines X-ray such baggage. There is no requirement, even on international flights, agency officials said.

John Lampl, a spokesman for British Airways, said he's surprised that most airlines choose not to X-ray their check-in baggage at Newark.

"At an international airport, everything should be X-

rayed, and we

X-ray carry-on and check-in luggage," Lampl said. "When it comes to safety issues, we don't nickel-and-d 2491051ime here. It's just too important."

"For an international flight, luggage should be screened," agreed Marty Salsen, senior vice president of the International Airline Passengers Association, a 400,000-member group that represents consumer interests on airline safety and other issues.

Baggage at other major airports receives much more scrutiny. All bags headed for international destinations from John F. Kennedy Airport, the nation's eighth-largest, are X-rayed, said high-ranking airline security officials working there. Likewise, security experts say comprehensive screening is standard practice at Chicago's O'Hare, the nation's busiest airport.

In contrast, the X-ray technology available in Newark's baggage areas is often unused. Once, when a Record reporter entered a secured baggage area, a large X-ray machine sat idle and covered with gray tarpaulins while hundreds of bags were being loaded, unscrutinized, on flights to Europe.

"That's not a good practice," said Lampl of British Airways, the primary user of the machine. "If it's an issue of expense for other airlines, the cost can be factored into the ticket price."

But other people say some airports need stricter security measures than others. JFK, for example, is considered a more popular potential target for terrorists and always has had tighter regulations than Newark, which has never been a victim of terrorism.

Many airline officials also believe that X-ray machines will do little to keep a bomb off the plane because they can't detect plastic explosives. Despite widespread agreement in the industry that high-tech bomb detectors for luggage are imperative, the FAA has continually failed to meet a *congressional timeline to install the advanced technology.*

That timetable was sparked by the terrorist bombing of Pan Am Flight 103 over Lockerbie, Scotland. That plane was destroyed by a suitcase bomb constructed of plastic explosives.

High-tech sensors are now being tested at airports in Atlanta and San Francisco, and Clinton has asked Congress for $20 million to increase the FAA's research budget. But the FAA has not formally embraced the technology for use in all major airports, and the powerful airline and airport lobbies have successfully fought such a measure because of added expense.

Most airline officials declined to comment on whether they X-ray or why they don't, saying any disclosure could provide ammunition for would-be terrorists.

"We do have other means of security screening that are not apparent," said Karla Villalom, a Continental spokeswoman who said the airline does not have facilities to routinely X-ray baggage.

"On security matters, we don't talk about specific policies," said Richard Martin, a United spokesman.

Both United and Continental, following FAA regulations for international flight, track passengers and their luggage: If the passenger doesn't get on the plane, the bag is removed. A directive issued Monday by Clinton would extend the baggage matching to domestic flights.

But this system is far from perfect, said an official whose company handles baggage for seven airlines: "If this was done properly, you'd never have any lost luggage, would you?"

FAA officials also refused to talk about X-rays or security at Newark, and stuck instead to scripted answers one official called "crib sheets."

"While the FAA cannot comment on the details of any specific measure, the FAA requires that all items transported on board a commercial passenger aircraft flying overseas be

subjected to intense screening and other control methods," said David R. Hinson, FAA administrator on aviation security.

Luggage left unguarded

But even beyond the scope of X-raying, other security measures at Newark's international terminal are questionable .

Once baggage leaves a passenger's hand, it moves by conveyor belt through the terminal on a short journey to one of several restricted baggage rooms. There, the luggage revolves on large steel carousels until it is loaded onto carts for transport to the awaiting jetliner.

No one guards the conveyor belt or the carousels for the majority of flights. Often, baggage is left unattended, numerous baggage handlers said. During one 20-minute period when a reporter walked around one baggage room, luggage from a pending flight was left revolving on a carousel while baggage handlers worked in a different part of the loading area.

The doors to the restricted areas have locks, but so many personnel are coming and going that it is easy to walk inside. Many doors have combination keypad locks, but the access codes are the same for the entire terminal, said employees who use the areas. Get that number, and you can get anywhere.

The Record reporter who walked into an area full of luggage did not have the identification badge issued by U.S. Customs that employees in restricted areas are required to wear on their lapels. On one occasion, a Port Authority security official was present but never questioned why an unidentified man without credentials was in the baggage area.

The FAA is well aware that such security breaches are possible.

In 1993 and 1995, undercover teams of federal investigators sidestepped security at a number of undisclosed major airports in the country. The investigators carried no ID but still managed to work their way into secure areas and onto empty aircraft, according to two recent reports by the U.S.

Department of Transportation, the FAA's boss.

During the 1993 sweep, one undercover agent carried a deactivated hand grenade undetected through a metal detector. The federal agents infiltrated 15 secure areas out of 20 attempts. In one instance, an investigator left a note for the flight crew in the cockpit.

"Right now, there are huge holes in security at every airport," said Salsen, of the International Airline Passengers Association."Luggage, cargo can get through. There are more people than ever with access to an airport."

One major problem, sources said, is that workers are poorly trained on security issues.

According to internal airline memos obtained by The Record, ticket agents at Newark have been specifically instructed to question travelers who pose the highest security risk. The agents have a checklist of sorts to determine which passengers meet that profile. But they were given no training in how to ask these questions or how to properly "profile" a potential terrorist.

Normally, when ticket agents notify supervisors that a passenger meets the "profile" of a terrorist, the passenger's luggage is hand-searched.

Ticket agents also have been instructed by the FAA to beckon a supervisor if a passenger's passport bears the stamp of Iran, Iraq, Libya, Sudan, Syria, Cuba, or North Korea. But both mandates have gone largely ignored at Newark, several sources said.

"Customers get frustrated because they think you are trying to accuse them of something," said a ticket agent who asked not to be identified. "So it's easier to not question them. Because of that reason, most of us don't."

And pay of less than $6 an hour, many ticket agents said, is not compensation enough to endure irate passengers who feel their privacy is being violated.

The low pay among ticket agents, baggage handlers, and other personnel causes high turnover and confusion.

"The training is bad and the pay is horrible," said one security official responsible for a half-dozen airlines. "So they get high turnover. You can't get dependable people that way. You're handing your bag to someone who's been here for a week. The guy who's telling him what to do has been here a month. I see it all the time. Maybe the guy wants to do a good job, but he doesn't know how."

The International Airline Passengers Association has been arguing for years that these workers need better training and pay.

"We feel these people shouldn't be minimum-wage earners with a turnover of six months," Salsen said. "They're being told to profile passengers. I can't imagine those people have the experience or training to be able to profile the right type of people.

"These people get a week of training class and are scanners. I was at a Denver airport and they were spot-checking people," he said. "They went through the bags of two college females, and I seriously doubt they were a security risk. I'm sure they did it to talk to them."

Salsen's group also has been critical of the skimpy background checks done on many employees who have access to planes or baggage. People such as ticket agents or anyone with access to the interior of an airplane must endure stringent screening that includes fingerprinting and criminal background checks. But for others including those who work in restricted areas who could gain access to the airplane the only requirement is that they be asked about pre 2491052vious employment, said many employees who underwent the checks.

In his directive Monday, Clinton ordered the FAA to require criminal background checks and fingerprint records for all airport and airline employees who have access to secure areas.

Tighter screening is more important than ever because airlines have less control today over who has contact with the plane. At Newark, most airlines have contracted with companies to run their entire operation, from ticketing passengers to preparing the planes to handling the baggage.

Contracting all the services required to get a flight off the ground means the security risk is enhanced, security experts said. It takes as many as 80 people to service an aircraft, including mechanics, maintenance crews, and caterers.

"Get one of these jobs and you can get inside," said George Lenz, vice president of the Sigma Group, a corporate security firm in New York City.

Federal investigators are examining the possibility that TWA Flight 800 was brought down by a bomb smuggled aboard the food cart.

Investigators also are examining the effectiveness of airline and airport security at Kennedy Airport, said a TWA security official who spoke to The Record under the condition of anonymity.

"Some of the [federal] agents have commented about how confusing the security operation is with all the different companies and parties involved," the official said.

One firm's record of risk

The picture at Newark is no different. The Port Authority is responsible for the public areas of the airport, including the roadways, runways, public lobbies, parking lots, taxi drop-offs, tarmac, and anything along the perimeter of the airfield. According to FAA regulations, airlines must purchase X-ray detection systems and hire security to screen passengers and patrol the restricted areas of the airport.

At Newark, Gateway Security of Newark was hired by the Port Authority to guard the tarmac. But the bulk of the security workers, including those in uniform who X-ray carry-on baggage at detectors leading to the gates, are employees of International Total Services Inc., an Ohio-based contractor with a history of security lapses at other airports.

In June, ITS airport guards at Albany Airport apparently failed to spot a .25-caliber gun concealed in a Pennsylvania woman's purse as she inadvertently carried it through a security checkpoint, according to the FAA and airport officials. After realizing she had the gun, the woman notified ITS guards, who at first refused to believe her.

In February, local officials said a disabled hand grenade fell out of a bag that had been checked by ITS security at an airport in Islip, N.Y., startling passengers. In August 1994, two ITS officials working at Tampa International Airport were arrested by the FBI after federal officials said they made off with $2 million in Federal Reserve Bank cash from an airplane.

It is unclear whether ITS, which was hired by all of Newark's international airlines and many domestic carriers, has encountered problems in Newark. ITS officials declined several requests for interviews, and Port Authority officials have continually refused to release any information about incidents with employees at Newark airport.

"You don't lay out what you do in the public anymore because you don't want to give anybody a primer," said John Kampfe, a Port Authority spokesman.

Aviation security experts, industry officials, and airline personnel at Newark all criticize the airlines' practice of farming out security work. They believe that airport security personnel should have law enforcement or military training and experience and that these security workers should be responsible for all ramps, cargo, baggage, and passenger checks. Bomb-sniffing dogs might help, too, until the better sensors are available in all airports.

"The biggest problem is the security force being used at

airports," Lenz said. "You can have the best equipment in the world, but it's just a hunk of equipment if the person who's operating it isn't trained. The people who do the screening at airports are among the lowest-paid around. They get training, but it's not sophisticated training."

A security official for a half-dozen airlines in the international terminal at Newark agreed.

"I wouldn't hire these guys to protect me," he said.

4 RETURN TO THE CRADLE OF LIBERTY

I am sitting outside the Liberty Bell, Independence Hall, FBI and the National Constitution Center in Philadelphia on a sweltering and humid night in August. I am with Jason Goodman, a friend who runs CrowdSource the Truth and we are prepping for my first 'on camera' appearance.

I have managed to keep my identity secret for more than two years but now I am going public. Mostly to silence critics and allow readers to know I am not done wreaking havoc on the FBI and DOJ and – to be honest – it's too complicated to run a news organization from the shadows. So, it is time to come out and into the sunlight.

I liked this interview so much because I was in a good mood and just talking straight. And I said many things I would have to rewrite in this book, so I decided to just take most of the transcript from the interview. The key parts. Goodman always gets me to say too much. He has evolved into a real pro.

MOORE: So I thought this would be a good place to start because this area was really an important area for the creation of True Pundit. I used to come here and just kind of chill out. This is Independence Mall and, Independence Hall's down there. The Liberty Bell when you opened up, the FBI building is there too -- some friends of mine, and the FBI and the DOJ, and then over there is the National Constitution Center, which speaks for itself.

Yeah, so welcome to Philadelphia.

GOODMAN: Yeah, man Michael, good to finally have you on camera.

Moore: They let me out of the cage, out of the box, and back in the weight room. You know, get things back together. I feel good man. I feel really good. I feel, you know, it's---I'm not going to minimize law enforcement or anything like that, but it is tough being undercover for like two years or two months.

Goodman: You feel a sense of relief?

Moore: Man. I really, I just, it feels good. You know, it's like, all right, now I don't have to do X, Y and Z, and we don't have to worry about X, Y, and Z. We can just be us and also feel that there's so many things I want to do, you know, if I want to go get somebody's face I can go get somebody's face, it's not like, "hey buddy, who are you"? and then I have to slink away or something like that. You know what I mean?

Goodman: It's going to change the style of reporting that you're able to do it at True Pundit?

Moore: Well, I think a lot of things are going to change. Some advertisers were holding money back. 'Well, we don't know who these guys are. What's this guy's story?' Then we had some morons in DC saying, oh, this guy, these guys are Russian bots. I still don't know what that means. The only Russian bots we know in Philly was in Rocky IV when he was fighting Drago. It's the closest we get to Russians around here. But no, I used to come down here, and that's the FBI building here, and then this is another federal building. This is where they (FBI) take you at, the big building there, where they take you at seven in the morning when they come into your house with guns pointed at your kids and decide that, you know, you're an arch criminal because you had a hobby and a side business or a consortium of people that were trading hockey videos, and had hockey websites, with highlights and things like that. This is where they bring you. They won't bring somebody like Hillary Clinton here. They won't bring somebody like Bill Clinton to a federal building and things like that. They bring the little guys who they can just squeeze.

Goodman: Hockey videos are worse than rape and destroying countries?

Moore: I mean, if you have a list of priorities of what the Department of Justice thinks, yeah, you know, you have this, our country is, is out of control with corruption and most of it comes from the top of Justice. They won't do anything about these big cases, but they find a little case and they will just squeeze you and try to destroy you.

Goodman: To me it wasn't about hockey videos obviously.

Moore: Well, they're going to make it like hockey videos. Oh, you know, it's funny. I wanted to go to trial. I was like, we're going to kick the shit out of these people at trial because I've done trial prep professionally, right? For other people. My lawyers were saying things look pretty good. Everything looks good. My wife said – you know this went on for eight years. Eight fucking years.

Q: So the lawyer costs and everything must have been outrageous.

A: No, no, it wasn't that. It wasn't bad because I figured out how to win in that category. We'll talk about that later, but my wife said I was talking to her once, telling her things are going really good. I just came back from Philadelphia. Great Attorney Kathy Henry few blocks over. She's a fantastic attorney. I said, Kathy thinks everything is great, and my wife said, "This has gone on long enough. You got to tie it off".

Q: She wanted you to end it?

A: I said what do you mean man? I mean, we're ready to rock and roll. This is a bullshit case, and she said, no, enough is enough.

Q: Too much toll on the family.

A: It's too much toll on the family. They (FBI) know that when you look at the Mike Flynn case, when Mike Flynn's family, they squeeze you. Now, Mike -- Mike had to pay for his legal fees so they squeeze you, right, and they ruin you financially. I mean he had to sell his house.

Q: That's crazy.

A: He's, you know, that's crazy, and, but I, I think from talking to people that are in the know, I haven't talked to the general myself but I've talked to some pretty close people. His wife said that's it...that's it. No, because in his case Mueller says, oh, let's go after the kid. Let's go after Mike Jr. That's like, well, and then the mom steps in and says, hey, a "mom's instinct" kicks in. No, no, no, no. This has gone on long enough. Cut the deal and get it over with. So for me, coming back down here (to Philly), right now, especially, it's like a dream come true.

Q: Wow, so because you're out of jeopardy, you mean?

A: Well, I'm out of jeopardy, but we've taken our resources, and our knowledge, and our angst -- there is angst -- by a lot of ex-federal agents, current federal agents, and we've turned the tides against these people. Right now, my life isn't in jeopardy, my life isn't coming unglued. Their life is on the ropes. I'm not on the ropes. I didn't do anything wrong. I've led a pretty good life. Everybody makes mistakes, right? I've made some mistakes, but it took the whole situation with the Feds for me to really say, all right, well we're going to come up with something to change things in a legal way. We're not going to do anything violent or anything crazy and threaten people. We're going to use what we have. National Constitution Center gives us the Constitution, which gives us freedom of the press, right?

Q: Well, sort of.

A: Well, First Amendment, so we're going to use that. So, I went back to what I had learned in college, and what I had worked in mainstream media, and I'm not blowing my own horn. I was pretty talented at it, right at an early age, and then I got out, I went into different things. I said, well, I'm at rock bottom after the legal case. They take your money. They take your job – I had a great job at Citigroup, good job. I was good at that too.

Q: You were doing fraud investigations for CitiGroup and probably at Citi the second anything comes up I would presume ...

A: You would think that, but Citi was really good to me, like they knew about this was going on and they were like, look, this isn't some kind of capital crime. This is some kind of rinky-dink thing. So, Citi while this was all going on, supported me really well, and I was surprised by that, right? And then Citi -- we did work for an affiliate, Our group at Citi got bought by another big company. They were great too, but I came down here for sentencing, and this is a great story. There's a lot of shitty stories in this whole thing, but this is a great story. So, the guy who was my judge his name was judge Schiller. An older guy, you know, really smart. Thank God for this guy because these jack asses wanted to put me away for 35 years.

Q: For hockey video?

A: Yeah, for hockey videos.

Q: What was it? Was it even like the NHL?

A: No, the NHL made a big stink about it, and they said I made all this money, you know, half a million dollars or something like that.

Q: Is that true?

A: It's not true. What had netted out, the judge had figured out with his people. This is probably a $40,000 beef over eight years.

Q: So why isn't it just a civil...?

A: It's basically $5,000 a year.

Q: But why isn't it just the NHL suing you for damages for that money? Why is it...?

A: Right, anyhow, you're getting ahead of the story. So, Judge Schiller says in court to the US attorney, -- they brought a US attorney from Washington D.C. too. It had nothing to do with Philadelphia. These guys were told to take the case out of Washington. The FBI was told to take the case out of Washington.

Q: Do you ever do anything in Washington? Sell the videos in Washington?

A: No, it came from the DOJ headquarters, the whole thing. So that tells you exactly what, what the hell is going on. If it was an organic case here, it would have started here, but instead, it started in Washington. So, there were two US attorneys in the courtroom and the judge said -- I'll never forget it. The judge said, "what did this guy do to the Department of Justice to be treated this way?" They were like, "Oh, I don't know, your Honor, what are you talking about? Oh, you must be ..." And the judge was like was like, look, I've been here a little while, and know what's going on. Earlier he had said, it was interesting, Judge Schiller said, I was at a Christmas party and every judge in the eastern district – that's all of Philly federal court -- came up to me and said, what is this piece of shit case in your courtroom where they're going after this guy for criminal copyright infringement?

Q: Two U.Ss Attorneys? How frequently do two U.S. Attorneys get involved?

A: The whole thing is anyhow, it's obvious what happened, right? So, they turn your life upside down. So, it was a big, big moment in my life where I could take a step back. They take everything, house, money, job, and the most incredible part – why I really got upset beyond the kids being threatened with the gun twice in my house. The day I was sentenced was the day I got home. My boss called and said, hey man, I can't do anything. We had to let you go, and I said, that's fine? My boss was a great guy. Still a good friend. I don't burn bridges professionally. I don't burn a bridge. He said this guy from the FBI called HR (human resources). He said you were sentenced. He made a big stink with HR. So, then he (FBI agent) called my boss after that and said, how long is it going to be employed for, and all this stuff. He went out of his way to make sure I got fired, but this is the best part. He asked my boss what they're doing with my job and what the qualifications are to work there.

Q: He was trying to get hired?

A: He was trying to get fucking hired in my job. You can't make this stuff up. It's completely insane, and so I was saying to my boss, are you kidding me? I mean, I mean my boss was a good guy. We played hockey together a long time you know, hockey teams, and we'd go hunting together and stuff like that. He's like, I can't even, I don't even know what to tell you. It's the weirdest whole string of events. Anyhow, I had to come down here (to Philadelphia) when I had to go over there (federal building) and play grab ass with these people and I would just sit and figure things out (in park near Liberty Bell), and this is where I came up with Thomas Paine thing. Because I'm sitting here and Independence Halls is in the back. Ben Franklin's hang out is back there and everything, you know, and where they signed the Constitution. And I came down here once and it was really crowded in the daytime. (Federal probation) is like you have to be here a certain time. So I come down here and there's nowhere to park. So the National Constitution Center had just kind of opened up, and they had this big parking sign. You go down into the parking garage, right? So there's a guy there like an attendant and the little shack. So, I pulled up and he came out, I rolled the window down. He said, "are you on the list"? I say "yeah, I think so." And he said, "Are you, Mr. Paine?" I'm not kidding, and I said, yeah, I'm Mr. Paine because I was running late. You know when you're under their thumb (FBI, Federal probation), if you're not there at a certain time, it's like, it's almost like you robbed a bank, right? It's like, "why weren't you here? Yeah, you have to wait for an hour and a half when you're here, but you have to be here on time."

So, I started laughing. I went home, I told my wife, I said, I guess I'm Mr. Paine now. So whenever I came down -- but you to pay to park, you didn't get anything for free -- but every time it came down I was like, yeah, Mr. Paine? "Oh yeah, come on in." So, I always parked at the National Constitution Center and then when we came up with this, uh, operation True Pundit I said: "I'm going to be Mr. Paine" because this is where it all started.

So, Thomas Paine came to Philadelphia in 1774. So, that's why I'm Thomas 1774 Paine because on Twitter because this is where it all started. So, that's kind of the genesis of, of this particular spot, you know, it's like the Bermuda Triangle to me really in a way. It's a National Constitution Center. You got Independence Hall and the Liberty Bell, and then you have the FBI and the federal buildings. And so it's really a microcosm of the whole story. I mean, you couldn't put these buildings together any better, right? And to illustrate my story, my struggle, it's crazy.

Q: Well, I'm realizing now why you were so adamant that we don't do this on Skype.

A: You know, why? Because everything we've done has been planned and thought out, and strategized, upside down and sideways. Two years ago, I say a year ago, when we got on a roll we knew that I would be outed eventually if I didn't come out of myself. So I said, well when that happens, we're going to do the shot down here (in Philadelphia). We're going to do a shot right down there because that's what I want to do because it gets so much more of the story than just being on Skype, you know, sitting on Skype, and it really is incredible when I come down here now, to know what a difference a few years makes or what way your life could go. Crazy.

Q: So I think a lot of people were pretty shocked yesterday when the surprise news came out and they didn't necessarily, nobody knew, obviously this story of ... let's take it back for a second because let's say you were selling, I mean, you've told us you were selling VHS tapes of hockey games.

Yeah, we traded and we sold games, absolutely.

Q: Okay. So ...

A: They weren't copywritten, but that's okay, that's a whole other story.

Q: Even if they were, even if it was a copyright violation, even if you stole those things, like why is somebody like Imran Awan being handled with such kid gloves, and you with hockey videos they're breaking in your house, pointing guns at your wife, your children. Why did they just show up with an FBI badge and handcuff you?

A: They never came to the house and talked to me or anything like that. It was just boom. I got indicted. There was never any like, you Imran, this whole drawn out stuff for Imran. I can't talk for Imran. You know, the guy's a Democrat is well connected. I was... I was a contractor, federal contractor. We did a lot of work for a lot of people, and I wasn't connected. I was connected to some people. I'm working on a book. People are like, well, what the hell did they come to your house for? What is all this for anyway? I'm going to tell people what it's all for. It's a shocking thing, and they wanted me to shut up, right? That's what this whole thing was about and I'm not the only person they did this too. Other people who knew (the reason Feds were harassing me) were damaged in different ways. That's a campaign to shut us up because we found out some things we shouldn't have, and here's the problem. A lot of times you find out stuff you shouldn't have and you just kind of gloss over it, but I was like, this is too crazy to be true. So I started like, researching because I'm thinking if this is true, what I found out -- I shouldn't be working for these people. These are not the kind of people I want to work for.

Q: So let's, let's clarify something because I think that

I'm guilty of perpetuating some rumors because although you and I have met in person before, and I knew your name and aspects of this story, there were a lot of things about you that I didn't know. There were details about the story and there's details that I still don't know, and I think that I got the idea and maybe shared this with people incorrectly that you had been a law enforcement officer that worked for the DEA.

A: We worked for the DEA, sure.

Q: But as a contractor or investigator?

A: They come to us when they needed stuff. We had an expertise. We can get information anywhere on anybody fast. We built an incredible network. When you look back when you read all this stuff about Fusion GPS, that's 2016 and 2018 everybody's talking about Fusion GPS. We were the first ones. We were the first Fusion GPS. Except we didn't tinker around and try to mess with the elections and set people up and things like that.

Q: But I think most people equate Fusion GPS with making crap up.

A: Well, Fusion GPS, they might, you know, they've definitely had an arm to do that, but they also investigated people. A Fusion GPS would subcontract with somebody like us. Fusion GPS probably would have been a client, and they come to us and say, we got $25,000, give us everything you got on this guy, and then we'd go to work.

Q: And then if they don't think that that's sufficient, then they embellish, they make things up. They...

A: We're just one source. They might have, they might have 10 or 15 sources. They come to us. We have an expertise, right? We had an expertise in telecommunications, right? We had a lot of expertise in telecommunications and finances, right? If you were doing something crazy with your finances we would know about it, we had contacts. If you were just calling people you shouldn't have been calling or calling strange people, we would find out about it because we had a lot of contacts. Former guys who made a career in telecommunications. Former guys who made a career in banking and things like that, and finances. So, they will come to us for that. Now, if they want somebody tailed, they'd go to somebody else. We didn't do surveillance. We didn't like hide the bushes and stuff. We did all our, our digging was electronic but we would find stuff nobody else could find because that's what you had to do when I was a reporter coming up and that's what made me stand out my career, stand out from the other slobs in the newsroom. And I call them slobs because that's exactly what they were, and they still, nothing has changed since I -- well, a lot has really changed about journalism, but, these slobs are still in the newsroom and worse, and they don't do anything. They only can do something that somebody hands them. There's very little digging going on. I mean, look at how lopsided the media is when it comes to the Left – it's like it's a candy store, like what are you waiting for? Obviously, now we know the answer, right? They're (the Left media) corrupt, so, there's nothing and they're not waiting for anything. This is how they are. I would sit around and think like, dude, this is your beat. You have a national security beat, why aren't you covering the FBI? What are you doing? If it was the way it was -- it was better than the 1990's. Now it's like "Oh yeah, did you see that story Breitbart or True Pundit did"? Well, yeah. Fake News.

Q: Well, they seem determined to have people believe that True Pundit is fake news. Even yesterday, the story was that your scoop on the Chinese having hacked Hillary Clinton's server -- a certain failing pile of garbage according to the president and me and I agree with him. The (Buzzfeed) said that that was fake news. But in fact, we find out today that came from the inspector general. You guys had that scope two months ago?

A: Over six weeks ago. Yeah, we took a lot of heat from it. Some of these quote-unquote fact checkers came out, and said, oh, that's not what happened. It's like; how the fuck do you know what happened?

Q: James Comey says that it was an unsecured server and very likely had been accessed by a multitude of foreign parties.

A: I don't. I mean, it's specifically about this story. I don't know what Comey said. I thought we had enough to go on. With us, it's very different than the way things are set up now with other media places. If I feel we have enough to go on, and it stands on its own there. Our sources are pretty good. It flies, man.

Goodbye, it's out the door and it's in print, right? These other places, they hymn, and haw, "I don't know, Let's talk to the lawyers, Let's do all this," right? That's great, but you're missing the boat, okay. I mean, that's a big story, and we took a beating on it. Now it comes out today and we probably get no credit for it, but here's the thing, right? This is a more important angle to talk about. People know what is going on, they're not dummies are dummies, whether you're left or right or conservative or not, or a liberal or in the middle. If you read something somewhere six weeks ago, you're going to say, "hey, I saw that six weeks ago with these guys (True Pundit) and it's pretty good." But when you keep reading things in True Pundit and a year later, two years, 15 months later, three weeks later, you see it other places, eventually, you're like "wait a minute, these guys are pretty good." You know what I mean? Well, let's go read these guys. Everybody's slamming these guys. Now they're saying that the guy who helped, you know, one of the founders is an arch criminal. Well, wait a minute. What about all these other people in the media? What about the New York Times chick who's whoring around with the source? Sex for journalism. I mean, what about all this? There are so many instances of professional malfeasance in journalism. What about these people? Oh, they get a free pass because they're the New York Times.

Q: What about the fact that the crime that you were, you know ... I guess what it was you pled guilty to? It was a minor thing that they, they basically got you in a position where you had no choice. I mean normally that's the kind of thing where it seems, you know, you always see that FBI warning on a VHS tape, but how many people?

A: There's never been another case. There's never been a criminal case, a copyright infringement.

Q: Really?

A: No, not like this, for trading and selling DVDs. There's never been one. That's what the judge and that's what the court told us, but that was a couple of years ago. I don't know what's happened since, right? The deal is this, right? It's a coming of age story for me because I was always on the other side. We're digging up dirt on for people or we're helping out certain agencies, and they're tracking people and kicking their doors and fucking up their lives, and who knows, maybe messing with their kids at gunpoint, right? I don't. I don't know that. When you're on the other side of the door, it's like, wait a minute, this is what you guys are doing with the Intel we're giving you?. This is it, I mean, and I'm talking about some arch-criminals that we helped background. This is what you're doing -- you're attacking -- you terrorize the entire family in the dark? That's what the Constitution is about, right? So, to flip everything now you're on the other side of the door, the other side of the table in the courtroom. Defendants on the left, prosecutors on the right. When you flip the sides of the courtroom, you go to the left and you're on the other side of the door that's coming in at you, and they have guns at your family. It gives you a perspective that few people probably have that I was able to say, hey, we need to do something about these people because if they're doing it to us, they're doing it to other people. Now we find out they do it to a lot of people. They do it to their own people.

Q: Oh yeah. Well, we've heard that from Robyn Gritz. We've heard that...

A: Robyn is a perfect example, and she's a great patriot, and she texted me yesterday after all this stuff started breaking, and she said, I think it says "fucking go, baby go". Because she knows me. She knew who I was beforehand. I told her everything. We were down in DC. I told her. She was outraged, and I think she's a very sensible person, and she was outraged, man. And I was like —when I left -- I was like, God damn, she was really mad.

Q: It's probably bringing back feelings for her. She got railroaded out of there too.

A: Not only that, there are stand-up people in the FBI, and there are stand up people in these agencies that have had it with the way things are done. When they treated me that way, these guys in Philly had to dance because it came up from DC. Even one of the agents told me, during the process, he was like, man, this is bad. It was bad.

Q: Who is the director?

A: Mueller, yeah. The agent said, "What they've done to you is bad." We even had two agents who told wife during the first raid -- you ready for this? "You have a lovely kitchen and a lovely home." My wife, she comes in, and she pulls me aside. She says, is this some television show I don't know about. She literally said that and she's like, is this some kind of weird television show that you arranged like that we're on.

Q: Like getting punk'd

A: That was completely insane, and then my wife was upstairs trying to console the kids because they just had guns pointed at their fucking heads.

Q: How old were the boys at the time?

A: 12 and 8.

Q: Do they recount their memories? What do they say about that?

A: I mean, it goes both ways because now my kids are older, right? So, and we break a lot of balls cause we're from Philly. Everybody breaks balls down here. So, it goes from dad that's kinda fucked up to -- if you're watching a movie and the FBI warning comes on they're like "Aw dad, man better watch out. They really mean it." Which is really cool. It's funny. Even though I'm getting my balls busted it's good. It's a good zinger. So, but the problem was for a lot of years, whenever somebody knocks on the door....

Q: nervous as hell kids, right?

A: That's right. It could be anybody. UPS.....

Q: Makes them not trust law enforcement.

[A: They do trust law enforcement because I told them even when they were small, look, your dad's got a dispute literally right there. Dad's got a dispute with these guys. It's all going to be worked out -- specifically told them this in front of (FBI) them. These are not bad people. We just don't see things that eye-to-eye right now. Eventually, it will be cleared out, but they're not bad people, they're just doing their job. And they're not really bad people when they come into your house and do that in a certain way because they've been told to do it by some fucking asshole sitting up on the top floor (of the FBI) like in DC, right? A lot of these FBI agents who did stuff -- rank-and-file guys -- were just taking orders. So that is true? They're not bad people. They're just doing things that they shouldn't be doing and I know people are gonna say, Oh, you're defending them because it's reality. I mean, it's reality. So, back to the other thing is, yeah, somebody knocks on the door. They freak out. Especially my youngest guy at the time, he has special needs, anxiety, and depression.

Q: So how's he doing now?

A: He's doing better now. But see they (FBI) knew this because the first time they came in and I lawyered up, everything's, you know, you're talking to them and stuff (negotiating). They knew this (he had special needs), they knew this, but they still came fucking back (with guns)...

Q: Because they're pressing your buttons.

A: They still came back, and they sent him over the edge. I mean, did they bloodied me in front of him, right. He was 11at the time (he was eight during the first FBI raid.)

Q: That's shocking for a kid.

A: They drug me out of the house, beat me down. I'm not complaining too much, but my face was bleeding pretty good. Anytime you get cut in the face it looks like, you know, you're in a WWF wrestling movie or something, but he's 11 freaked out, and they're trying to break the door down. You know, I'm making him breakfast...

Q: Why not just knock?

A: Here's the deal. They knock on the door, right? You know, it's the fucking FBI. Nobody knocks on the door like that unless they're crazy or some kind of late night party got out of contra, and I'm like, as soon as I hear the knocking I'm thinking: Shit, okay, they're back because I know right in my head. Right away. He (my son) is freaked out because of the noise. He's 11. So I give him a hug, and I'm like: come on buddy, everything's all right. I'm hugging him. They could see right through the windows, and I'm hugging, right, but because I don't open the door right away, they try to break it down. So, I come over to the door. What the fuck are you guys doing? I'm right here. I'm like this, you know, right here. Pull up my shirt right here. (hands up, pulling shirt up to show no gun or weapon) I opened the door. You would think they would be like, okay man, we're here to arrest you or something like that.

Q: Punched you?

A: Well, I got three guys on my back taking me outside, rubbing my face against the cement. My kid is down the hallway. It's a straight shot from the front door to the family room, and he's just like--- I got up, and I got a glance of the kid, my youngest son and he's just a mess -- just brutal.

Q: That's just shocking for a kid. So we've been talking a lot about the hockey videos, but I want to emphasize that that obviously wasn't the motivation. It was what you had learned in your investigations as a contractor with federal agencies that they wanted to silence.

A: The problem is I push things a little bit too much sometimes, you know, I admit that, and uh, I've always been that way though. If I find something out, I want to find out what's going on specifically. I know this is gonna sound crazy, but kind of like religion, I was born and raised a Roman Catholic, right? So, I have a certain set of values that I like to try to maintain. Doesn't always work out right. But was telling my wife at the time … she's always like, "Why don't you tell me anything? Why don't you tell me anything, why don't you tell me anything for like 20 years (about Intel)." So, I'm like, you don't want to know.

Q: It's for her safety.

A: Well she's just ... you don't need to carry around certain baggage, right? So, I told her: there's some heavy shit going on, man. I think, uh, I can't work for these people (Feds) anymore if it's true. So, I want to investigate and see if it's true. If somebody gives me a big story like that, I'm going to -- just as a journalist -- I'm going to investigate it because ... I can't explain it. It's Something inside me, that's just the way it is.

Q: And you don't want to take it on face value. You want confirmation?

A: Not only do I want confirmation, right? But I'm working for the Feds. I got my own crew, right? I can worry about them in certain situations now because if I know about this stuff what does that jeopardize them? What if we take a job and if there's something nefarious going on? I have to know about that. And then there's part of me that will always be a journalist no matter what, who says, Hey, this is a pretty good story. I want to know more about it, and like I said, I can't explain why I'm like that. I just am like that. It's just like, let's see, let's get to the bottom of it. So you start poking around about it, and all trouble breaks loose. A lot of trouble obviously, right? To shut me up. But we've come back full circle. Because I'm right back to the same story. I'm going to fucking tell it.

Q: FBI corruption?

A: It's worse than anything you could imagine. People are like, what are you working on? What's going on? Give me a hint, even Robyn Gritz, some other people. I said, Nah, I'm not telling you. You know, I've had conversations with some congressmen, and they're like, "When are you bringing us this thing"? I said, "When it's right, then I'll bring it to your desk." So, when it's right, it's almost right. People say if you have something, you should just put it out. That's one of the dumbest things I've ever heard, right? Because things don't work that way. There's a process.

Q: What is the process?

A: The process is if you have 10 people to talk to, right? Then, you know, you have 10 more people to talk to, and you've only talked to five of them...

Q: You put it out the other five won't talk.

A: No, you have to talk to the other people because the story can change, right, and when you talk to these people, maybe you get another person to talk to so the list always grows. It's like it's an ever-changing list, you know, it's like the national debt clock. So you want to try to get as much as you can because the story gets better the more people you talk to. So, the story is interesting on its own, right? I think it's the biggest national scandal in American history.

Q: And this is what your book is going to be about?

A: I'm going to drop a couple chapters....here's how the book is going to be. We're going to open up with what happened to me and my kids because I think that's very compelling. I wouldn't want somebody to miss it, and the stuff I wrote yesterday, it's okay. I left out some really key details on purpose because I don't want to scare the living shit out of people. You know the book is, in other words, when I came out, I'm not going to be like so hardcore. I'll freak people out, right. So, it was a little tame. So, the book is going to be -- yesterday was rated PG -- but the book is rated R. I would say it's definitely rated R.

Q: Well, we were just talking about when the story's ready, and the list of people that you've got and how you're going to bring it up.

A: I said it's the biggest American... I think it's the biggest scandal in American history. I really do, and I think that now that I'm out, I feel a lot safer. I feel like, thank God, because it was hard to work on it. It was really hard to work on it. Knowing if something happens to me, not only does the story not get out, but something happens to me; like if I get hurt or something.

Q: Is it still a danger. I mean, people know that you know this stuff, right?

A: I don't think so. I mean, I, I think that you're safer in the sunlight than you are, and you know? I had dinner a few days ago. I talked about it yesterday with a congressman, and he said, the good guys don't hide. The good guys don't hide and that really just struck me.

Q: It happened serendipitously.

A: Well, I mean I had to come out sooner or later, but

I don't want to take away from the work that we're doing because I really think, and I've talked to a lot of journalists offline, mainstream journalists, Fox, and other places. Folks from all over the place. People think, oh, we just sit around. We have folks all over the place who said the stuff you guys are pumping out is crazy. I had one guy telling me who I trust really well, who has been with Fox for a long time, he said in 2017 the work you guys did on the FBI is a career body for a national security reporter. And I feel that way, you know, but like I said if it's good we're going to pump it out and if it offends people, I don't really fucking care because that's how I'm built too. I'm from around here, so...

Q: You don't think poker players are more accurate than True Pundit who tried to sling shit online? I don't mean to bring him up.

A: I don't know anything about poker, but bringing up poker – THIS is kind of a game. If you look at it as a game, and you want to be in the game talking about games now, right? If you want to be in this game, and you want to sling arrows for a living, you better be fucking willing to take some arrows, and you better be able to dodge some with a smile at the same time, right? This is a nasty game.

People are playing for keeps, and obviously...

Playing for keeps, and I tell you what there's going to be a lot of problems when this book comes out, and they know that because I've been running my mouth because that's what I do. I, if I've got something to say, I'm going to say it right. Somebody told me today, a PR guy told me less balls, more poise. So, I'm trying to tone it down a little bit but, and I told you before the market will decide whether the story is credible, you know, and, one of the main things I wanted to get through to people is that we started with a couple guys and $35 for our server fee, okay?

Q: $35 a month?

A: $35 a month for the server, and I think we paid like 60 bucks for a crappy design. I think True Pundit is one of the worst design sites I've ever seen. This thing makes drugs look like some kind of a church picnic. It's so bad, and we'll work on that. Maybe it's a re-design, right, but, the emphasis wasn't on flash or anything like that. It's just, look, the reason we got the site was like 65 bucks. So our buy-in was like 100 bucks or something like that. So, we started with 100 bucks, and the first week I think we had 45 people looking at it, first week, 45 people. I was psyched. I was like 45 people care what I have to say, and now this month will probably be four million.

Q: 4 million?

A: 4 million.

Q: So see, this is what is really frightening to a CNN, Washington Post...

A: And I haven't even started doing video. Now Let's start doing some fucking video. It's like, you wanted me out of the box, surprise motherfucker! Sorry for my language. You know, I'm out of the box now. What are you going to do about it? I can be a bigger menace out of the box, believe me in my career and Intel and journalism. I'm a street reporter; really I think is one of my strengths. So for the last two years, I haven't been able to be on the street, and some of the guys like, don't go on the street because every time you go on the street, you know you can have somebody else do it. I said, yeah, but nobody's got like....

Q: Your instinct...

A: I just want some answers. You see these videos and people were like, hey, why did you do it, and they're like, they're walking away. I'd be like, "Hey, the fuck is wrong with you?" You know, you were put in office to do these things and you've done nothing. What is your problem? You know you want to be like, I never understood why there had to be civility. They're almost like you have to be almost like a linebacker. It's like, "Hey Yo, where do you think you're going?' Because I'll come to your house next, right?

[Q: People might be realizing now that some of my endeavors have been inspired by consulting with you.

A: Yeah, but I mean it's...some people are like, well that's bullshit. Is it really because I left my house to get an answer, right? I left my office to get an answer. I didn't come down here to be treated like a piece of garbage because when you watch politicians, the way they treat reporters, sometimes they're like, you can't ask that question ... the congresswoman can't answer that. You know, you see these things where the people roll up on Debbie Wasserman Schultz...

Q: She's busy running out the back door.

A: Who do these people think they are? And as a reporter, you want to represent the people at home who want answers. If I see some reporter get turned away or something, I'm pounding my fist. Why can't we get answers; go after this person, right? That's what you're supposed to do. Not sit at your desk and wait for the president to Tweet, and write a story on it or write a story on why a flag isn't at half mast or whatever. Or even write a story about my sorry butt, but I mean I'm not a big player, right? We're not big players. I guess we're making some noise, when they start slamming you, I guess you're making some noise or you have people worried. Well, that's great because they should be worried.

Q: Well, there's a story that's been worrying a lot of people that I did a little something on today that ruffled some feathers. I wanted confirmation on this Jenny Moore story, and I know that you guys had reported on it. You're one of the only outlets that reported on it. George was talking a lot about it of course, but I wanted to speak to the cops, and get their official determination partly because I just didn't know what was going on and there are people involved in this that are trying to implicate me in things, and trying to hang me up in certain ways. A lot of people have been asking me, you know, Michael Moore, are you related to Jenny?

A: Jen and I, we're not related, but...

Q: You worked with her somewhat?

A: It's terrible. The whole thing is terrible.

Q: Do you suspect that she was murdered?

A: I don't know the answer to that, and it's like, for me, that's not what the story was about. The story was about. I thought people needed to know what she was working on, okay? It keeps making circles. Yikes! (Responding to a helicopter hovering over the interview site outside the Liberty Bell, near FBI).

Q: We're still good, I think.

A: Now listen with Jenny, okay, I was in Los Alamos and Santa Fe. We're doing a lot of these interviews with a lot of former federal agents, retired guys, and some good sources. They live out there, and or they're out there in the summer. I don't know why, but it's the place to be. Well, there's the National Laboratory. It's a good reason.

Q: Particle Colliders.

A: It's a spook fest out there, so I was out there doing some interviews when this whole Jenny Moore thing happened. I had no internet, none, okay; cellular I think I had one bar. Cellular I think I had a one Gs, two Gs, and I think I had one of those Es. Remember, we used to get a E for Edge. It was showing me an E. I'm thinking what does that mean? I'm looking at a battery – is it like empty or something. We had a satellite out there and satellite Internet. Dish Network. It was the worst satellite I've ever had. Okay, so, I had no contact with anybody, really anybody and this whole thing with Jenny breaks. So, I'm trying to process this. It was actually a good place to process it because it's quiet and it's away from everything so I can process her death. So I sat on it for a day, the Jenny story when it first broke that she passed away, and try to get some facts. There was a two-hour time difference out there. So, I woke up like three in the morning, and I said, I've got to write the story. What she was working on. I have to write it because what if it plays into what she was working on, you have to write it. Like, I have to, I have to write it or it would bother me because that's what she was working on. I went up to North Jersey. I told you all this was happening at the time I was …

Q: There was a moment where I was supposed to do the interview and then the guy got squeamish.

A: This guy was in such bad shape. You wouldn't believe this guy.

Q: The victim?

A: The witness, alleged victim, you know, he was in such bad shape, vomiting all over the place, okay, and shivering. He had a blanket on the whole interview, like a child. I've never seen somebody that bad, and I'm sitting there thinking this is pretty heavy for a Sunday. I went up there on a Sunday, I think it was

July 1. That's one of those interviews when you get in and you're like, fuck, I want to go home because you're like, this is really heavy, and I don't like doing a lot of this stuff about, you know, children being hurt because it's just really difficult to.

Q: It's just so ...

A: You have to be in another league. You have to get to another level and you had to be built for that. So, it's hard for me to do a lot of this stuff about the children. So I did the interview, and her plan was this, right, and I agreed with it. Okay, whatever you want to do, because I'm not going to do anything to disrespect the kid because he's gone through enough already. I could have put the story up the next day with the video, you know, hour and a half interview saying, Oh, this guy claimed he was raped by Bill Clinton but he didn't want that done. And she didn't want it done that way. So, there has to be, when you're dealing with sources, a level of respect. There has to be a level of respect. Otherwise, you're not going to get another interview.

Q: Also the guy could get hurt.

A: The guy is an eggshell, literally an eggshell, okay? He can barely sit there. What would happen if somebody came after the guy? I told my wife, I said, I can't even believe this interview I had, this guy was so busted up. So, I thought it was important for people to know that is what Jenny was working on that, and it was a Bill Clinton story. That's all I wrote. That's all I wrote about. She was working on this... she is dead.

The police said she had a seizure. We didn't say anybody killed anybody, and we didn't say anything like that. We just gave the facts, right? The kid is 26 now and he alleges that he was abused on yachts and passed around by political elites. So I didn't come out with the video, look at this guy, boom, boom. You know, that would have been sensational. Something you would do if you're only interested in traffic or shock value. I still have the interview and if something happens to the kid then the interview rolls. People asked why don't you release to the interview. So it's because that interview was probably the only thing keeping that kid safe.

Q: Why is that?

A: I think that when they know you're dealing with, from what I've talked to people when they know you have something in the can, right? It's more powerful than releasing it out of the can in certain instances. I think when it comes to this kind of thing when it comes to child endangerment, how would it look if this guy got roughed up right now, after the Jenny Moore story? Whether Jen died of natural causes or she had a heart attack or whatever, that wasn't my point. I think when we did get in touch from New Mexico, I told you this isn't the point. The point of the story is that I just had to say what she was working on because if it does tie into it, maybe a story like that breaks and a cop says, we need to look at this a little bit differently. We need to take a step back, and look at some facts and see if maybe we're missing something, right, and the, the way that they come to that approach on a case is that information has been shared, that she was working on something politically volatile, right? So, that was my point, to put it out. Not only that, I think, you know, knowing her and some of the work we had done together that I owed that to her. I don't think you should sit on information like that. I just don't think you should do it, and, and for me personally, it would have haunted the hell out of me because what if I'd be sitting here with, well, what if we didn't put that out? What if we didn't put it out, you know, and it could have made a big difference in the investigation when, when a body is found and I'm in a forest 5,000 miles away, right? What do I know about the case, right? So, you put it out, and you see where it goes. That's what I did. Then we were attacked for that too. The mainstream media said she wasn't working on this case.

Q: What? How do they know that you were with her?

A: What the fucking are you talking about? What are these people talking about? They just make shit up. No, it's not been "unconfirmed." Well, nobody called me and talked to me. Why don't you call me? I'll tell you it's confirmed. And then these are little tactics they use, so maybe you play the video then if something does happen to the kid, they'll put it around your neck like an anchor.

Q: Right.

A: "Oh True Pundit ruined this kid. He would still be alive if they didn't play the video." Do you understand how this game works?

Q: Well, I'm starting to understand. I'm learning about it firsthand.

A: But you have to know this stuff on the fly, otherwise somebody is like "Put the video out, put the video up, put the video out. Why are you holding it back? You're suspect."

Q: I mean, it seems to me they're always trying to come up with a way of doing something that you're damned if you do and you're damned if you don't. They're trying to get you into checkmate situation.

A: What's the word sanctimonious? Is that the word?

Q: It's A word.

A: It's like they did this. True Pundit did this. Well, wait a minute. Buzzfeed comes out, True Pundit did this. This guy who runs True Pundit did this. What about you? You guys with the Trump dossier, right?

Q: Yeah. I don't understand how they have any credibility.

A: Why are you even still in business? And who are the cement heads reading this site for news?

Q: And they think it's great.

A: I mean, we did a story about a year and a half ago. Buzzfeed said the FBI never looked at the DNC computers after the hack, right? So, they came out that the FBI never examined the DNC computers after the hack. It's like I said, this is, first of all, the first trigger was why is Buzzfeed writing an FBI story, right? These guys blew up a water balloon with a -- I mean of watermelon with rubber bands or something like that.

Q: I don't know why. I mean, isn't Buzzfeed, like, where's the best place to get a double-decker burger?

A: What's the best place to get a fake dossier to ruin the president; the top 10 places you can dish a dossier? No, so I called a couple of (FBI) sources and they well, the Buzzfeed story is not right because we asked (to examine the DNC servers) but they never gave it to us. See, that's different. When the FBI asks for your servers, and you don't give it up. That's a different story than the FBI not looking at them. So, you know, little things like that where you just destroy this huge, I mean, NBC has got $200, million dollars invested in this Buzzfeed thing.

Q: Really? I didn't know that.

A: NBC Universal's last stake was $200 million. They might have another up for another $65 million, whatever. We are eating Ramen Pride noodles and I could pick up the phone and say this Buzzfeed story is bullshit. So, when they graduate from these little lies into this big massive Trump dossier lie, and then whenever somebody gets traction on the other side like us, they try to bring a sledgehammer down on your head.

Q: Well, I found it interesting that one of the things

that they were really specific on was that, you know, the notorious pro-Trump fake news website. It's like, they throw all that out there and it's like, what?

A: Okay, but they're only, you have to understand that, in this media environment – They're only writing for their cement-headed readers. Our readers, for the most part, are going to read anything they write with a grain of salt if they read it. The other thing is they don't, there's nobody keeping track of, of our track record at Buzzfeed. They're just going to write that because it's easy, and it's lazy, and they don't have to look through the research and what we've been right about. I still don't know what the hell we've been wrong about. I don't know because everything we write about comes true down the road. So, I mean the last time I checked, if you're first in, you win in journalism, right? I mean even the right media is not much better than the left media when it comes to that. When it comes to us, they take our stuff. There's no attribution. Then they're like: "Breaking News" It's like, wait a minute, we broke that eight months ago. What the fuck do you mean breaking news on Fox? I mean, who are these people? Who are these people, right? They just take stuff from you and they won't … because they're competitors and they're insecure and number three is they can't duplicate the sources we have because we're such a hybrid, weird thing. We went back and we invented our own journalism. This is like you don't have to go find sources. You have the sources when do you start. Usually when you start a beat -- when I was working for mainstream media. Have we got time?

A: I'm not checking the time. I'm making sure the static isn't coming through.

Q: Whenever I started a new beat in journalism when I was young, the first thing I'd do is go to a barbershop. Editors would say, "Alright Moore, you're covering this town." Okay, I'm gonna go hang out at the barbershop and I'm going to go there at the busiest time. Wanted to be the last in line right? So, I can listen to these guys and then I'm going to go back to the barbershop. Maybe I'll take these guys some coffee. Maybe I'll take some donuts and I'll start fucking hang out at the barbershop. Then I pass out my card after a couple of weeks. You don't want to walk in like the jackass with the car like, hey, like gave me now. Yeah, some people need to be massaged. So, you develop a beat that way and then you, it's literally, it's from the ground up, right, and then when you, after a while after you worked the beat for a while, people start giving you information. Well, the way we created this, as we already had the goddamn information, let's just put it out, and other people that know that their identity will be protected, sources would be protected, right?

Q: The thing that's becoming clear to me, that there's kind of a new paradigm, right? I mean obviously, True Pundit can get started for 100 bucks, and put out stories with law enforcement sources, and FBI sources and stuff like that. That's irritating the mainstream. We've heard about the Church Committee's hearings and Operation Mockingbird and everything. I've been talking a lot about how I feel like there are people trying to control the flow of information over social media. Buzzfeed to me seems very much like the mainstream media's version of Four Chan. They can put out a piece of a crap story, and you know, they're not the New York Times, so people sue Buzzfeed, whatever. But the New York Times can then say, oh, Buzzfeed is reporting that you know, prostitutes pissed on Donald Trump or whatever, and then that becomes a story.

A: The Left is very well organized. The mainstream media, okay, what they do is, it's really a thing of beauty. And if the right media got its head out of its ass, it can be a lot more powerful, but the right media is ego driven with a lot of people who don't understand that there's greater strength in numbers. So, what we have to do, True Pundit, we have to sit back and say, we don't need a Breitbart. We don't need Drudge, right, and we don't need Daily Caller, and we don't need Fox News because we have our own forum. We don't need them to retweet our stuff, right? Our stuff doesn't have to be pure enough and washed down enough, watered down enough, for us to get retweeted by these places. Because what the hell is the use of getting into journalism if you can't do things the way you want to do it? Like I got out of journalism because I couldn't get stories in the paper. There were always lawyered up. I got chased out of town because we're chasing the guy running for Senate.

Q: Really?

A: Like my family was threatened back then. I get real nervous, not nervous, but I get a little antsy when my family gets brought it into. Yeah, and, I'm Irish, so we tend to wear our heart on her sleeves a lot. It's like okay fucker, you want to come at me? Maybe I am not in a position to come at you right now, but I haven't forgotten about you, and when I get in a position to come at you, you're gonna wish you didn't mess with me because it's like the Liam Neeson thing. Remember he said, I have a certain set of skills. I do have a certain set of skills. Okay, and we haven't even started using those skills yet. This is just almost like a hobby. This is what's crazy. When people say, well, what kind of investment do you need and how hard are you working? I think we're working at about 30 percent of our capacity. If we got funded and we took off, it could be a national nightmare. Now, the people behind what's going on at the DOJ, they know because they know what kind of work we did for them. They know what we did for the DEA.

MISSING TEXT.

Q: Robert Mueller, he knows you personally? He's aware of you?

A: Absolutely. Because our body of work was exemplary. I mean, how do you leave journalism at 28 years old think I was? The next day, let's say literally the next day, you're working for the FBI on your first FBI job. Usually, if you left journalism, you'd go on vacation. You know, get a sandwich for a week, hang out with the family. Your career is over, and the next day you're working for the Feds. So, you know, the thing that the Feds are good at, is seeking out talent and you can say what you want about Fusion GPS and places like that, but these guys were talented. They had a certain set of skills that get the job done, right? So, they're gonna make a lot of money now. We didn't make anywhere near that amount of money. This is a long time ago, but we've made good money. I mean, you can make 75 grand a month.

Q: Wow, yeah, doing political opposition research.

A: Doing political opposition research, doing competitive research. I woke up one morning, our company was on the front page of the New York Times.

Q: RIght.

A: "Information Nightmare" or something like that, and Sen. Barbara Boxer was going to subpoena us. Alright, so, so Barbara Boxer says we're going to put these guys in front of a Senate committee, right? Senate subcommittee on how they can get all this information. How are these guys getting all this information?

Q" Cause they figure somebody is leaking something to you or whatever ...

A: Are they breaking into phone companies or what are they doing? They get all this information, and why are they selling it to corporations. We not only did business with the Feds, we do business with corporations, big corporations, you know, we're hired guns and this still goes on today, except today it's rampant. Like people don't know, they think Fusions

GPS is the only place. There are hundreds of places like Fusion GPS. Hundreds. So, Boxer says, Mr. Moore is going to come in front of the Senate subcommittee and he's going to talk about it like you're on the seat, you know, you see these guys like Zuckerberg? So I tell her lawyers to tell fucking Boxer we just did her campaign. We just did the dirt for her campaign on her opponent. Never heard from Barbara Boxer again, okay? So, I mean, this stuff goes on, it's rampant, and what we did now we've internalized that and turned it into journalism, and it's threatening. It threatens a lot of people because it works

Q: And now you're out. You're out of the hiding, out of the shell ...

A: Out of the box, man.

Q: How are things going to change now for True Pundit that you're Michael Moore and not Thomas?

A: We'll see. I don't try to read too much into it. We have a certain mission. We had like a two and a half year game plan. Our mission was, and people say, well, you're out of control, you're partisan. Everybody's partisan. Isn't it time we just admit that we're partisan? Everybody has an agenda.

Q: CNN is not partisan?

A: CNN would be better off if they just said, look, we don't like Trump, so we're going to report like we don't like Trump. Why are they pretending? Oh, we like him. What do you think people are? Maybe people are, maybe people don't get it, but we have a certain time frame and certain things we want to achieve, and so far everything's gone perfectly. Literally perfect. Everything including this thing with the coming out. I had to come out before the book because if we didn't come out before the book, it would have been too much of like, well, what's going on? This guy, they tried to mess up his family. So, it's like a stage, right? This is the first part of the story. Well, this has been planned. People have to know, they have to identify, say, hey, this guy was wronged, and now he's on kind of a warpath and my contention is what's more American than that? Getting even. Getting even is American.

Q: Getting justice.

A: Yeah getting Justice because it started in the 1700s here. The English were pushing everyone around, and people said fuck this. And it all started right here (pointing to Liberty Bell, Independence Hall)

Q: You're happily married still to the same woman.

A: Great woman. Wow. I don't know how she's done it, but my point is, what changes for us is we have a plan, we're sticking to the plan. Anybody who wants to fire arrows, it's like, fine, do what you want because we have a plan and the book is part of the plan and then what happens after the book? I don't know. I mean, we'll probably still be in the news business. I imagine there'll be serious problems for a lot of people after the book, and we'll go from there. I mean, for me the book is the greatest story that I will ever have a chance to tell people anywhere. There can't be a bigger story than this to me. So, for me, it's very exciting.

Q: You know, the psychology of the whole thing is really interesting because when I saw the story yesterday, you know, I saw your story, and then I saw the Buzzfeed story and I think everybody, you know, we had some idiots on the internet saying, "Oh, Thomas Paine doxxed and this and that.

A: Whatever doxxed, you know, we released our story first. I mean, you're not going to scoop me on my own story.

Q: Yeah, yeah, yeah.

A: Who's going to scoop me? If you could scooped on your own story when you have like 20 or 30 years in journalism. It's time to get the hell out of journalism, right? You have to control the story. Especially your own story. The fact that somebody came, and said we're going to do a story on you is all part of the plan. right? Like we had a contingency for that, right? So, the original plan was you and I are going to do this Thomas Paine unmasking in a couple of weeks.

Q: Sort of what we're doing now.

A: Right, but we were going to do it in a couple of weeks.

Q: Yes.

A: Okay, because to coincide with the book. So, the contingency was if somebody comes up before that, right, and wants to be Johnny badass of journalism we will just put the story out. We don't care. Like it's not, that Oh, he's been hiding for two years, right? No, no, no. That's not it at all. This was part of a plan, right. You can't tell this story without a following. You have to build the following first man because I had a mentor who told me -- my buddy Dick Callahan passed away when all this was going on. He could have -- this is the best part, he said, "You want me to fix this for you with the Feds? He could have fucking fixed it with a couple of phone calls, gone away.

Q: Wow.

A: He was sick at the time. He lived in Santa Fe, New Mexico. Then he fell down the stairs. He got sick. One of those things where you, if you go into the hospital, and one thing leads to another, you know, so he was in a rehab at the time and I said, Dick, don't bother yourself with it. Once you get healthy -- this guy's like a father to me. He told me a long time ago though, that you have to plan things out, right, and you have to be methodical, especially when dealing with the -- he didn't trust the FBI. He told me not to work for the FBI, don't do any work for the FBI, don't have anything to do with the FBI. We done?

Q: No, not at all.

A: So, you're moving this camera thing around like a

maniac.

Q: I'm trying to keep my arm from falling off, change the shot a little bit. He was smart to not trust the FBI.

A: He didn't trust the FBI. I mean he had a saying I'll put in my book. I can't put it on here. It's a little bit too raunchy, but he was just such a great guy and he was well respected by everybody and he was a former U.S. Marshal. You know Donnie Brasco? Okay, Donnie Brasco was a federal agent, FBI. So, Dick was the NYPD version of Donnie Brasco, but he never wanted to do a movie. He never wanted to do anything like that. He gave me his files. I have his files. Probably a thousand mugshots of gangsters. They hunted down for Marshal's and for working for the Justice Department. Anyhow, so he taught me to be very methodical, and if you're going to go against these guys, he told me when we were building the case for trial, be methodical, don't be rushed, plan everything out 10 times, take your time. So, when I sat down after everything happened to me, that's what I did, right, because when they take your job from you...

Q: You got a lot of time on your hands.

A: Then they take your side job from you, right, and you can't leave the house for a year. Okay, give me a legal pad. Start writing down. Okay, here's my list of people. Here's what happened to me. Why? You know, what happened starts in D.C. Why? Everything comes back to the fact that certain things myself, and other people had learned while in the employment of the federal government in one aspect or another, right? Had been turned into bad things that happened to them afterward, and pressure that had been put on them. So, I took his advice and there's a plan and we're following the plan, and it's absolutely perfect. I mean, I couldn't be happier with the way things are going. People think, "Oh, you got big problems now" because you're going public. No, no I don't.

Q: Well, that's what I mean. The psychological aspect of it and like being here, talking to you, seeing you.

A: That's why I came the next day.

Q: Yeah.

A: Because it's like, hey man, you fucking think I'm going away. I'm not going away. What do you think this is? Buzzfeed said this is a grudge. Grudge? This is way past a grudge. This graduated from grudge a long time ago.

Q: What is it?

A: This is an Op. This is a mission, and here's the thing. Look at these guys (the FBI). They're dismantled, but our goal was not to put people in jail or not to get people...

Q: Why not?

A: Well, because it's a false goal in journalism.

Q: Why? I want certain people to go to jail.

A: You have to understand if putting people in jail is your goal on journalism, as a journalist, you're going to be disappointed because not many people in D.C. ever go to jail. The goal was to dismantle the FBI so that Americans would take the FBI off their mantle and say, these guys are corrupt. There's something wrong. That was the goal. It wasn't to get anybody fired. Now, that's going on a long time. This is a corrupt organization, right?

Q: Yeah.

A: So, Americans would take them off of the mantle and say, no, these guys are not everything we see on TV. They're not everything that we see in the movies. There are problems here that need to be fixed. My thought was somebody would come along and say, let's fix this broken thing, and put it back up on the mantle, but that hasn't happened yet. So that amplifies what we're doing because now they're saying, everything's fine. This isn't broken. Don't look over here. This is not broken, right?

Q: They point the finger at you.

A: This guy is the problem. Here's the problem. He's got a grudge. Yeah, but maybe so, but...

Q: These are facts.

A: What have we done that's been wrong? We get it right every God damn time. The facts speak for themselves. I mean, if you to go from 45 readers to 4 million to 4.5 million and we don't spend any money on marketing, we don't spend any money on advertising. We don't spend any money on Twitter advertising or Facebook advertising. I mean, when you see a lot of these guys on the right, I won't mention any names, but they have 10,000 retweets. Come on man, you got...

Q: That's a lot.

A: You've got 100,000 people, and you've got 10,000 retweets. You're pumping that up with a credit card, right? Because they do because they think that, okay, if I can portray myself as being more...

Q: Sock puppet accounts.

A: If I could portray myself as being more mainstream than I am, then hey, great, right? Because I get more credit online. We don't do that. If you retweet our stories because you want you. If you can even find our stories. Now they're buried.

Q: Shadowbans and all that. Well, the thing that I find refreshing...

But they keep doing that though, but here's the thing real quick, they keep shadow banning, and they're just crushing us different ways, but it's like putting a water hose in a bucket of running water and trying to put a lid on it. The water is going to find its way out. So, if you're writing good stuff and it's true, they can't keep the water in the bucket. It's going to find readers, find your site anyhow. It's useless, all this banning and stuff. If the source is good, the market will decide that, hey, I don't care if it's presented to me in a convenient manner, I'm going to go find it on here. So, they come to the site.

Q: I was going to say that it's refreshing to be here with you, talking to you, doing this interview, and see how yet again, you know, the opposition seems to try to trip you up or trip me up or trip Trump up or whatever, and it sort of seems to keep exploding in their face. It's not working the way they want it to.

A: What Callahan told me back in the day, the truth is like water. The truth will find it.

Q: The path of least resistance.

A: Path of least resistance. You can go up against a Buzzfeed or even a Fox, you know, Fox is full of shit these days. I don't know why people watch it. We've run stories that they won't run, anti-Obama stories. And pro-Trump stories – Fox has a culture there now where they won't do it -- but the truth wins with very little money, very little money. The truth can compete in an environment where billions of dollars are spent or millions of dollars are spent to try to suppress -- but the truth finds a home. It really does.

Q: And that's what's frustrating, and that's what's driving them to put out these, you know, Buzzfeed things.

A: Well, there'll be more, you know, we like it. I mean, people don't understand that like this guy does, right? I grew up right down the road in Delco, okay. If you want to come at us -- if you were in school or something right, and you had to have two things in grade school. This is grade school. I moved here from western PA when I was in grade school and I was like really sharp wit. The first day I gave somebody a nice zinger, and the whole class laughed. I got a bloody nose at recess and I'm thinking what's going on out here? This place is crazy, right? So you have to learn that if somebody is going to punch you in the face, what are you gonna do about it, right? Somebody wants to kick your door in and they want to point guns at your head. What are you gonna do about it? You gonna do something about it or are you just going to roll over. So, my story is that I'm doing something about it, and that's just the way it is and it's going to get worse because I don't feel that I am done. I've talked about this book coming out and it's not just a sales thing. I don't care if I make $5 on this fucking book. I don't care and when it's done, it'll be a weight off my shoulders, but it's part of what I wanted to do and we're going to do it.

Q: No, you're pumped up. That's what I mean: their efforts keep exploding in their face. True Pundit...

A: They don't know who they're dealing with.

Q: No, they don't.

A: Because when you've been at rock bottom, they take everything away. It's really -- they do it not just to me, they do it to everybody they deal with. They squeeze them to prove their point, and it's not just us out here. Contractors or whoever, journalists, anybody -- like Cherly Atkinson, she's no different. They just say, hey, we're going to do what we want against you and you know, go do something about it, but they do it to their own people.

Q: Sick.

A: Right? So, the world now knows what's going on, and more people are coming to us now with information. Now is when we get real dangerous. Like this is like a buildup. Last two years. It's like, okay, let's see what we can do. Let's stay behind the scenes and we stay behind the scenes because of what these guys (Founding Fathers) did down here (Philadelphia), when Common Sense was published. It wasn't Common Sense by Thomas Paine. It was Common Sense by, I don't know who the hell wrote this, but it's pretty good. Let's go kick somebody's ass. I mean that's who it was. It was written by "Anonymous." So, people the last two years were like these guys (True Pundit) aren't legit because they don't put an author name to their stories. This is how this country started. Do some basic history, and do some basic research where we went all the way back to 1775, right, and we said let's do it like these guys did it. Let's see what happens. And all along the way people are prodding you that you have to put your name to it, you have to put your name to it. I Don't have to do a fucking thing that I don't want to do. It's my shop, our shop. The only thing we're going to print. The only rule I had Jason, during this whole thing was, we're not going to bullshit people because it won't work. It won't work. If we make some shit up about this place, about the FBI, it won't work. Sustained. Maybe one or two stories. It's like, yeah, okay, right, but every time one of our stories comes true, right. I say comes true. They're true when they come out, but it comes true (air quotes) every time. People were like, wait a minute, now it's been two years of this. It's not just like, oh, we broke three stories. We're talking about dozens of stories, big stories, you know, so...

Q: Well, you're building your legacy right now, and I think that...

A: I don't think I'm building a legacy. I think I'm making up for things that I've done. Almost like a penance sometimes. I'm not proud of a lot of stuff I did for the federal government. A lot of the jobs. I'm not proud about that, and I have like a debt to repay. Does that make any sense? Yeah. Because like I said, growing up Catholic, that's just kinda the way you're taught. I don't agree with all the tenet of Catholicism with a lot of stuff has gone on in the church, but we went to Catholic school out here in Philly in Delco. There's a discernible difference between right and wrong and when I'm in my twenties, right, making crazy money, and I came from nothing. So when you're making $75,000 a month slinging research for somebody, at some point you're like. During some months you may make maybe $100,000. So, when you're making that kind of money, you look the other way, when it might be ... because you've never had a taste of it growing up with nothing and all your family is like, wow, this guy's made it. So, now there's a whole thing going on. So, when you look back though, time gives you wisdom. You look back on it and you say, I didn't have to do it that way. There were things we did. I'll say, you know, jobs we did, we shouldn't have done.

Q: But you're talking about the method by which virtually everyone in that system is seduced. They don't want to be the guy who is giving up that payday and disappointing the family and all that.

A: For like 50 grand...60 grand. I'm talking about ... You can make that much money in a month, right? If I was making 65 grand or $70,000 (a year), I'm selling my soul to the devil? That's not much of a soul.

Q: There are other ways that those guys might be seduced. The money and the power, you know...

A: They liked the money but it's mostly the power.

Q: On that note, I'll say is there. Is there anything you want to leave everybody?

A: Nah, that's good. So we have unfinished business. I personally have unfinished business, and somebody -- Buzzfeed said -- this is some kind of vigilante journalism. Hey, sounds good to me, man. Whatever you want to call it. I like vigilante journalism. You know, if somebody out there wants to register a site for me and we'll give you a couple of bucks, but you know, and whatever you want to call it. I mean this is why we have a Constitution. It was signed in this city. People should know that you can for 35 bucks and a dream, you can make a difference and you can try to right the wrongs in this. And that's scary to people who spend billions of dollars to try to control a message to know that some maniac -- the way they're portraying me now -- some maniac with journalism experience and, and I won a lot of awards, probably 30 awards, some big awards in The New York market. It's not easy to win an award in New York. Some guy could come back from the dead in journalism and start rocking the boat. But it's just not me. There are other people that we work with. We have great sources and these people put their ass on the line too, and there's no -- if people think there's a lot of money being exchanged, there's none. There's nothing. I mean when they come at you, they ruin you financially so you quickly learn...

Q: Their first move.

A: You quickly learn that you're ruined financially. Like you either figure out a way to get your house out of foreclosure or file for bankruptcy. They ruin you. There's no -- that's the first thing. That also gives you perspective. I don't want to drone on, but when you lose all your money, and you start to have to sell the things you worked hard for or get rid of -- that gives you perspective. Where you're like, hey, maybe I should be on another path. So, everything gets jumbled up and then you have to sort it out. So, anybody who thinks that we're making crazy money and stuff like that, we're not, and anybody who thinks that we're in this to make money, I guess can think that. It's pretty bad planning, considering we (True Pundit) didn't take any advertising or make any money for the first 15 months we did this. So, I'm excited, man.

Q: It's really just a newfound freedom.

A: Well, it's newfound freedom, but our plan is, it's so perfect man. It's like there have been a little bit of bumps along the way, but it's gone really well and I'm happy. Everything, everything has gone well, I also want people to know that, that when this comes out, you know, and you see it on these big other news organizations that have the guts to run it, which I don't know how they won't. We started it. I don't want credit for it. I just want people to know that we started it because if we take credit all of ourselves, it can't catch fire and take off, you know? Just to know that we had a role in it, so I'm excited. I'm excited. If anything happens, bad happens to me, you'll know because you got the interview, you'll know, and there are other people that know what's going on. What I'm working on that will step forward. I'm talking about some high profile people will step up. Just say, Yo man, this isn't some BS conspiracy. This guy was working on X, Y, and Z. So, that's why I feel like I'm protected, you know because I think there are people that have my back that have power. That's what this story is about, and we're gonna see how it plays out. So, when you're talking about legacy, I don't feel like it's a legacy. I just feel like it's, it's unfinished business, and almost like a penance, so to speak, right? Because if you've done bad things, you have to do good things and make up for them. So that's where I'm at.

Q: Well Mike, I got to thank you for allowing me to be along this journey with you. You've been super helpful to me. Your guidance, advice, and participation.

A: You need it.

Q: I know.

A: So no, I, I appreciate it, man. It's good to have you in Philly and you know, this place is special to me even though it sounds crazy, right? It is special to me. It's a special place. You got the FBI and you got everything. You know, we explained it. It's a special place. So it's good to do it here, and I wanted to do it here and I envisioned this a year ago and now, like I said, as part of the plan for me it's when things fall right into line. That's awesome. I love it. So thanks.

Mike Moore

5 THE AL-QAEDA
HACKERS CLUB

The FBI was in the catbird seat. It's 2000 and Bill Clinton is President. Louis Freeh is FBI Director, and things are going swimmingly for an undercover FBI operation that has cracked and infiltrated al-Qaeda. That is no easy feat, mainly because these FBI agents and operators haven't even left the United States. Instead, working on a little-known and top-secret operation FBI Intel folks have finally convinced Osama bin Laden's henchmen and terror captains that they are radical Muslims willing to wage Jihad in the United States in the name of the terror mastermind.

After working three years undercover, exchanging thousands of emails and online chats with Al Qaeda's hierarchy in the Middle East, one FBI operator has really stood out to Al Qaeda management. Showing true disdain for American infidels and all the hallmarks of a radicalized Muslim, the undercover FBI operator has conned the brightest terrorists in the business. And that's incredible news for the FBI and CIA who – at the time – were struggling to find a foothold and HUMINT (Human Intelligence) peg inside the global terror faction and its related cell known as Al Qaeda.

But that had all changed now.

In fact, the FBI was not only finally inside Al Qaeda, its undercover moles were invited to join its board of directors. And yes, Bin Laden did run the radicalized group much like a corporation, insiders confirm. But Bin Laden wanted to expand and he had big plans for the United States. First and foremost – beyond the killing of innocent Americans, he tried to domesticate millions of Al Qaeda funds in banks and brokerage houses in the United States. And by domesticate, we mean laundering money. Bin Laden recognized the challenge of financing terror and propaganda campaigns in any country absent domestic payment routes. Blind Sheik Omar Abdel Rahman learned this the hard way after masterminding the 1993 bombing of the World Trade Centers in New York. The "first" strike in lower Manhattan. The warm-up strike. Sheik Omar Abdel Rahman used German banks to finance the 1993 bombing, and it was one wire from a German bank that helped lead the FBI to the Jersey City, NJ doorsteps of the men who blew up one of the twin towers. And also lead them to Sheik Omar Abdel Rahman. I was there as FBI executives negotiated with newspaper's brass to keep that Intel quiet – about the German bank – until they could trace the wire and its proceeds in a journey to find and arrest the perpetrators.

This was my newspaper at the time, so I had a front-row seat. It was the first time I saw how the game was REALLY played. Wait, media companies cut deals with the Feds, I thought? My newspaper is playing nice with these guys? What was that about? If you have dirt on terror suspects, I was adamant, print it and let the Feds sort it out. Scoop the FBI. Fuck the Feds. I was a rookie. I remember the FBI executives from the New York field office laughing as they exited the conference room. And I thought about those same agents chuckling less than a month later when an FBI "negotiation" torched children in Waco, TX. And these editors thought they cut a favorable deal with the FBI, I thought? This was sharks and minnows, and I was employed by the minnows.

Newspapers and television always buckle to the FBI, State Department, et al because these agencies threaten to jail editors and publishers over "national security" breaches if they do not do exactly as the Feds say. And the cowards in the media almost always buckle. I would see this scenario play out time and time again during my newspaper career. When we had eyewitness testimony from DOZENS of New York residents who reported a fast-moving projectile was flying at TWA Flight 800 seconds before it went down – that story was killed too, just like the World Trade Center story. The State Department had threatened to lock me up personally on the TWA 800 story. And the newspaper bosses killed it. The FBI and State Department (CIA) were steamed I had, a day earlier, snuck in an eyewitness account of a major in the New York Air National Guard who flew sorties in Vietnam. He was flying maneuvers at the time Flight 800 went down and told me he too spotted what appeared to be a missile strike the TWA flight. And we printed that and it set off a shit storm in D.C. The source – who was on the record – was all but put in the federal witness protection program and the Feds leaned on the paper for a retraction and correction. And clamped down on my ass after that one. I had scored one for the good guys sneaking his testimony into the paper. But it was one of the last statements the Major gave. I don't believe he ever spoke of what he saw in the July sky that evening. They shut him up faster than they did my newspaper.

NBC's Bryant Gumbel was standing beside me during the same interview on the beach dunes in East Moriches, New York. The sun had just come up the day after the crash. And the sunrise that morning was indeed a beautiful thing that day, a strange backdrop as first responders were fishing ----400 bodies out of the water and putting them in refrigerated trucks.

Gumbel never did run that bombshell interview on NBC News or the Today Show. Is anyone surprised? That was a smoking gun and NBC buried that probably somewhere on the beach near where the teddy bears, suitcases and personal belongings of the downed passengers were washing up with the morning tide.

If the world had Twitter back in 1996, I could only imagine my Tweets as a frustrated mainstream media reporter who believed the journalism game was about telling the truth and not playing paddy cake with the Feds. Perhaps something like this:

1996 version of Tweet:
"These cowards I work for are hiding eyewitness accounts of a missile or projectile striking #TWAFlight800. Have Loeb Award and Pulitzer nominations. Anyone hiring? #NoSellOuts"

Let us get back to the German money behind the first World Trade Center attack. That $50,000 wire led the FBI to the terrorists and their leader. Bin Laden feared this years before. Absent a network inside of shell companies making wire transfers and deposits inside the United States banking infrastructure, this was bound to happen time and time again.

In fact, per emails -- exchanged between undercover FBI operators posing as radicalized Muslims poised to wage jihad in the United States -- with Al-Qaeda lieutenants and captains, the terror conglomerate was desperately seeking to branch into the United States, employ U.S. banks and also enhance its online backbone of servers so that emails could be shrouded from the NSA, CIA, and U.S. Intel apparatus. And do you remember that undercover FBI agent I described earlier who had caught the attention of Bin Laden and his boardroom of terror bosses?

Word spread through Al-Qaeda leadership circles in the Middle East. They had found their guy in the United States. He had brains, contacts, a disdain for his country, and the connections to help plan Bin Laden's expansion into the U.S. – both financially and radically.

Al-Qaeda had found their man.

Except their man was actually a woman.

Her name is Alijandra Mogilner

The irony here is thick, obviously. Women can't even show their faces in public in the Middle East – and are often treated and beaten like dogs -- but the biggest, baddest terror group in the world had just been compromised by a female FBI operator.

And when Al-Qaeda fell for Mogilner, it fell

hard. For the Feds, it was a grand slam, with terror leaders offering her and unknowingly the federal government of the United States the keys and recipe to unravel Bin Laden's entire operation. Al-Qaeda wanted Mogilner to handle the money laundering in the United States AND help Al-Qaeda to migrate it's emails and international communications to an offshore server. And she would serve as the administrator and maintain the server. In essence, Mogilner – who was believed to be a radicalized U.S. male – would have every email written to and from top Al Qaeda management. This bombshell – plus the oversight of Al Qaeda's money laundering inside the United States. Three years of undercover work had struck gold, and this was the motherlode.

"The FBI … we had the opportunity to have Bin Laden's server and have everything Al-Qaeda did online go through our control," Mogilner said. "And he wanted us to be his treasurer in the United States" to launder money and make state-side payoffs to and for his terror cartel.

"But the FBI thought it was not worth the $50,000 a year that it would cost to do it," Mogilner told me during an interview.

Mogilner and her FBI commissioned crew had infiltrated the biggest terror cartel in the world, posing as Muslim males and would-be jihadists. And the FBI walked away from the Op once she and federal operators had broken through a once-impenetrable wall to have an insider's seat at Al Qaeda's big table. The FBI walked away from a goldmine of Intel that could have changed the course of history. Literally.

One year later – after the FBI walked away -- the Twin Towers crumbled, Pentagon walls tumbled, and a hijacked commercial airliner headed for the White House crashed in western Pennsylvania. All within a matter of an hour on Sept. 11, 2001.

The FBI had sold out. Again. A recurring theme now for decades. Back then FBI executives could blame it on Bill Clinton. And he indeed was to blame.

But it was the FBI, Bill Clinton's FBI, that took its own fox out of the Al Qaeda henhouse. And stunned undercover operatives who broke their asses to pull off what was previously considered impossible.

Mogilner details her groundbreaking undercover work for the FBI:

"They were looking for their own server. Al Qaeda was, so they could have security and have got an exclusive server. And then we had the offer ... we ended up being part of their board of directors. Essentially, the heads of each of al-Qaeda's departments were organized just like a big corporation. They wanted us to be treasurer for all of his money in the United States and to provide the server to keep tabs on Al Qaeda."

Mogilner said between 1999 and 2000 FBI executives calculated it would cost the equivalent of a mid-level agent's salary to pull off this coup, or roughly $52,000 a year.

"They said it wasn't worth it," Mogilner recalls with disgust.

Mogilner's famous -- and now infamous -- Op and group were dubbed the 'Muslim Hacker's Club.' It doesn't have a rock-n-roll ring to it like 'Crossfire Hurricane,' but the difference here is one was an actual operation, and one was a fabrication of the mainstream media and corrupt FBI brass running for cover.

Mogilner had brought Bin Laden's operation on a silver platter to her FBI overlords, and they punted.

"I was basically on al-Qaeda's board of directors and invited to be its U.S. treasurer," she said. "We volunteered to provide bin Laden with a computer server. I said we'll provide you with a server and we'd make it look like it was located outside the United States, Canada or Mexico.

We would have known everything al-Qaeda was doing, what they were planning. But the FBI decided bin Laden wasn't very important. We were (already) inside for two years, beginning in 1998. We did obtain a lot of their emails."

But Mogilner stresses the FBI and the U.S. intelligence apparatus could have had ALL al-Qaeda's emails. That's a massive difference compared to merely a small sampling of emails. And the difference between Intel gleaned from such emails could literally save lives and help put a severe dent in al-Qaeda's global terror network and radical mayhem. And potentially pinpoint many mainstream players linked to Bin Laden who were hiding in plain sight, in "normal," traditional careers.

"The guy who was doing their (al-Qaeda) online stuff, money laundering and running their online presence actually worked at JP Morgan in London," she admitted.

Mogilner would not identify the subject but said he was a key IT worker for the bank who was fired after the financial conglomerate learned of his alleged connection to al-Qaeda. Stunningly, however, Mogilner said the FBI did not pursue the man, nor did British Intelligence arms MI5 or MI6 who are tasked with investigating terrorism. She said he took a job with another company and was never charged – or even interrogated to her knowledge.

"He was a member of al-Qaeda, running their money laundering, running their empire if you want to call it that," she said. "It was all very international and very large. They (FBI) weren't interested in him and never did anything that I know of."

How in the hell would the FBI or CIA walk away from such a gem, like the JP Morgan connection?

"Well, they just didn't care," Mogilner said. "They didn't want to spend the money. Al Qaeda wasn't important, and they said that everybody knew bin Laden wasn't important. Bin Laden had other operations going that were considered, by the FBI, to be very unimportant. But that he (Bin Laden) considered tremendously important. And I think Bin Laden was correct."

And the FBI, again, was on the wrong side of yet another case to protect America's best interests. And on the wrong side of history. Again.

"Bin Laden had big propaganda, publicity programs going in Bosnia, Chechnya, and many other locales like the United States," Mogilner said. "He was trying to turn public opinion about his operations, and he did a pretty darn good job of it."

But this wasn't merely any public relations firm prepping news releases and coaxing reporters to shower a political figure with good press. Quite the opposite. Bin Laden was running a cartel of skullduggery, planting fake news, and putting cash behind his causes. Hired muscle to steer his "propaganda" campaigns via force and good old-fashioned terrorism.

"For example, in Bosnia they backed Hezbollah and Chechnyan fighters that came in," Mogilner said. "They would put out "news" stories. They attacked people. They saw that there were going to have to be new leadership, so they backed people they wanted for leaders after the war and did all kinds of things. And to a great extent, it worked."

Sounds like many U.S. Democratic politicians might have read Bin Laden's guide to political skullduggery. And what you're reading here folks indeed is a rare look behind the curtain. Very rare. Don't let this gem slip through your fingers. Mogilner, the American woman who infiltrated Al Qaeda posing a Muslim man, was interested in pursuing Bin Laden's connection to politics and politicians – and elections – in countries that included the United States.

But the FBI didn't want anything to do with Bin Laden's potential infiltration of Washington D.C. or to ascertain if portions of the news media – and elected officials – were receiving terror-backed financing. Is this why Bill Clinton's administration and his FBI walked away from the 'Muslim Hacker's Club?' Was Osama Bin Laden financing U.S. politicians and news agencies or public relations firms? Or even worse: Was bin Laden using his banking contacts – in companies like JP Morgan – to dig up dirt on politicians worldwide to use the damaging information to blackmail politicians? Or media executives?

The FBI pulled the plug on the operation that could have answered all those questions. It's appears to be another case where the FBI and it's Deep State overlords did not want such vital intelligence to fall into the hands of the Bureau's rank-and-file agents. That is always a concern during institutionalized corruption. Honest agents could blow the whistle on malfeasance and wrongdoing.

But the Feds did not want the keys to al-Qaeda's Kingdom, as a key player like Mogilner attests. And lives were lost, the unfortunate yet familiar cost of poor or deliberate – or both -- FBI decisions that stretch over the last 20 years. At least. (Many of these gaffes are intentional. No one – not even the FBI – could prove this chronically feckless. Mathematically, it's almost an impossibility. It defies advanced mathematics if these mistakes were by chance or just happenstance.)

And in 2001, Americans watched in sheer horror as the country and world changed forever on September 11. As the media looped footage of the planes crashing into the World Trade Centers before they crumbled to the ground like sand castles washed away by a high tide.

Meanwhile, al-Qaeda was, of course, a household name and global threat. And the FBI had walked away from controlling and crushing Bin Laden's terror conglomerate just months earlier. Like cowards. Or traitors. Or both.

I can attest to this statement personally. Before, during and after 9/11 – while my group was working for the FBI and Feds – we were also working for America Online (AOL). Its director of security was a former CIA spook and friend. And we loved doing AOL's dirty work. And it was easy money really, because folks, AOL was flush with cash and more importantly, we had access to AOL's resources which certainly augmented our federal work. Feds need to crack an email address without the hassle of a warrant? Or they need it in 30 minutes because they're up on a wire or surveilling a target, they come to us, we backchannel the Intel and make a nice dime. AOL's legal folks approved of the arrangement until the web giant fired its head counsel during its decline. And my contact followed. To this day, somehow I still get blamed for his demise but – spoiler alert: AOL sunk faster than the Titanic. And there are no golden parachutes on a shipwreck.

My point here is this. We knew the al-Qaeda terrorists who hijacked the planes to carry out the 9/11 attack were employing AOL and its AIM (instant message) chat to plan the strike. If the FBI had listened to Mogilner and her groundbreaking 'al-Qaeda Hacker's Club' – the FBI would have known this too BEFORE the strikes. I can hear folks now saying: "Oh, how did you know the terrorists used AOL. Anyone can make a statement like that." Actually, that's a valid point. And why I decided to document it within 48 hours after the 9/11 attack in 2001, a fact that angered FBI brass. But I had seen them cover so much shit up in other Ops, I had to put them on notice – as well as the general public – that if the FBI had been monitoring al-Qaeda's communications – like Mogilner illustrated in this book – perhaps things would have been different.

At the time I knew the FBI had dropped the ball on this and my group issued this intelligence publicly in newswires on Sept. 13, 2001, and it is documented. Forever. It was the first real public confirmation that Osama bin Laden was linked to the 9/11 attacks.

PR Newswire
September 13, 2001, Thursday
E-mails Link Osama bin Laden's Terrorist Network
to Tuesday's Bombings
SECTION: DOMESTIC NEWS
DATELINE: NEW YORK, Sept. 13

The following was issued today by DigDirt.com:

Federal agents have developed what they believe is the first concrete evidence linking Tuesday's deadly terrorist attacks on the World Trade Center and the Pentagon to the terrorist's network of Osama bin Laden, according to U.S. intelligence officials.

Federal agents have successfully tracked e-mails and electronic correspondences (AIM) regarding Tuesday's hijacking bombings to known associates of Osama bin Laden, the Saudi exile and known terrorist, who has waged Jihad, or holy war, on the United States.

The FBI served search warrants on Earthlink and America Online Tuesday, targeting electronic correspondences both before and after the bombings by approximately 10 subscribers linked to bin Laden's terrorist network, sources said. Numerous messages were pinpointed through e-mails, and U.S. intelligence officials said the transmissions were not encrypted and according to certain content, the users believed their messages were stealth and completely untraceable.

By late Tuesday, sources said, agents had been provided with full transcripts of all recent e-mails generated on the accounts of the targeted subscribers.

DigDirt.com has been commissioned to launch private-sector inquiries into the recent terrorist attacks, with company personnel immediately dispatched to New York City on Tuesday.

DigDirt.com, an e-commerce investigative information and

public records website, offers global access to critical intelligence searches in 106 countries and access to more than 500 billion records worldwide, ranging from in-depth background and highly specialized intelligence searches in the United States and abroad.

Company founder and CEO Michael Moore is a national award-winning investigative journalist and has covered the TWA Flight 800 explosion, New York City subway explosion, the aftermath of the 1993 World Trade Center bombing, and uncovered serious security lapses at Newark International Airport after working undercover to gain undetected access to planes, the tarmac, baggage areas and other facilities.

6. THE SWEDE LOOKS
TO 'BAG' BIN LADEN

Tom Orest put together a "network of part-time and one-time" federal agents and international intelligence scofflaws to hunt, track and kill bin Laden in Iran. A rogue bunch for sure, but more than capable.

Orest's Intel and bin-Laden hit squad included intelligence contacts in the U.S. and Iran, including high-ranking former operatives of Savak and undisclosed political, military and civilian attaches in Pakistan, Iran and globally. Orest served many masters in U.S. intelligence, including NSA work and the United States Army Security Agency (ASA). Orest cut his teeth in military intelligence, monitoring and interpreting military communications in the Middle East, China and the Soviet Union. The ASA was under the control of the NSA.

Orest was also a federal contractor for the military and Dept. of Defense, among numerous other government and private concerns.

"I had heard from three different sources he had gone to Iran for kidney treatments," Orest said. "Dialysis. It was interesting because they put him in a safe house, an old Savak safe house."

The Savak was the secret police, domestic security and intelligence apparatus in Iran, established with the assistance of the U.S. Central Intelligence Agency and the Israeli MOSSAD. Savak was known for its vicious and brutal tactics and operated until the Iranian Revolution when the prime minister ordered its dissolution.

Savak has been dubbed Iran's "most hated and feared institution" as it was quite fond of torturing and executing dissidents absent any trials. During Savak's power, the group boasted many thousands of agents serving in its ranks – some insiders estimate as many as 60,000 throughout Iran. Orest noted Savak hideouts and safe houses were still being utilized by the Islamic Revolutionary Guard in Iran.

"The property where he was installed had hardwired phones because they knew our intelligence service had picked up his use of mobile and satellite phones," Orest said. He noted the Iranians and bin Laden's al-Qaeda entourage learned about the U.S.'s phone monitoring by politicians who were bragging about monitoring bin Laden's communications – by reading American newspapers like the New York Times.

Orest said bin Laden and al-Qaeda were elusive in Iran, as he and his deputies moved around between cities and villages whenever there was a rumor that a U.S. hit squad might be coming to grab him. Some rogue posses of Iranians too wanted bin Laden's head on a stick, Orest said. After all, there was a $25 million U.S. cash reward for the terror mastermind. That cash can buy a whole lot of Toyota Land Cruisers – the vehicle in the Middle East that had earned equal cultural status with camels and prized hunting falcons among royal families.

Orest himself had assembled such a hunt-locate-and-kill squad. And he was going after bin Laden. And Orest was very plugged in and had informants in the region pumping him great Intel – the Intel the CIA had too but was ignoring.

Orest said when things got hot, bin Laden would duck into safe houses in remote villages. That supports intelligence from other insiders who attest to bin Laden spending the majority of his time in larger cities. He had reportedly shaven off his trademark beard and dressed in business suits or business casual attire as well.

Orest hatched a plan to extract bin Laden from Iran.

"With our own resources we planned to engage his security support to take back a head or two," Orest said. "Because of the logistics of getting in and out, we planned to bring back only bin Laden's head in a bag. The head was so easily identifiable; there would be no problem with identification."

And collecting that $25 million reward.

Orest had logistics prepped and his own squad of former agents and ex-military ready to roll. In fact, he said the team would use Tehran as a base, and a U.S. Congressman had agreed to help the group gain entry into Iran. The Congressman, as stealth diplomatic envoy, also agreed to stay in a hotel and hold everyone's identification in case the Op went bad. Orest said all they needed was to do was launch and dismember bin Laden.

Orest said his group knew where bin Laden was: The exact building he was living in. But he might relocate so he intended to move quickly.

"The problem was the Company came in – the one in Langley," Orest said referencing the CIA."

During the first of multiple meetings, high ranking CIA officials met with Orest, team members and also visited the Congressman who agreed to help capture bin Laden. Orest said everyone was threatened with arrest if they left the United States or made any moves to snatch bin Laden or his severed head from Iran.

Keep in mind, according to research and interviews, both the CIA and FBI had more than a dozen other informants at this exact time, relaying intelligence linking bin Laden to Iran. Orest was the only one with the chops -- and the local muscle -- to handle the terror boss' extraction himself. After decades of working in Middle East Intel, Orest converted to Islam so he was not considered a 'non-believer' by the Muslim locals. He blended in and was embraced and that was worth its weight in gold – hopefully $25 million worth.

One of the additional sources relaying intelligence at the time to FBI and CIA brass was Alijandra Mogilner, who previously ran the FBI's successful "al-Qaeda Hacker's Club" Op for the FBI under Bill Clinton's White House.

Mogilner said she was working for a CIA front company at the time as a cover for Agency Intel work and notified her old bosses at the FBI – Robert Mueller's FBI – about bin Laden's location in Iran. Neither Mueller nor any of his deputies reached out to her for additional details. There was never even any follow up. She was taken aback by the cavalier attitude.

"Did they want to find this man or not?" she asked.

Apparently they did not. Just like Tom Orest.

The CIA threatened Orest and his Intel crew, along with may have been a select group of lawmakers helping these patriots pull off an operation that federal agents had gone out of their way to avoid. CIA and State Dept. officials pledged they would be indicted for violating the Logan Act – the Deep State's faithful federal felony boogeyman statute for many decades.

The Logan Act, on the books since 1799, is the federal law that criminalizes negotiation by unauthorized persons with foreign governments having a dispute with the United States law, positions, and policies. Only two poor mopes have ever been indicted on charges of violating the Act, in 1802 and in 1852. The federal government lost both cases at trial, and both men walked.

I spoke to the Congressman implicated in this rogue Op, who asked to remain anonymous. He said he was threatened with criminal prosecution as well from the Justice Department.

But Orest – known as the big "Swede" for his Nordic heritage and 6-foot-eight towering stature -- and his crew believed they were legally empowered by the Fed's offer of reward for bin Laden's capture which did not stipulate he could only be hunted on a playing field approved by bureaucrats and policy wonks inside the CIA and State Dept. Osama bin Laden, Orest believed, was fair game. Most would agree. Orest's argument was rooted in common sense.

The federal government disagreed, saying the Operation and any unauthorized actions would clearly undermine the U.S.'s position in Iran.

But what position was that? That tenet even baffled lawmakers who were familiar with the proposed mission. Even seasoned select lawmakers who were not aware of any U.S. position in Iran that would be violated for trying to grab Osama bin Laden and perhaps one or more of his lieutenants – say maybe a man like Ayman al-Zawahiri?

There was a $25 million price on his head also. That's $50 million in rewards right there. And Orest recognized he might have to tote home two heads in one bag. He would need a charter flight. Even in Iran, you can't bring severed heads onto a plane as carry-on baggage.

"It was a nasty situation where they would prosecute under the Logan Act," Orest recalled. "You know, it's never been used, the Logan Act. It hasn't been used."

But the U.S. intelligence brass had made a diplomatic gaffe here, revealing such a mission would have violated the United States' "position" in Iran. Up until that point – in the early to mid-2000s – America's position was that Iran was a terror regime and sworn enemy of the United States.

"This was the first time they slipped, the CIA and State (Dept.) slipped and mistakenly revealed there was some type of policy in play (with Iran)," one Congressman said. "I didn't know of any U.S. position during the Bush administration that would prohibit killing America's public enemy number one. Perhaps there was a policy. You'd have to ask the White House staff at the time and guys like Dick Cheney.

After all, this was the same crew from the

Weapons of Mass Destruction fame in neighboring Iraq. Good luck getting a straight answer from these Bush White House players.

And from research conducted for this book, we do know that the highest ranking members of the Bush administration knew where bin Laden was – as well as members of his family – yet failed to do a damn thing about it. In essence, as you will learn, the GOP White House was no better than the Democratic White House to follow. Both allowed bin Laden and al-Qaeda a free pass.

How Orest and his team's Intel were treated are indeed the poster boys for the Bush White House's live seminar in government malfeasance, malfunction and malpractice.

Orest and his crew, along with Congressional personnel and Intel informants were called to additional State Dept. and CIA-sponsored sit-downs. One such roundtable was held in Paris, France. There, U.S. bureaucrats informed the team that they were wasting their time looking in Iran for bin Laden because the high-ranking government officials said he was in Pakistan. French intelligence echoes the sentiment of CIA.

But wait, until that point in time – which was six to seven years before bin Laden was killed – the U.S. government had only acknowledged that bin Laden was hiding in Afghanistan. Now he was in Pakistan? This was news to all concerned parties.

"They were trying to sway 'The Swede' and his squad from going to Iran at any cost," one Congressional source said. "In the process, they slipped up again and admitted he was not in Afghanistan, in some dark cave. Some U.S.

ambassador said too much at the meeting from what I understand. I got very heated and some of these (political) appointees fall apart when that happens."

But Orest knew these "official" contentions – that bin Laden was touring Pakistan -- were pure bullshit, based on recon work he had already privately commissioned in Pakistan and its border with Afghanistan. But he took the information from the State Department and began re-combed Pakistan to find traces of bin Laden. And what the hell was French Intel involved for? The French were tight with Iran. What was at play here, he thought.

"I had teams going through and sweeping the tribal lands, and we had contacts in hospitals, everywhere you can imagine," Orest said. "He wasn't anywhere in Pakistan. We searched high and low and did not find him or any trace he was there."

Orest had particularly great contacts from American-speaking medical personnel At Christian Hospital in Tank, Pakistan and medical facilities throughout the country.

Orest said bin Laden at that time had not been spotted in Pakistan per local source and informants, a stark contrast from what the State Dept. personnel had told him. Orest believes the State Dept. was posturing to keep his crew dormant in Iran.

Orest said he had better sources than the State Dept. anyway telling him specifically bin Laden was being harbored in Iran. What better sources did he have? The same contacts in Iran that tipped him off to bin Laden's residency in the country. And the same contacts who blew the whistle on an IED smuggling Op that was killing and maiming U.S. soldiers in Iraq. Iran was building and shipping IEDs to Iraq to employ against U.S. forces and soldiers. That bombshell Intel came to Orest from Iran's 'Committee of Nine.' (Go ahead and Google it, you won't find a shred of information about it.)

The Committee of Nine was the terror Sanhedrin in Iran, a clandestine group of radical leaders that selected targets for terror who planned out deadly attacks on the unfortunate recipients of mayhem and misfortune globally. The committee, a private death court of sorts, may still be operating today though it is not clear. But Orest and Congressional Intel sources said the Committee was running during bin Laden's stay in Iran, and it made some committee members uneasy, though most approved, including Khamenei.

"I had a source on the Committee of Nine supply that intelligence to me," Orest said. "He was directly a member of the committee. My source said bin Laden was in Iran. It was 100 percent correct, there is no doubt. The Supreme Leader of Iran sits atop the committee."

That is Sayyid Ali Hosseini Khamenei, Iran's Grand Ayatollah since 1989. Khamenei is Iran's head of state and its commander-in-chief of Iran's armed forces and, in his spare time, radical terror boss. Khamenei is considered the most powerful politician in Iran – and the Middle East -- many would argue. Orest said all things terror-related ran through Khamenei's stewardship of the Committee of Nine in the early to mid-2000s.

"This was a death squad, run separately from the Iranian government so that only trusted Muslims would know what was being planned, the terror attacks around the world," a congressional source said.

Another well-placed military source vetted Orest's story and confirmed the details – including the information he provided the State Dept. and CIA on bin Laden in Iran.

"Mr. Orest had served his country throughout the globe with distinction in many intelligence roles," the source said.

"If the CIA was serious about getting bin Laden, the Swede had him nailed," a Congressional source said. "They were not serious because they could have had him, the Swede would have brought his fucking head home in a sack. It was all arranged."

Orest agreed.

"We pinpointed the actual building he was in, the safe house in Tehran at the time," Orest said. "We knew exactly where he was and they didn't allow us to go after him when the whole world was looking for him. They didn't even try."

The U.S. government was not interested.

Orest said military contacts that were his friends – who were still on active duty during the time Orest was planning the bin Laden operation were interrogated to see if they were connected to him and what they knew about the operation. One good friend was demoted to base chaplain, he said and removed from a career in military intelligence. He actually liked the chaplain gig better and rode the post out until he retired.

Beyond hassling Orest's active duty pals, The CIA and State Dept. never did follow up on the Intel supplied by Orest, his team, lawmakers involved in the rogue Op or seek a meeting with the member of the Committee of Nine that divulged bin Laden's whereabouts.

Orest offered to make introductions in Tehran to U.S. agents.

The U.S. government was not interested.

7 MUELLER, THE DEEP STATE HITMAN

A firefighter's worst nightmare is arson, a crime committed by someone who understands how to torch a location, causing harm while remaining anonymous.

GOP Congressman Curt Weldon, a former firefighter and lifelong supporter of first responders, knows those are some of the hardest fires to put out and hardest to prove. And in his career in Washington, Weldon witnessed another version, too: political arson.

In October 2006, three weeks before Election Day, FBI agents raided Weldon's home, his eldest daughter's house, and attorney John Gallagher's Philadelphia law office.

Weldon was stunned at the raid, not only from the shock of it happening, but that it had taken place only weeks before an election. The U.S. Justice Department had had a long-standing policy to not initiate raids or aggressive legal action that might adversely affect an election.

But despite his shock, Weldon knew, too, that he

had made enemies inside of the beltway -- most notably within "deep government" -- after he had published a book exposing how intelligence communities failed to share information with each other that could have prevented the 9/11 attacks.

Congressman Weldon made the same mistake I made. In 2007 I set out somewhat informally to put meat on the bones of disturbing Intel I had gleaned from a sitting and powerful Democrat in Congress.

Osama bin Laden was hiding out in Iran. And the leaders of our country knew about it and where. Bombshell revelations. But remember how D.C. operates. This was a high-ranking Democrat spilling the beans about the Republican Bush White House in 2007. If that Congressman knew a Democratic president would succeed Bush – and keep this scandal alive – I may have never learned this in the first place.

Years earlier, Congressman Weldon was on the exact vision quest, seeking answers from CIA Director George Tenet about bin Laden's residency in Iran. In 2003, Weldon wrote an explosive letter to the CIA chief, inquiring about bin Laden in Iran.

"On April 25, 2003, I met in Paris, France with [REDACTED] a former high ranking official under the Shah, who claims to be well connected to knowledgeable and high-ranking sources in Iran's present government," Weldon wrote.

Weldon continued, detailing Intel gleaned from the Iranian whistleblower: "The government of Iran is giving refuge to Osama bin Laden is a safe house located near Tehran, in the northern suburb of Pasdaran."

"I urge the CIA to interview [REDACTED] and assess the credibility of his allegations," Weldon continued. "This assessment should be done by the CIA independently, not relying upon any foreign intelligence service, such as the French Ministry of Interior, that may have ulterior motives in accessing [REDACTED] allegations."

Weldon had done what at least a half-dozen other Congressmen didn't have the guts to do: Put the intelligence on paper and run it straight up the CIA's flagpole.

And what did Tenet do?

His CIA handed it off to French intelligence.

Weldon took the move as a major slight and began making noise all over Capitol Hill about Iran harboring al-Qaeda terrorists – and bin Laden living in Iran. Too much noise, in fact.

And on Oct. 16, 2006, Weldon felt as though he was facing an arsonist. He was campaigning in Swarthmore Borough that Monday morning when his beeper and cell phone started buzzing: his daughter Karen's home and Gallagher's office were being raided, each surrounded by news crews that had been tipped off in time to set up and film agents carrying boxes out to vans and trucks.

The scene was further enhanced by helicopters flying overhead and dogs sniffing materials to create the impression of a massive criminal operation. And it all came on the heels of a national story carried by McClatchy News several days earlier, with headlines shouting "Congressman in tight race for reelection comes under federal investigation."

Weldon immediately canceled the rest of the day's scheduled appearances as reporters, cameras, helicopters, and media vans parked outside of his home and offices. His opponent's supporters also descended, gathering with protest posters and declaring Weldom a crook and a criminal.

Fearing his daughter might need to mount an expensive legal defense, Weldon canceled all campaign TV commercials to conserve funds, and then watched as his opponent flooded the market with his own television ads and mailings, claiming that Weldon was a part of the corruption in Congress. There was no time to counter. The heat was fast and intense and couldn't be extinguished before extensive damage occurred.

Weldon had been poised to become the chair of the House Armed Services Committee if elected to an 11th term. He had served as vice chairman of both the House Armed Services Committee and the House Homeland Security Committee, and he had a long and storied resume to bolster his chances at the chairmanship.

It included authoring and sponsoring legislation to mandate a national missile defense system, which required the abrogation of the ABM treaty passed by a veto-proof House majority; drafting and creating a bilateral strategic plan for U.S./Russia relations, which was endorsed by Mike Pence and Bernie Sanders alike; and organizing and leading an 11-member bipartisan Congressional delegation to Vienna to lay the foundation to end the Balkan War.

Weldon had successfully fought to prevent the closing of the local Boeing plant in Delaware County and save 5,000 jobs; garnered a veto-proof bipartisan vote in Congress on his missile defense bill despite opposition from President Bill Clinton; and defeated Secretary of Defense Dick Cheney's attempt to slash the budget, instead restoring funding for the Marine

Corps' V-22 aircraft program

Weldon prided himself on never backing down from a fight, from his days as fire chief and Pennsylvania state fire instructor, to those as mayor in Marcus Hook, when he took on the Pagan motorcycle gang as well as negative perceptions of his beloved town.

But this one was different.

"No battle in life could prepare someone for the pain and agony of relentless attacks on your character, but even worse -- relentless attacks on your family," Weldon said in his book, Awakening the Sleeping Giant: The Political Empowerment of America's Heroes.

Weldon felt empty, unable to explain what was happening, and genuinely concerned for his daughter. He had cameras, and microphones thrust in his face every day, asking for comment, to which he could only reply, "It is what it is" and "I have done nothing wrong."

Weldon's instincts were to fight in spite of the long odds. And why not? He had faced down Kim Jung II and Paek Nam-sun of North Korea, Zoran Dindic of Serbia, King Fahd of Saudi Arabia, and Moammar Qadaffi of Libya, not to mention Vladimir Putin and Saddam Hussein.

But when your door gets kicked in for asking questions, the curious mind starts to churn even faster. They didn't kick your door in for just any reason. And certainly not for hockey tapes.

And when you discover they kicked a U.S. Congressman's doors in for the same reason, your hunch quickly grows from conspiracy theory to government conspiracy. Especially when it cost him his seat in Congress and Mueller was the man behind the curtain – a man whose FBI covered up Intel about bin Laden hiding out in Iran safe houses. A man who is currently investigating President Trump whose firebrand style of governing could expose this scandal for what it is: A massive betrayal. Even a preschooler could put those puzzle pieces together.

I spoke to Congressman Weldon who did not want to get involved with giving Intel for this book because he said "my family has gone through enough. I want to talk, there is so much to say, but I just can't do it to my family. I can't. These people in D.C. are evil people. You can't even imagine. That's all I want to say at this time."

After Mueller targeted Weldon for asking questions about bin Laden in Iran – things turned really ugly – worse than FBI raids on Weldon and his daughter and business associate in Philadelphia. That was bad because it cost Weldon his job and traumatized his daughter. But those casualties pale in comparison to what happened to Weldon's son.

Weldon kept speaking at events and kept responding to the questions, though it all seemed like a bad dream. Thirty years of public service, and now this: ambushed with no explanation and no advance notice, no consideration for his family.

The election had been poisoned and still, Election Day couldn't come fast enough. Weldon knew he couldn't win this one against the anonymous governmental bureaucratic arsonists.

On Election Day, he spent most of the day in Marcus Hook visiting old friends and stopping at polling places in the borough hall where he had served as mayor, the firehouse where he had spent countless hours, and the community building just two doors from his family's home.

That night, he gathered with his family and his wife's extended family -- the Gallaghers, of no relation to John Gallagher -- to count the returns. Unlike the two dozen times they had done this before, whether for County Council, national delegate to the Republican National Convention or for Congress, this night was different. They all knew ahead of time that the ending would be a sad one.

They watched as towns Weldon had won easily in previous elections reported neck-and-neck results or losses. Within an hour of receiving the early results, Weldon called his opponent to concede.

He held his granddaughter Reagan, then 2 years old, and told his supporters and the national television networks and reporters that his public career "had been a good run," then wished his opponent well.

The political arsonists had succeeded: the smear had worked, and Weldon's public career was over.

Weldon's son, Curt Jr., was triggered.

Weldon's son was a strapping young man, a former ice hockey player, raised in one of the toughest neighborhoods in suburban Philadelphia. And a loyal son. Close friends of Weldon and former Congressional colleagues recount this saga. After Mueller and senior Justice Department prosecutors trashed his father's career, Weldon's son "went off the rails" and informed his father Congressman that he was heading down to Washington D.C. to personally take care of the lead prosecutor who had signed off on the bogus search warrants that targeted his sister and father.

"He said he was going to kill this prosecutor," a family source said. "And he left the house in Pennsylvania in a rage and was headed to D.C. to thrash this guy in the Justice Department."

Mueller's illegal antics had triggered Weldon's son. And Weldon could not stop his son from departing the house. In a panic, Weldon called the Pennsylvania State Police who intercepted his son en route to Washington, D.C. Congressman Weldon had stopped his son from assaulting – and likely much worse -- Mueller's counterpart in the Justice Department but at a steep price. He was arrested.

"Curt's son never forgave the Congressman for what went down," another family source confessed. "It was such a mess. Just a mess."

Congressman Weldon's son, Curt Jr., -- a vibrant and robust athlete who dominated on the ice rink and baseball diamond -- turned to opioids to help cope with the depression following the arrest and the aftermath of the televised bogus federal raids orchestrated by Mueller. He spiraled deep into an addiction to pain relievers, Oxycontin, and benzodiazepines, which was prescribed for his anxiety.

In 2016, Police found Curt Jr. on his couch in his apartment, dead from a drug overdose. He was 35.

Curt Jr. left behind a 7-year-old son.

I looked up Curt. Jr.'s obituary. In part, it reads:

"Curt was interested in every one of his father's campaigns for Congress, attended three national conventions, and worked for the U.S. Chamber of Commerce and Delaware County Homebuilders Association. Curt also worked in construction, hospitality, and started his own small business. Like too many

people, Curt struggled with addiction to prescription opioids and benzodiazepines and worked through several rehab programs, but could not shake the negative spiral that is common to people suffering from addiction. Curt's love for his family and his son never wavered as he strived to control the disease that confronted him on a daily basis. Curt was a hardworking, fun-loving person who enjoyed life but fell victim to the same epidemic that has had disastrous effects on families and communities nationwide. Curt would want his legacy to be that his early death might save but one person struggling with addiction. We ask that those who wish to pay tribute to Curt do so in their own private way with someone currently afflicted with addiction. If you touch one life at risk and give that person a sense of hope and caring, Curt would be grateful! Every life has meaning; as difficult as it sometimes is, we must never give up hope! Curt is survived by his greatest love and personal treasure, his seven-year-old son, Bennett Curtis Weldon. Curt idolized Bennett in every way imaginable for a father."

The parallels here are strange for sure; the personal parallels between Weldon and me. Curt's son played at the same hockey rink my son skated at for years for the Philadelphia Little Flyers. Their high schools played against each other as well. Curt Sr. and I both grew up in Delco. He taught school in Darby. We drank beers in high school and hung out in Darby, Havertown, and Folcroft. And it was Mueller who dispatched FBI agents from the same field office in Philadelphia to disrupt both of our lives for poking around and seeking answers about the same story: What was Osama bin Laden doing in Iran.

But the bigger picture, the broader scope concerning the national political landscape and how Congressman Weldon's railroading fits – is even more bizarre.

Justice Department sources divulged the fake raids to sandbag Weldon's Congressional career were approved by Attorney General Alberto Gonzales, who had notified the Bush White House of Mueller's intent to serve a search warrant on a GOP Congressman two weeks before his re-election vote.

"This was ok'd by (Dick) Cheney," the high-ranking Justice source revealed. "The Vice President gave the approval to what amounted to ruining the career of a GOP member of Congress and to lose the seat to a Democrat. I don't think this has ever been done by a party in the last 100 years where GOP leaders ensured Weldon would be removed, silenced."

Weldon, behind the Congressional curtains, had been lobbying for powerful committees to investigate why Osama bin Laden was tucked away in Iran and how al-Qaeda was rebuilding its terror infrastructure under Iranian protection. Many of Weldon's colleagues were spooked, as were the sentinels of the Deep State. Weldon also publicly pledged – upon reelection – to call FBI and CIA officials, as well as NSA and military leaders, to the Hill to testify what they knew about bin Laden's living arrangement in Iran, which he likewise alleged was brokered by the Saudi Arabian government.

"I have never seen the GOP cannibalize its own House member like it did to Curt, days before an election," said one Congressman who asked to be kept anonymous. "In all my years, I have never seen anything quite like that."

To summarize, the Bush White House's savagery of Weldon was truly remarkable, even by Washington D.C. standards where betrayal is almost as famous as the Cherry Blossoms.

A GOP White House, led by Cheney, gave the Attorney General of Republican-led administration permission to the FBI director to ruin one of the longest-tenured GOP Congressman in the county and ultimately forfeit his seat to a Democrat.

"They were terrified of Weldon," one FBI source said. "Mueller was not a fan whatsoever."

Philadelphia attorney John Gallagher's office was a raid target as well. To me, he described the FBI-linked events of that day as a shit show.

"They closed down Market Street in Philadelphia during morning rush hour," he said. "There were 75 federal agents involved and helicopters hovering over buildings and the office. Every single media agency was there, and the streets were closed."

This was the same Philadelphia FBI field office who took its marching orders from FBI HQ to kick the door of my house in too. The similarities are startling and equally alarming.

"Mueller was worried about Weldon getting control of intelligence oversight," one well-placed Bush administration official said. "He ranted about Curt after many floor speeches and press conferences and when his book came out. He (Weldon) had many powerful people worried and truly wanted to clean up the intelligence community."

Weldon's book hammered the dysfunctional intelligence community and accused the CIA of failing to act on Intel pinpointing bin Laden's whereabouts. Before 2004, for instance, Weldon asked CIA Director George Tenet to work with a well-placed informant dishing details of bin Laden's activities in Iran.

Tenet said he would act on the shocking Intel but then reneged.

Weldon then called out Tenet on national television, throwing him under the bus on CNN in June 2005.

WELDON: *Well, Soledad, I was on "Live on CNN" on September the 11th right after the attacks, and I said, "Today our system failed the American people."*

And back then -- for two years I had been pushing, and the CIA had resisted establishing a national collaborative (intelligence) center. That capability exists today.

The CIA has not always been right. They didn't predict the fall of Communism. They didn't get it right when North Korea launched a three-stage missile. And they didn't predict 9/11, even though we told them what they should have been doing.

I was approached by a Democratic member of Congress two years ago about information about the location of bin Laden, and not from one source, but from several sources. I went to the CIA a week later, gave it to George Tenet. He assigned one of their top operations people to work with me.

One of the sources I gave them -- the first meeting he had wasn't with the U.S. intelligence officer. It was with a French intelligence officer in Paris. And when my source called me, he said, "Congressman, I had a meeting, but it was French intelligence, and they told me not to talk to an American member of Congress."

Now, that's not the way our intelligence community should operate. If they didn't think this guy had any credibility, they'd come back and tell me. But don't send someone from French intelligence to tell this guy not to talk to an American member of Congress when over the past two years we've seen that Iran, Ayatollah Khomeini, has been causing major problems for us in theater, in the region and around the world.

Weldon had just called out the former CIA director, who stepped down a year earlier, on CNN. In essence, Tenet had placated Weldon and passed the bin Laden informant off to French Intel. Clearly, the CIA was not interested in Intel about bin Laden in Iran.

Ignoring intelligence at CIA was a recurring theme, even though, as early as 2003, informants and federal agents were reporting bin Laden sightings in Tehran and other parts of Iran. And that doesn't even include the Congressional chatter in the beltway. Sure, other Congressmen were fielding similar reports, but no one had the balls like Weldon to publicly flame throw Bush administration members on live television or in print. Even the Democratic Congressman who initially tipped me off to the Iranian bin Laden information explicitly told me if I outed him in any way, it would set off a shit storm.

"I never out anybody, you know that by now," I said.

"I know that otherwise, I wouldn't have told you," he said.

I kept my mouth shut. Like I always do, as far as linking his name to the information. But I still got that shit storm regardless.

Meanwhile, Weldon was on a path to big trouble too, but he didn't yet realize it. He was being monitored – just like the Trump campaign in 2016.

Looking back, Weldon realized he had made a lot of enemies inside the beltway, particularly during his last term. As recently as September 2006, the National Journal had published a front-page story declaring Weldon "The Troublemaker" for his investigations of numerous and serious Clinton scandals, pre-9/11 intelligence that had gone ignored, bilateral U.S,/Russia stupidity, and the whereabouts of Bin Laden.

Weldon had fought the "deep state" bureaucracy, especially intelligence operatives, and created anonymous enemies who were eager to remove him from office. He had publicly criticized the CIA's leadership for its lack of a coherent policy to deal with Iran in his 2005 book, "Countdown to Terror."

In that book, Weldon had presented evidence of Iran's secret plan to undermine and control local civic groups throughout Iraq and the Middle East.

But the biggest bombshell was when Weldon revealed, publicly for the first time, his unsuccessful efforts in 1999 to establish and fund a national data mining center through which the intelligence agencies could collaborate with the Pentagon and share raw intelligence data. His proposal for what was deemed the NOAH Fusion Center (National Operations and Analysis Hub) was rejected by the FBI and the CIA.

Weldon's book also said that pre-9/11 intelligence had been largely ignored by our agencies and bureaucracy. During its investigations, the 9/11 Commission had refused to interview anyone associated with "Able Danger," a top-secret program created in 1999 by Hugh Sheldon, chairman of the Joint Chiefs of Staff, to collect actionable intelligence against Al Qaeda worldwide. The commission's 9/11 report contains no mention of the Able Danger program.

Military intelligence officers from the Army and Navy told Weldon that Able Danger had identified Mohammad Atta and the leading 9/11 masterminds in the U.S. two years before the attack, but was prohibited from passing that information along to the Justice Department -- and were now instructed to remain silent.

That conclusion matched information contained in the national bestseller "Horse Soldiers," also published in 2005, in which Army Special Operations General Geoffrey Lambert admitted that within seconds of the 9/11 attacks, he knew who was behind it. Lambert said he knew it was Atta because he had been briefed about him by Able Danger several years earlier. He described his involvement in the decision to block the transfer of military-collected intelligence to the Justice Department as one of the worst decisions of his career.

The information in "Countdown to Terror" had not been the ramblings of a conspiracy theorist. It had been vetted by former CIA intelligence analysts, and former CIA Director Jim Woolsey as well as Al Gore's National Security Advisor, Jack Caravelli, both endorsed the book.

After the book was published and Able Danger was revealed, former FBI Director Louie Freeh said in the Wall Street Journal that we might have been able to prevent the 9/11 attack if we had allowed the transfer of Able Danger information to the Justice Department.

It was shocking information, but any furor was bound to die down eventually as some other crisis grabbed the country's attention. What Weldon's enemies would not have been able to wait out would have been his ascension to the chairman of the House Armed Services Committee.

If that had happened, Weldon would have had unlimited subpoena power regarding any investigation involving national security.

And it was no secret that, as chairman, he would have convened formal hearings on pre-9/11 intelligence, Able Danger, and the whereabouts of Bin Laden. He would have issued the subpoenas necessary.

It was crystal clear: the only way to prevent that from happening was to thwart Weldon's re-election. His career needed to be burned to the ground.

As a side note, while I remember to mention:

Let's jump ahead 11 years and discuss the 2016 election briefly. After we started breaking stories on the FBI – and exposing corrupt pieces of the Bureau – internal emails show Andrew McCabe wrote James Comey at FBI HQ and called True Pundit a "heavyweight source." We received some props from our readers as the docs were released on the FBI Vault by the Bureau. True Pundit was a "heavyweight source." Sounds good coming from the top tier of the FBI. But … I read between the lines. To me, McCabe was busting my balls, and the FBI released those emails so I would know McCabe's thoughts: I was a piece of shit. A rookie. That's how I interpreted the "heavyweight source" comment. So, I'm always up for a fight. We had been honing the best McCabe Intel for some time, adding to it. Enhancing. My thoughts were: if you want to go to that much trouble to bust my chops – and you're calling me a lightweight – we'll just open up the tap and let it all start flowing out. And we did. Big league. We were producing one breaking story after another on McCabe, and then we moved onto his associates.

Where is McCabe now? The lesson? Be careful who you poke a stick at. They might take that stick and shove it up your ass.

Back to Weldon.

Weldon was learning this lesson too. The Deep State turned on Weldon in 2004-2005. According to intelligence sources, Weldon was the target of wiretapping of phones and emails as well as internet activity. Likewise, his computer use was being monitored both in D.C, his office outside Philly, and his home.

"This looks like it was a FISA sweep involving the FBI or they (the Deep State) tapped him without any warrant," one source revealed to me. "I don't see how this could have been approved any other way. They were looking at everything on this guy. His file looks pretty bad going back to 2003."

The same time Weldon began asking questions about bin Laden's whereabouts in Iran. Purely coincidental, I'm sure.

That is Intel from one of my "heavyweight" sources. One of the same folks who helped get McCabe and his pals fired from the FBI. Irony.

But wait, the Deep State was using FISA warrants and illegal wiretapping as political weapons in 2003 and 2004?

Who in Mueller's FBI and the Bush Justice Department signed off on spying on a member of Congress? Or was Weldon surveilled without any warrant? This was a Republican serving a Republican White House. A Republican administration spying on a Republican Congressman. Then ordering FBI raids on the Congressman's family and associates two weeks before an election.

And still, no one in the federal government had lifted a damn finger to see if bin Laden, in fact, is or was living in Iran at the time.

Again, we fast forward to 2018. So the FBI played a role in the illegal surveillance of a U.S. Congressman circa 2004 and now the man who was FBI director at the time – Robert Mueller – is investigating Trump who was also the target of illegal wiretapping under FISA by the FBI under Mueller's best friend forever, James Comey. There seems to be rather large conflicts here, to say the least. And proof that FISA and wiretaps have been a weapon in the Deep State's arsenal for more than a decade – more likely almost two decades.

Congressman Weldon was out of a career spanning two decades in Congress and set on a path to a rough journey -- burying his son who was collateral damage of the Deep State rainmakers in D.C. who play for keeps when it comes to protecting the D.C. Swamp.

There was no time, of course, to analyze and draw attention to the questionable FBI raids at the time it all happened, but some interesting facts became clear afterward:

- No one agent from the FBI ever questioned Weldon or his daughter Karen
- Attorney Gallagher had been working on highly sensitive initiatives for the U.S. government when the FBI raided his law office
- The National Congressional Committee emailed Weldon's campaign chairman in September 2006 to advise the campaign that Weldon's opponent had decreased his weekly Philadelphia TV purchase by $463,000 for one week only during the eight weeks before Election Day. That one week wound up coinciding with the week following the raids -- which garnered substantial national and regional media coverage.

Weldon would contrast his treatment with that of former Illinois governor and Congressman Rod Blagojevich, indicted on Dec. 9, 2008. When U.S. Attorney Patrick Fitzgerald announced the indictment, he said that he could have indicted Blagojevich before the election but waited until December because of the Justice Department's policy of not taking public action that could affect an election.

In Weldon's case, the planted news stories and public raids all took place three weeks before the election and directly led to a defeat. There was no indictment, no arrest, and neither Weldon nor his daughter was questioned.

Weldon said he doesn't blame FBI agents for what happened and has the utmost respect for them and for their profession. During his career, Weldon had worked alongside FBI agents to fight organized crime, including the Pagans motorcycle gang, and to fight terrorism and foreign espionage.

He was outraged, however, at the anonymous political arsonists who ordered his takedown and who caused harm to his daughter.

And his son.

The Deep State had sent a clear message to Congressmen and Senators who may have considered picking up Weldon's bin Laden-lit torch in Iran. That subject was clearly off limits and caveat emptor to any lawmaker who wanted to broach it on national television.

Or they may find themselves picking out a casket for their children too.

For me, Weldon's story struck several nerves, and I was better suited to understand just how nefarious Deep State players are, including Mueller.

"Mueller hates Weldon," an FBI insider said. "There is real hate there. He wanted to take him down."

I am no expert in Middle Eastern affairs nor do I ever want to be, only because most of the pundits and experts have rigid ideologies and opinions that will remain unswayed regardless of exculpatory proof. While many experts are indeed passionate, they are entrenched and shackled by religious doctrines, others by rivalries based on heritage. Nefarious entities exploit this. These are weaknesses, the inability to process new intelligence because it doesn't match previous experiences, knowledge, and analytics. This is how governments and their players hide frauds and scandals in plain sight. This is textbook Deep State.

This is textbook FBI and vintage Deep-State Mueller.

A relevant example is to discount the factual

landscape of this work based on the premonition that the Saudis and Iranians are sworn enemies and would never work together, especially to hide Osama bin Laden. Such supposition heavily discounts the fact that Muslim dogma requires believers to protect and aid their brethren against all infidels, especially those in the United States, according to Intel officials who cited this as one fundamental motivation to hatch the deal to warehouse bin Laden – and al-Qaeda – in Iran. Among many other reasonable reasons. Pallets packed high with cash. Influence. Safety. Weapons.

Likewise, both countries had just formulated a security pact in 2001 work with each other instead of against one another. It was a landmark agreement. That is a fact and trumps all arguments that "these two countries hate each other."

This is why reporting facts and testimonies prove far more superior to pontificating personal opinions which are inherently flawed and biased. And therefore, the "non-expert" on a topic who showcases facts, documents as well as dates and times is likely more qualified to add new dialogue to any complicated debate, compared to regurgitating talking points honed through decades of analysis and observation.

Broken down, what does this mean? I'm a simple man reporting simple facts to explain complicated stories. And facts do matter. Especially facts like in the case of Weldon's political death.

If you present viable, correct pieces to a puzzle, certainly you have likewise added inherent value to help solve complex issues and the big 'picture.' It doesn't matter if you have all the pieces to the puzzle and can connect them all, it only matters that the pieces fit. The experts are then better suited to move the pieces around and find their matches.

The puzzle was coming together.

Before I forget, I talked to Gallagher for the book. He said Mueller's FBI took one file from his office during the raid. Gallagher was representing a Russian citizen who had family members in Philadelphia and who begged John to take the case.

So why did Mueller want the file?

The Russian was run over by a drunk driver and confined to a wheel chair. That drunk driver was a station chief for the CIA on duty in and around Moscow. He was on his way to a strip club. And he was blasted.

But it wasn't the first time the CIA officer mowed people down with his car on duty. Drunk.

And Gallagher had compiled affidavits from other State Dept. employees attesting that they man was a menace and should be fired. Gallagher said this man was likely a friend of Mueller or a friend of a Deep-State friend.

"Mueller wanted the file because the guy was a CIA station chief but he was also president of the Communist Party over there in some regards," Gallagher said. "We had pictures of him in the file dressed in a Nazi uniform at one of the meetings. So I think that was the reason the FBI raided my office, to get that file for something Mueller wanted to keep quiet as a favor."

Another side note here I must add before it slips my mind. At the same time Mueller was silencing and ruining Weldon, the FBI was covering up Intel on bin Laden in Iran. These are insane facts.

Former FBI Ops leader Mogilner said she was working for a CIA front company at the same time as a cover for Agency Intel work. She notified her old bosses at the FBI – Robert Mueller's FBI – about bin Laden's location in Iran. Neither Mueller nor any of his deputies reached out to her for additional details. There was never even any follow up. She was taken aback by the cavalier attitude.

This means U.S. Special Counsel Robert Mueller -- former director of the FBI -- failed to act on intelligence confirming al-Qaeda leader Osama bin Laden was in Iran for years after 9/11.

Mueller was FBI director spanning the time bin Laden had been tucked away in safe houses in Iran with his family. But Mueller ignored intelligence from well-placed informants that bin Laden was in Iran.

Another informant from Europe who had done contract work for the CIA and FBI -- was also blowing the whistle on bin Laden but no one on Mueller's FBI would follow up, according to interviews I conducted. He had peppered federal agents with deauls on bin Laden's activities and travels in Iran – sending tips for nearly 36 MONTHS – THREE YEARS.

Mueller never followed up. The informant was ignored.

During the same time that FBI executives were sitting on the bombshell information about bin Laden's whereabouts, Bob Levinson mysteriously disappeared in Iran in 2007. Even after Levinson's capture in Iran, FBI executives still took no action to act on intelligence pointing to bin Laden's residency in Iran.

More alarming, Levinson vanished from Kish Island in Iran and bin Laden had been spotted at the same place by other informants, though it is a popular resort area.

Instead, under Mueller, the FBI covered up the bombshell Intel pouring in from federal agents and informants. Meanwhile, bin Laden was public enemy Number One, at the top of the FBI's Most Wanted list, yet the FBI did nothing to pursue credible intelligence he was living in Iran.

And now Mueller is investigating President Trump.

Levinson, a former FBI agent, and CIA officer is believed to be held captive in Iran.

Even Barack Obama's $151 Billion ransom paid to Iran in the form of a "nuclear deal," freed all other American hostages held in Iranian captivity, except for Levinson.

Why? Does Levinson too know the details of the Saudi government's secret deal with Iran to safeguard bin Laden and his al-Qaeda deputies after 9/11 in Iran?

More importantly, were efforts to bring Levinson home intentionally botched by high-ranking FBI executives? The operation was spearheaded by now-disgraced FBI deputy director Andrew McCabe who is under federal investigation in late 2013. By then James Comey had taken the reigns of the FBI from the retired Mueller.

Comey and McCabe. The FBI duo who allowed Hillary Clinton to skate, now in charge of a hostage recovery operation in Iran. One can guess how this turned out.

FBI agents said FBI bosses tampered with the Levinson rescue case and it went sideways, despite the tireless efforts of the Bureau's rank-and-file to bring him home.

Eight months after the Boston marathon bombing, FBI agents experienced problematic case meddling by FBI bosses, sources said.

Levinson is a former Drug Enforcement Administration and Federal Bureau of Investigation agent who disappeared in Iran in 2007, where it is believed he remains captive today.

U.S. officials believed Levinson was grabbed by Iranian intelligence to be dangled as a bargaining chip in sanction negotiations with Washington. After, of course, he was interrogated and likely tortured. Levinson was likely working an OP for the CIA at the time of his arrest, according to numerous public sources.

When FBI team members pitched other ways they thought they could help free Levinson from Iran, the ideas were shot down, squelched or stalled by bosses.

Now, after revelations shine a light on the U.S. intelligence agencies ignoring credible intelligence about bin Laden living in Iran -- and operating al-Qaeda from Iran -- are we to believe that the government didn't leave Levinson in Iran because he knew this too? And presumably would talk about it publicly if and when he was freed and back in the United States.

Mike Moore

8 CIA & HILLARY SAFEGUARD BIN LADEN, AT ALL COSTS

Intelligence folks report that after Tenet left the CIA, his successor Porter Goss too pledged to look into the reports – trickling in from other Congressional sources -- that bin Laden was indeed living in Iran. Goss was new on the job in late 2004 and assigned the task to select deputies. In fairness to the CIA, Goss did press for status reports on the Iranian intelligence. New reports were filed from informants in the Middle East and Europe, mirroring what Weldon said.

"Goss was in over his head at CIA," one well-placed intelligence source admitted. "It's not that he couldn't handle the job, that wasn't it at all. He wanted to change the CIA, reform it. He came from the legislative side and believed the company (CIA) needed retooling."

Goss' reforms were met with serious blowback by the agency's Deep State sentinels and liberal

Clintonian gatekeepers. Goss' demands for agency personnel to ferret out the bin Laden intelligence was ignored, and his underlings placated Goss by telling him it was being looked at. It is quite doubtful any such assurances were true. The CIA hadn't lifted a fucking finger to pursue bin Laden in Iran or even develop more intelligence. Goss was being lied to at the same time Weldon was being spied on.

Goss lasted seven months as director of the CIA.

Any semblance of a CIA inquiry into bin Laden's activities and living situation in Iran left the building with Goss.

The Deep State had whacked Weldon and Goss and iced CIA assets in Europe and the Middle East which continued to report bin Laden sightings in Iran from 2003 thru 2007. In fact, federal agents were told informants would no longer be paid for any tips or information linked to Osama bin Laden or al-Qaeda deputies hiding in Iran. Uncle Sam closed his fat wallet and eventually, informants clammed up.

Makes sense. Why do you need to pay informants giving intelligence on bin Laden's whereabouts if you already know of his locations? And if you want him hidden in Iran, the last thing you need is another Curt Weldon poking around and demanding answers. I mean, how many Congressmen or Senators can you illegally wiretap before word gets out about that? Perhaps we should ask Mueller and Comey.

Shutting off the American cash pipeline to bin Laden informants and rats who pump HUMINT to federal agents was the brainchild of the man who took over the CIA after Goss quickly packed his bags and got the hell out of Langley. Michael Hayden, the boisterous anti-Trump analyst for CNN, took the CIA reigns from Goss. Another Bush appointee. And another Deep State general who had little tolerance for any intelligence linking bin Laden to being holed up in Iran.

Now, Hayden was a strategic appointment for Bush. If Bush wanted to keep a lid on any Iranian-linked bin Laden scandal, Hayden was a key appointment. Hayden was a retired four-star general and more importantly, former director of the National Security Agency, from 1999 to 2005. If the NSA had pinpointed any chatter – from anywhere in the world – about Osama bin Laden or his al-Qaeda deputies in Iran, Hayden would know, as the NSA monitors terror networks worldwide. And damn near everyone else too from school teachers to mob bosses. I mean, just ask Hayden.

Hayden was the father of warrantless wiretapping when he ran the NSA, the byproduct of supposedly trying to keep the United States safe from terrorists after 9/11. (Unless of course, you receive intelligence that the mastermind of 9/11 is living in Iran).

Even a rudimentary online search in Wikipedia pinpoints Hayden's involvement in what emerged as one of the biggest government scandals in U.S history:

He was Director of the National Security Agency (NSA) from 1999 to 2005. During his tenure as director, he oversaw the controversial NSA surveillance of technological communications between persons in the United States and alleged foreign terrorist groups, which resulted in the NSA warrantless surveillance controversy.

NSA warrantless surveillance (also commonly referred to

as "warrantless-wiretapping" or "-wiretaps") relates to the surveillance of persons within the United States, including United States citizens, during the collection of foreign intelligence by the National Security Agency (NSA) as part of the Terrorist Surveillance Program.[1] The NSA was authorized to monitor, without obtaining a FISA warrant, the phone calls, Internet activity, text messages and other communication involving any party believed by the NSA to be outside the U.S., even if the other end of the communication lay within the U.S.

Soon after the 9/11 attacks President Bush established the President's Surveillance Program. As part of the program, the Terrorist Surveillance Program was established pursuant to an executive order that authorized the NSA to surveil certain telephone calls without obtaining a warrant (see 50 U.S.C. § 1802 50 U.S.C. § 1809). The complete details of the executive order are not public, but according to administration statements,[5] the authorization covers communication originating overseas from or to a person suspected of having links to terrorist organizations or their affiliates even when the other party to the call is within the US.

In October 2001, Congress passed the Patriot Act, which granted the administration broad powers to fight terrorism. The Bush administration used these powers to bypass the FISC and directed the NSA to spy directly on al-Qaeda via a new NSA electronic surveillance program. Reports at the time indicate that an "apparently accidental" "glitch" resulted in the interception of communications that were between two U.S. parties. [6] This act was challenged by multiple groups, including Congress, as unconstitutional.

The precise scope of the program remains secret, but the NSA was provided total, unsupervised access to all fiber-optic communications between the nation's largest telecommunication companies' major interconnected locations, encompassing phone conversations, email, Internet activity, text messages and corporate private network traffic.[7]

Remember Edward Snowden? He blew the whistle on Hayden's Stellar Wind program at NSA after Hayden had the bright idea to fire government employees and hand the country's most valued secrets to outside contractors. Like Snowden. And companies that operate like Fusion GPS, and many sources surmise Fusion GPS itself. A fantastic way for your friends to land lucrative contracts. In fact, it's a fair statement that without Hayden, there would have been no Edward Snowden debacle.

But now – after a tenure at NSA where Intel officers used the Constitution like a dish rag -- Hayden was running the CIA. Even after the NSA failed to flag any actionable intelligence al Qaeda telecommunications involving plans to wage jihad on America – leading up to 9/11. Perhaps Stellar Wind would have served as a more appropriate name for Bush's cabinet and intelligence post selections.

So if Mueller's FBI did not apply for a FISA warrant to wiretap and spy on Weldon, Hayden would have been the point man on monitoring such communications in 2005 at NSA. And he didn't need any pesky warrant to do so. Hayden has lashed out at President Trump on Twitter in defense of fellow former CIA Director John Brennan in recent months.

You can at this point make a safe wager that given Hayden's history at NSA – and the possibility he wiretapped at least one Congressman for speaking out against the Deep State -- he likely was not interested in any actionable intelligence pinpointing bin Laden in Iran. And you would be right.

Despite the Deep State's best efforts to curb bin-Laden tips about Iran, they just would not die. The information kept filtering its way through the State Department, FBI to the CIA. Even U.S. Senators now were getting involved, including top Democrat Rep. John Murtha and GOP's Weldon and Sen. Olympia Snowe had all given Hayden heads up, relaying information from their sources that bin Laden was in Iran. Now, Hayden had a chance to redeem himself for a disastrous tenure at NSA and perhaps pursue this intelligence and develop an Op to seek and catch bin Laden.

What would Hayden do? Patriot or puppet?

Deep State puppet.

"Hayden received tips from Congress about Iran (and bin Laden)," one well-placed intelligence source said. "His blanket response was to instruct them not to share the intelligence with staff members and other members of Congress."

One senator wrote Hayden multiple times revealing, based on independent information and federal informants, bin Laden had been spotted in Iran on several occasions in 2006 and 2007

"Hayden instructed the Senator not to mention this among colleagues in committees because they didn't need that information spreading. He was in damage control."

Now there's a leader who is going to reform the CIA. And find bin Laden. Unless, of course, the CIA already knew where bin Laden was.

Hayden had spooked select lawmakers, telling them if explosive intelligence like this leaked to staffers and through Congress, it could spread quickly through the beltway. Like wildfire. The alarming revelations were already making rounds on the D.C. elite cocktail circuit. That was dangerous enough. But also relegated to many of the old guard, both Democrat and Republican, who knew how to keep a secret, and put it in a vault for a rainy day for leverage. Like a squirrel stockpiling nuts for the winter, D.C.'s electorate busied themselves finding such nuts and hoarding them for use at some unknown future date during some yet-to-be-determined political crisis.

But this intelligence was no ordinary nut. In fact, it could burn down the entire forest. A big plug like this, when pulled, could drain a large portion of the prophetic D.C. Swamp. Quickly.

There was no chance to find, kill or place OBL in custody. He wasn't in the country at the time.

"The betrayal at play is tremendous," a former State Department official said. "If you take the information about him (bin Laden) and go looking for him in Iran, but fail to bring him out, at least you tried. At no point did we really follow up. There was always some type of excuse."

That revelation in a nutshell truly speaks volumes. More facts can often be deduced from what the government failed to do and why they failed to do it. In this scenario that is trying to confirm bin Laden was in Iran. Even applied to basic principles of human behavior and motivation, if you do not know where someone is, you conduct a search for that individual based on any and all tips and information. If you genuinely seek recovery. But if you know where someone is – even if you're claiming you do not -- you do not need to conduct any search.

And for patriots who believe in truth, justice, and

the American way -- things were about to get even darker.

Let's recap on how, so far, CIA directors handled the bin Laden in Iran Intel. And remember, this is based on the intelligence I have assembled without access to documents, cables, witness testimony – all the goodies a Senate committee or the FBI would have access too. So we are literally just scratching the surface.

Tenet: Failed to act or even search for bin Laden in Iran.
Goss: Wanted to act, tried to respond, was lied to and forced out of CIA in seven months.
Hayden: Failed to act or even search for bin Laden in Iran.

Enter Leon Panetta, who took over the CIA for Hayden in 2009.

"Panetta is an institutional worm who lives in the pockets of the Clinton family," one Congressman confided with me. "I didn't trust him when he was in the House (Congress), and as CIA director, he became even worse. Don't forget, he then became secretary of defense under Obama."

Of course, I am talking to the Congressman about Panetta's response to how he handled the specific intelligence that made it to his desk that Osama bin Laden was living tucked away in Iran. And the Congressman flies off the handle about Panetta, firing off examples of his political malfeasance and corrupt history doing the bidding for the Democrats and particularly anything that needs to be performed to protect the "Clinton Cartel."

But then — somewhere in the middle of his rant - - ... I mean it's a rant where the Congressman gets those little white things in the sides of his lips because he's talking so fast and animated that his mouth cannot produce enough saliva to keep up. But he says, you need to ask your sources about Bill Richardson.

"The governor of New Mexico?" I responded? "What the fuck does he know about bin Laden?"

"He knew bin Laden was in Iran. Just ask your sources. See what you can dig up."

Now, this is a new wrinkle in the story. A Democratic governor tossed into the mix here. This might get interesting, I thought. Richardson was a former U.S. Ambassador to the U.N. and Dept. of Energy Secretary under Bill Clinton. We're moving up the chain of custody here, I thought. He also sought the Democratic presidential nomination in 2008, with his sights on becoming the first Latino president.

Now I was already scheduled to travel to New Mexico and chat up many spooks, so this might dovetail nicely to see what could be found. And Richardson was the longtime governor and Obama buddy. If you consider Wayne Newton Mr. Las Vegas, then Bill Richardson is Mr. New Mexico. I was really intrigued.

The Congressman was right. Richardson was in play. But I am at a loss here because on limited funds. I have trekked to New Mexico and it is far too early to pull a Mike Wallace on Richardson in Sante Fe at his home or office. It's August, and the book isn't coming out until the Fall. I can't light a fire yet with a loyal member of the Democratic machine like Richardson, or it would spark a bonfire, and that would give the machine months to prep to take me down. And this story with it. Now, I know I am going to light some fires out here in New Mexico regardless, but they are small fires with ex-spooks – that frankly, you can never fully trust. These guys are some of the best liars you have ever seen. Learning to deceive and lie, after all, are part of the tradecraft and the tools to keep you alive while on the job. After a while, at least for me – it was hard to discern between truth and lies, after performing spook work. So I understand some of these sources will double cross me – but it is a smart play.

They fail to recognize my upside. I am banking on getting double-crossed because such leaks will allow others to contact me after they are debriefed by colleagues – and in essence, rat them out. I expand my reach, again, on a limited budget by investing in the notion that spies will be spies. And they have to report Intel to someone.

It's late October as I write this and by now Richardson already knows what I was working on. So knocking on his door like CBS' Mike Wallace would have been a rookie move in this pursuit. That's a Big Media play. And I am small media, wielding a big stick.

In 2011, Richardson was on the short list for a position in Obama's cabinet. It was a foregone conclusion that Obama would wipe the floor with Mitt Romney in the 2012 presidential election so Richardson's name was being floated for months to be appointed to a cabinet slot and it could have happened even before Obama's reelection. That is an essential backdrop for the coming intelligence on Richardson.

Another critical factor in understanding the political landscape at the time is to look at the public comments of Panetta during the exact time frame we are discussing involving Richardson.

We turn to the June 28, 2010 transcript of a conversation between Panetta and Jake Tapper on This Week on ABC:

TAPPER: What's the latest thinking on where Osama bin Laden is, what kind of health he's in, and how much control or contact he has with al Qaeda?

PANETTA: He is, as is obvious, in very deep hiding. He's in an area of the tribal regions of Pakistan that is very difficult -- the terrain is probably the most difficult in the world --

TAPPER: Can you be more specific? Is it in Waziristan, or?

PANETTA: All I can tell you is that it's in the tribal areas, is all we know -- that he's located in that vicinity. The terrain is very difficult. He obviously has tremendous security around him.

But having said that, the more we continue to disrupt al Qaeda's operations -- And we are engaged in the most aggressive operations in the history of the CIA in that part of the world, and the result is that we are disrupting their leadership. We've taken down more than half of their Taliban leadership -- of their al Qaeda leadership. We just took down number three in their leadership a few weeks ago.

We continue to disrupt them. We continue to impact on their command-and-control. We continue to impact on their ability to plan attacks in this country. If we keep that pressure on, we think ultimately we can flush out bin Laden and Zawahiri, and get after them.

TAPPER: When's the last time we had good intelligence on bin Laden's location?

PANETTA: It's been awhile. I think it almost goes back, you know, to the early 2000s that it went -- you know, in terms of -- actually, when he was moving from Afghanistan to Pakistan that we had the last precise information about where he might be located. Since then, it's very difficult to get any intelligence on his exact location.

During 2008 through 2010, Richardson approached Obama administration officials and CIA Director Panetta directly to relay information he had developed showing Osama bin Laden was living in Iran. According to intelligence sources, Richardson provided Panetta with details of bin Laden's whereabouts soon after Panetta took over the Agency from Hayden.

Add this to the other intelligence that kept filtering into the American intelligence apparatus – both via front channels and back channels – and you quickly see Panetta was flat out lying to Tapper. Keep in mind that Panetta had already been briefed by Richardson about bin Laden's location in Iran.

By this time, the United States government had been delivered credible intelligence time and time again that bin Laden and family members had been tucked away in safe houses in Iran. And bin Laden himself had been either spotted or placed at crucial meetings in cities Iranian strongholds, including:

Shiraz
Qom
Natanz
Yazd
Isfahan
Tehran
Kish Islands

Yes, that's the same Kish Islands where Bob Levinson – former FBI and CIA operative – was kidnapped in 2007. And hasn't been seen since. That seems like an important detail the Feds would want to leave out of the public discourse about Levison's plight. Intel insiders report that few if any, Intel leads were coming in from paid Taliban and al-Qaeda informants placing bin Laden in Afghanistan – not even cave drawings put the terror leader there at the identical times sightings in Iran were pouring in.

"Panetta was told bin Laden might have shaved his beard and often wore business suits when traveling in Iran," one intelligence insider said.

Regardless, Panetta was sticking to the Deep State narrative that bin Laden was in a deep, dark, damp cave in Afghanistan. Even though Richardson – who was up for becoming Obama's Secretary of Labor at the time – specifically supplied intelligence, directly to Panetta, that bin Laden was in Iran.

"The problem for Richardson was that he wouldn't let it go," one intelligence insider said. "He didn't get an answer, and he kept asking Panetta what the CIA was going to do about bin Laden (in Iran). Bill can be like a pit bull, and he was upset about not hearing back about explosive information he provided."

Panetta had little intention of rounding up a posse and extracting bin Laden from Iran, either physically or diplomatically. The Deep State had traveled well past the point of no return by now, and even though Richardson was a newcomer to this journey, it was still a ship to nowhere. It's just that when you're on a CIA ship that swaps out captains during the trip, no one informs whistleblowers like Richardson that he might be in for a rough ride. It just happens, like when the FBI kicks your door in and terrorizes your family.

In 2009 Richardson soon found his New Mexico Governor's Office hit with a grand jury probe and the subpoenas started flying. He was the target of a fraud investigation for a pay-to-play scandal now, and it was leaked far and wide to the media – at a crucial time in Richardson's storied political career.

1. There was talk he was on the short list to become the next secretary of state.
2. He was a lock for secretary of commerce, a cabinet position in the White House
3. If all else failed he still boasted a stellar political resume as his tenure of as governor was winding down.

Richardson did not yet realize his political career was over. Every time folks tuned on the television or read the newspaper in New Mexico, pundits and reporters were talking about "Bill Richardson" and "grand jury" and "scandal."

"He was hung out to dry by Obama for pressing the bin Laden issue," said a White House confidant who served under Obama and Bush. "There is no question."

The intelligence assessment, according to insiders, was even more stacked against Richardson. He had served in key positions under Bill Clinton's White House and was thought to be a loyal Clintonian. But he angered the Clinton Cartel when he endorsed Obama in the Democratic primary when he was facing off against Hillary Clinton. Hillary was serving as Secretary of State and working hand-in-hand with Panetta.

You do the math.

Richardson, the five-time nominee for the Nobel Peace Prize for mediating dicey foreign dilemmas, was being railroaded for doing the right thing. Richardson in Feb. 2009 was asked, behind the scenes, by Obama to withdraw his nomination for secretary of commerce. He did. Richardson then lost the governor's race by 7 points after his approval rating went from 60 percent to the about 30 percent.

The Daily Beast described Richardson's epic spiral from political grace with the headline: "The Man Obama Double-Crossed."

More like triple crossed. (The Daily Beast seldom gets anything right.)

Incredibly, the undaunted Richardson still kept dogging Panetta about bin Laden in Iran.

"You have to credit this man," an intelligence insider said. "They unraveled a solid career in politics, and he would not walk away from this. I don't think he understood what he was up against until much later. Richardson wanted to help the United States negotiate with the Iran to release bin Laden into U.S. custody. This is why he kept going back to Panetta. Richardson could have pulled it off too, if anyone could have, and he kept asking for permission and a team to open up talks with Iran."

In late 2010, after he approached Panetta with what might have been his final plea to follow up on his intelligence about bin Laden, he soon found his answer.

"Hillary Clinton and Panetta shipped Richardson to North Korea to get him out of their hair," one well-placed State Department source said. "They wanted him to handle the negotiation for hostages."

With all the distractions – the grand jury probe and a faltering economy in New Mexico due in part to Richardson's attention to clearing his name – the long-time and faithful Democrat was battling for his political life. He had been term-limited as governor and had to step down anyway on Jan. 1, 2011, but what about political life after the governor's office?

Richardson was still wrestling with the pay-to-play criminal investigation which was beginning to look like a cooked up smear. Then in 2011, Obama and pals upped the stakes. Richardson was the target of a new federal grand jury probe.

The New York Times, the Deep State's house organ, was more than happy to leak the news:

"Bill Richardson, the former governor of New Mexico who ran for president in 2008, is being investigated by a federal grand jury for possible violations of campaign finance laws, according to people with knowledge of the inquiry.

Defense lawyers and others briefed on the investigation said one of the accusations is that Mr. Richardson raised

$250,000 from supporters to quiet a woman who had threatened to file a sexual harassment suit against him.

Kenneth J. Gonzales, the United States attorney for New Mexico, said in a statement that he could "neither confirm nor deny the existence of any grand jury investigation into alleged criminal conduct" by Mr. Richardson.

Obama and pals had reached back into the Democratic playbook to put the nail in Richardson's political coffin: pulling the sex card and coupling it with a federal investigation. This tactic was recently on public display in the Brett Kavanaugh Supreme Court confirmation hearings – except the Democrats didn't have enough time to cook up a federal investigation before pinning the accusations on Kavanaugh. Instead, they pressed for an FBI probe during the smear – a new wrinkle in an old playbook.

Neither Richardson -- nor any member of his staff -- was ever indicted for any alleged crimes from either federal investigation.

"It was just politically motivated charges that went nowhere, but when they're broadcast, they stick in the public's mind," Richardson said in an interview with the Los Angeles Times.

Richardson told the LA Times that his relentless style might have worn out the public.
"People get tired of politicians," he said.

Especially ones who keep poking a stick in the CIA director's face about Osama bin Laden hiding in plain sight in Iran.

Richardson never served in political office again.

While Richardson was being ostracized and politically equalized – fancy terms for trashed and ruined -- Panetta and Hillary Clinton were running a sweet side Op.

Clinton, running the State Dept. at the time, and Panetta again running the CIA. A formidable Democratic duo. Generals of the Deep State, no doubt.

Enter the little-known Rewards for Justice Program. A simple Wikipedia search explains the foundation of this program where anyone can submit tips to help capture America's most wanted terrorists and receive a hefty cash reward if they are arrested. Or at least that's how it is supposed to operate:

The Rewards for Justice Program (RFJ) is the counterterrorism rewards program of the U.S. Department of State's Diplomatic Security Service. The Secretary of State is currently offering rewards for information that prevents or favorably resolves acts of international terrorism against U.S. persons or property worldwide. Rewards also may be paid for information leading to the arrest or conviction of terrorists attempting, committing, conspiring to commit, or aiding and abetting in the commission of such acts. The Rewards for Justice Program has paid more than $145 million for information that prevented international terrorist attacks or helped bring to justice those involved in prior acts.[1]

The program was established by the 1984 Act to Combat International Terrorism (Public Law 98-533), and it is administered by the State Department's Bureau of Diplomatic Security. Rewards for Justice was formally known as the Counter-Terror Rewards Program the name was soon shortened to the HEROES program. In 1993, DS launched www.hereos.net to help publicize reward information. Brad

Smith, a DSS special agent assigned to desk duty due to illness, served as the lone site administrator and program manager running the operation from his home.[2] [3] By 1997, the site was getting more than one million hits a year from 102 countries.[4] Smith is also credited with the idea to put photos of wanted terrorists on matchbook covers.[2] DSS agents assigned to embassies and consulates throughout the world ensured that the matchbooks got wide distribution at bars and restaurants.

The Director of the Diplomatic Security Service chairs an interagency committee which reviews reward candidates and then recommends rewards to the Secretary of State. The committee includes members from the staff of the White House National Security Council, Central Intelligence Agency, Department of Justice, Department of Defense, Department of Homeland Security, Department of the Treasury, and the U.S. State Department.

After the September 11 attacks, the list of wanted terrorists increased dramatically, and rewards were also increased, as part of the U.S. efforts to capture al-Qaeda leadership. However, the plan has been largely ineffective against Islamic terrorists.[5] The largest reward offered was $25 million for the leader of al-Qaeda, Osama bin Laden, which had "attracted hundreds of anonymous calls but no reliable leads."[5] Osama bin Laden was shot and killed inside a private residential compound in Abbottabad, Pakistan, by members of the United States Naval Special Warfare Development Group and Central Intelligence Agency operatives in a covert operation on May 1, 2011.

Per intelligence sources, numerous tips linking bin-Laden's location in Iran were flowing into the State Dept.'s program with whistleblowers looking to swap the Intel for a $25 Million reward.

Tom Orest said he provided information to the State

Dept. that had bin Laden's location pinpointed down to the city and street in Iran. Another intelligence source said he too had sent FedEx letters to the program with the detailed analysis of bin Laden's travel through Iran, spanning several years after Sept. 11, 2001. And they weren't alone.

"The program received a number of tips about Iran," a state department insider said. "Normally you see all kinds of wild submissions with people taking a shot in the dark with a guess or disseminating rumors."

Not with the bin Laden Intel, however, with anything and everything concerning Iran.

Useful tips and detailed tips that filter into the program are forwarded up the chain at the State Dept. The top of that chain is the Secretary of State: Hillary Clinton and John Kerry during Obama's White House and Condoleezza Rice and Colin Powell during George W. Bush's White House.

But what if the U.S. government wasn't really interested in "capturing" bin Laden until the time was right?

Things were going swimmingly for both administrations when it came to crushing individual liberties under the ruse of fighting terrorism and finding bin Laden – dead or alive. The Patriot Act trumped an individual's Constitutional rights granted by the U.S. Constitution and 225 years of federal laws. Due process had been sold out in exchange for the government's hype that they were keeping you safe from monsters like bin Laden and his al-Qaeda terror network. All you had to do was surrender liberty, agree to have your civil rights trampled on – and Americans acquiesced in droves. Without hesitation. And it is still happening.

Now the FBI and federal agencies could work through the NSA to get warrants on your phones, your emails, your web traffic without any authorization. No federal judge was required any longer, not that it mattered much. A 'good' fed could always shop a warrant around to a compromised jurist. The courts in D.C. and beyond are packed with them.

Americans shuffle like cattle in U.S. airport 'security' lines – barefoot and beltless -- with their pants falling down. They allow the government to fondle their genitals in the same airport line: children, elderly, handicapped. No one is exempt from the security theater put on by the feckless Transportation Safety Administration.

Meanwhile, the international arms business was booming for military contractors and conglomerates, including the United States government. Fighter jets, missiles, weapons, tanks, ships, nuclear submarines. The D.C. insiders were getting even richer – filthy rich. Finding and killing bin Laden would be very bad for business. After all, fear sells.

With these elements in play – allowing the government to steal and trample civil liberties in the name of national 'security' – it is no wonder what was happening behind the scene of the Rewards for Justice Program.

American citizens or retired federal agents who were hunting Osama bin Laden became government targets. If their tips and Intel were credible – at least under Hillary Clinton – their submissions became a license for surveillance. That included any information filtering into the program about bin Laden living or being spotted in Iran.

"Any information about Iran was handled by the people at the very top of the State Department," one intelligence insider with knowledge of the program's working said.

Another intelligence official went even further, alleging credible tips pinpointing bin Laden in Iran were not only NOT paid because they were never followed up – but the whistleblowers were wiretapped, spied on and monitored to see what they were doing with the information.

"There was a concern about leaking details to the press or having people rail against the government for ignoring their ticket to a $25 million reward," one insider said.

Instead of using the information to seek bin Laden, State Dept. and CIA resources were being expended to keep a close eye on the whistleblowers who dared to try and collect a public reward for bin Laden's capture. A status report on each such person and entity was being forwarded to State Dept. brass on a "weekly" basis, one insider confirmed.

The intelligence program was operating like a counterintelligence program, with the Obama administration – Clinton and Panetta – pulling strings to safeguard and kill any information regarding bin Laden in Iran. A sophisticated cruel misinformation campaign dreamt up and implemented by sinister actors.

Remember "See Something, Say Something?"

In reality, it was more like: "See Something, Say Something, Have the Government Crawl Up Your Ass With A Microscope."

In somewhat of a foreshadowing of what promises to become a significant issue – perhaps later in this work or indeed outside the scope of this work – I wanted to make sure to post this current Reward for Justice description which currently adorns the RewardsforJustice.net website. I trust this will come into play sooner, rather than later, as many wheels and gears are moving behind the scenes as the research for this book progresses -- and beyond.

WANTED:

Information that brings to justice…
Ayman al-Zawahiri
Up to $25 Million Reward
Ayman al-Zawahiri is the current leader of the al-Qa'ida terrorist group and a former leader of the Egyptian Islamic Jihad. He was indicted in the United States for his role in the August 7, 1998, U.S. embassy bombings in Kenya and Tanzania which killed 224 civilians and wounded over 5,000 others.

With Usama bin Laden and other senior members of al-Qa'ida, al-Zawahiri is believed to have also plotted attacks on the USS Cole in Yemen on October 12, 2000, which killed 17 US sailors and injured another 39, and helped coordinate the September 11, 2001 attacks in which 19 al-Qa'ida terrorists hijacked and crashed four US commercial jets —two into the World Trade Center in New York City, one into the Pentagon near Washington, D.C., and a fourth into a field in Shanksville, Pennsylvania—leaving nearly 3,000 people dead. While al-Zawahiri now leads a small but influential cadre of senior leaders widely called al-Qa'ida Core, the group's cohesiveness the past few years has diminished because of leadership losses from counterterrorism pressure in Afghanistan and Pakistan and the rise of other organizations such as the

Islamic State of Iraq and the Levant (ISIL) that serve as an alternative for some disaffected extremists. Nonetheless, al-Qa'ida and its affiliates in South Asia, Africa, and the Middle East remain a resilient organization committed to conducting attacks in the United States and against American interests abroad.

Al-Zawahiri continues to record and disseminate messages, while al-Qa'ida has advanced a number of unsuccessful plots in the past several years, including against the United States and Europe. This highlights al-Qa'ida's ability to continue some attack preparations while under sustained counterterrorism pressure and suggests it may be plotting additional attacks against the United States at home or overseas.

We can just leave this here ... for now.

.

9 PETRAEUS THREATENS OBAMA

I have to pause for a moment really, after following recent news about the death of al-Qaeda linked 'journalist' Jamal Khashoggi. And what does his death have to do with David Petraeus? All these matters are dovetailing as many of the key puzzle pieces revealed in this work fit each other and other lonely puzzle pieces to the overall truth. Not the government's narrative. But the truth, as told by insiders and documents.

The outrage of the mainstream media and the Lib rainmakers in D.C. about Khashoggi's death is quite telling. For one, he was not an American citizen. Secondly, he was linked to al-Qaeda and was good friends with Osama bin Laden for decades. But that's only the surface. And Khashoggi is such a bit player and Deep-State pawn, he's not worth exploring further. What is essential to focus on here – is the utter lack of parallel outrage by these same American entities over the death of U.S. Ambassador Christopher Stevens and three American heroes who tried to save his life in Benghazi. There was no Liberal outrage for these poor souls when their own country abandoned them and left not only them to die – but dozens of other Americans who were saved by more heroes. Yet, we are forced to read all this ginned up outrage for a terrorist whose cover was to write for the Washington Post. More proof that these large newspapers and their publishers are generals in the Deep State war against America and her Constitution.

Like many Americans I once thought Petraeus was the 'real deal,' a rarity in the beltway. I am once again disappointed, like many of you. From speaking with Intel sources and federal agents, I do believe Petraeus threatened to blow the bin-Laden whistle on Obama. Those details unfold below. After listening to these accounts of insiders, it appears Petraeus and Obama were in a mad race to ruin one another. Can you imagine if Petraeus – the director of the CIA -- would have ratted out the administration for harboring bin Laden in Iran as well as other al-Qaeda terrorists?

Petraeus might be president today. But Obama struck first and again, we see a pattern where insiders were punished for threatening to expose one of the most heinous scandals in American history.

"The official story floating around the beltway is that Obama made a rude comment to Petraeus about Petraeus' wife," a well-placed intelligence veteran said. "The unofficial story is that Petraeus threatened to kill Obama in a very heated argument. Not to physically kill him but to knock him out of the White House, kill him as a political God and icon."

Things began to sour after an operation to rescue the folks in Benghazi went awry, not from operational difficulties on the ground but from political skullduggery from Obama's White House, Secretary of State Hillary Clinton, FBI Director Mueller and

Petraeus himself.

We journey now back to "the other" 9/11 -- the disaster on Sept. 11, 2012, in Benghazi, Libya.

When distress reports reached U.S. Intelligence in Langley and the Pentagon that the American ambassador to Benghazi and dozens of his diplomatic personnel were under terrorist attack in Libya on Sept. 11, 2012, CIA and Defense Department officials scrambled an immediate response.

Officials moved quickly to assemble a counter-terrorism team of professionals to dispatch to Benghazi. That little-known but elite squad, known as the Foreign Emergency Support Team (FEST), is, in fact, the government's sole inter-agency, on call and short notice team trained to respond to any terror-related incident in the world.

But not this time. Not in Benghazi.

FEST agents intent on rescuing the stranded Americans from the siege on the U.S. diplomatic compounds in Benghazi -- including Ambassador J. Christopher Stevens – were told to stand down, according to shocking revelations by FBI agents and CIA sources who spoke to True Pundit.

Robyn Gritz, a decorated FBI agent who previously served as the Bureau's official attaché to the CIA before Benghazi, recalls the troubling details surrounding the stand-down order.

Gritz details the FBI counter-terrorism division's initial emergency meeting to discuss the unfolding events in Benghazi. In the session led by now FBI Deputy Director Andrew McCabe, he briefed agents about the violent attacks in Benghazi. McCabe was assistant director of anti-terrorism at the time but running the FBI's response to Benghazi, sources confirm.

Gritz was already briefed by her Defense Department contacts who instructed her to prepare FBI personnel for the FEST plane.

"I said I got a call from DOD, people that actually put the FEST plane together and I was offered six slots for FBI, but I can probably get eight," she said, recalling the FBI's initial Benghazi meeting. "McCabe said: 'No, we don't need your help with that Robyn or help from DOD.'

"I explained to him that I was the only SSA (Supervisory Special Agent) sitting in this room that has deployed FBI on a FEST plane to a U.S. Embassy under major attack. In Yemen, terrorists were driving around blowing shit up. And it didn't stop when we got on the ground. And the same thing happened in Beirut. But McCabe told us all in the meeting the FBI was standing down."

Gritz led the FBI's FEST contingency in 2008 in the terror attack on the American Embassy in Yemen. The al Qaeda-affiliated attack – almost four years to the day of the Benghazi siege -- killed 18 people.

After the 2012 meeting where Gritz was spurned by McCabe, the FBI veteran said she was barred from further Benghazi briefings and the FBI's anti-terrorism email chain on the Benghazi attacks. While Gritz was not directly assigned to McCabe's task force, CIA had sought out her expertise to staff FEST for Benghazi and Gritz happily volunteered to help McCabe and Mueller in the Bureau's response. But she was basically told to mind her own business. Regardless, FBI agents quietly sought her counsel on Benghazi but did so in secret away from McCabe and Mueller.

For seasoned FBI agents, McCabe's stand down order was hard to process. McCabe told the room – after several emotional eruptions -- then-FBI Director Robert Mueller had approved the official "stand down for now" stance, another FBI official familiar with the meeting confirmed.

A second FBI agent familiar with McCabe's initial Benghazi meeting confirms Gritz's account.

"It left me shaking my head and ready to put his (McCabe's) head through a wall. He was going on and on about the violence in Benghazi having to do with a video on the internet or something. Nobody knew what he was talking about and why we would not load up (FEST) and respond."

The decision to walk away and merely sit idly made no tactical sense whatsoever.

"Why would you stand down when you can get Special Forces Operators there in one plane and FBI and CIA Intel as well?," the FBI insider said. "Wheels up in less than 90 minutes. Been done before."

The Benghazi assault, in fact, was the exact scenario FEST was created and funded for.

"We used FEST when I served on the NSC's Hostage and Personnel Recovery Working Group where we regularly discussed deployment of the FEST," Gritz said. "For example, when our embassy in Sanaa (Yemen) was attacked, a FEST plane took off with personnel and supplies. For it to not go to Benghazi was a real surprise. It was an incident that seemed like the FEST was made for. But it wasn't sent. Just like help from other resources weren't sent. Why?"

The now-retired Gritz and her FBI colleagues weren't the only agents dismayed at FEST's nondeployment. A high-ranking Defense Department source who was involved in Benghazi prep for the team echoed the collective FBI frustration. The career spy said the orders to stand down came directly from CIA Director David Petraeus, via National Security Advisor Tom Donilon in the White House.

"This is something that haunts me to this day," the DOD insider said. "The families of these fallen warriors need to know that there were people trying to get to them to help. That is what we do. But we can't fuel up a jet and load it with Operators without a green light."

The DOD insider said he wanted to "come clean" to let the families of Americans killed in Benghazi and survivors know that there were people in the United States working to rescue them and deploy Operators and resources to help them fight. However, they were denied the ability to do so "at every turn."

The official said when he was notified FEST was scrubbed, he cross-referenced with the Pentagon sources to determine if any U.S. Marine-led FAST companies had been scrambled to Benghazi as a replacement for the scrubbed Intel-based FEST. These Marine teams, called Fleet Anti-terrorism Security Teams (FAST) are part of the Marine Corps Security Force Regiment. FAST soldiers are highly-trained and reinforce security at US Embassy hot zones around the world. Each FAST Company consists of 6 platoons of around 50 men each, and there are two companies located near Benghazi.

FAST Company Europe is stationed in Rota, Spain, approximately 2,500 miles west of Benghazi and Fast Company Central is headquartered in

Manama, Bahrain which is roughly 1,800 miles southeast of Benghazi.

Plus, the DOD insider said Charlie 110 Company, a unit of approximately 30 U.S. Special Forces and assets was training in Croatia at the time, about 900 miles north of Benghazi, Charlie 110, typically based in Germany, could have also been dispatched to Benghazi quicker than any team. And, in fact, it eventually was sent, but far too late to save any American lives. By the time American Special Forces arrived, the deadly standoff had ended.

Well into the siege, no military personnel had been deployed to Benghazi. Neither FAST companies or the FEST unit were sent. From the Beltway, FEST could have been in Benghazi roughly twelve hours after takeoff, if its transport had been re-fueled mid-flight, sources said.

One hour into the Benghazi attack, No Intel or military reinforcements had been dispatched, according to the DOD insider and Benghazi timelines.

Then two hours elapsed and still no official movement of Intel or military reinforcements by the White House, Secretary of State Hillary Clinton, or Defense Secretary Leon Panetta.

Then three hours.

Four.

Five hours.

And still, no military personnel deployed to rescue Americans. By then, we now know the American consulate in Benghazi had been torched, and all diplomatic staff had been evacuated while Operators trekked back to a nearby CIA annex to continue fighting off waves of terrorists to protect

Americans evacuated from the consulate. Ambassador Stevens was also missing by that time. Presumably dead. Or worse.

During this time lapse – where many FBI, CIA, DOD employees lobbied feverishly for resources to be dispatched to Benghazi -- the exact whereabouts of President Barack Obama and Hillary Clinton remained mostly unknown. There are hours where the duo remains unaccounted for and absent from a crisis response which was seemingly formulated on the fly by understudies like Vice President Joe Biden to address the attacks, according to documents, testimony, and records.

Obama was missing for the first six hours after the attack was reported, some internal military documents show.

During this bureaucratic limbo, Gritz said she likewise worked contacts in CIA and Defense Department sources in AFRICOM to see who, if anyone, was being deployed after her FEST Op was grounded. No one had been given clearance to deploy to Benghazi, Gritz said she learned from her limited fact-finding.

"They were told to stand down," Gritz said.

Typically, the highly-skilled FEST deploys to assist, advise and coordinate U.S. government crisis response activities and includes representatives from the State Department, Defense Department, and the Intelligence Community, specifically the Federal Bureau of Investigation among other appropriate agencies.

FEST personnel are tailored to the specific international incident, and particular U.S. Embassy needs, according to its federal charter.

But not in Benghazi. That talent was grounded by Robert Mueller, then-FBI director and David Petraeus, then-CIA director. But who ordered U.S. agents to stand down? During the attacks, Hillary Clinton served as Secretary of State, answering to Obama. Are you beginning to see the pattern?

Yet after 70,000-plus pages of documents and 38 hours of House and Senate hearings about Benghazi and Congress' much-heralded Benghazi Report, there has never been any details about FEST and how its mission was scrubbed despite the outcry from FBI and CIA personnel who were prepping for its deployment to Benghazi.

Who scrubbed it? Until now, its existence in the Benghazi dialogue wasn't even acknowledged by Intelligence and military officials. It's one of many missing puzzle pieces, this one surfacing six years after the deadly Benghazi standoff.

No Congressional investigators ever subpoenaed or interviewed Gritz or critical State Department personnel. How can you compile a comprehensive report on Benghazi and not probe FEST?

Perhaps Congressional investigators and FBI need to independently determine what transpired with the FEST debacle.

State Department sources fingered Patrick Kennedy as pulling the plug on the FEST mission. Kennedy, now retired, was a State consigliere for Hillary Clinton, his boss at the time. Kennedy's name and emails surfaced in Wikileaks files, where he allegedly "pressured" the FBI to downgrade the classification of one of Hillary Clinton's classified emails as part of a "quid pro quo." Kennedy, the Undersecretary of State, offered the FBI more agents in countries where they had previously been forbidden.

But as stated earlier, a DOD insider said the White House disbanded the FEST Op.

It is important to note too John Brennan, during Benghazi, served as chief counterterrorism advisor to President Obama. Brennan's title was Deputy National Security Advisor for Homeland Security and Counterterrorism.

Brennan, working inside the White House, reported directly to Obama.

Six months after Benghazi – with the full government cover-up in motion – Brennan was promoted to Director of the CIA to replace Petraeus who by that time was embroiled in a personal scandal of his own with paramour Paula Broadwell. He was forced to resign from his CIA post months earlier.

And Susan Rice was promoted from U.S. ambassador to Obama's new national security advisor.

Two integral members of the Benghazi cover-up promoted for their allegiance. One could argue otherwise.

It must be noted that between Benghazi and Nov 9, 2012, when Petraeus resigned -- just two months after Benghazi -- from the CIA, according to sources, the general had an "ugly" running dispute with Obama sparked by comments the president reportedly made about Petraeus and possibly his wife. At one point Petraeus threatened to go public with details about Benghazi that would "soil" Obama's presidential legacy, DOD insiders confirm.

"Petraeus even threatened Obama during a meeting," one DOD source said. "It was bad. Very ugly stuff."

It came as little surprise then that Petraeus was

forced from office after an extramarital affair was soon leaked to the media and later, the unthinkable: Eric Holder's Justice Department indicted Petraeus for leaking classified documents to his paramour. Petraeus struck a plea bargain to stay out of prison.

"The General (Petraeus) should have exposed Obama like he planned," a DOD insider said.

What was Petraeus going to reveal? A sweeping stand down policy crafted by Obama? Or was this merely the by-product of a commander in chief who was AWOL during an international crisis?

Or did Petraeus plan to expose the entire bin Laden was in Afghanistan ruse?

Petraeus did not respond for comment.

With or without Petraeus' testimony, the FEST debacle points to the White House, especially since the National Security Council, by charter, green lights or red lights FEST missions. That would take the responsibility away from Hillary Clinton's State Department and Kennedy and place the decision to abort the FEST mission on the White House.

Did the national security advisor – with or without Brennan's urging -- converse directly with President Obama regarding scrapping the FEST deployment to Benghazi? Was it Obama who scrubbed the Op?

These are pertinent questions that have seemingly eluded Congressional investigators and Intelligence agency brass. And Obama and Clinton as well.

To summarize: Despite the best efforts of many Intel agents and military officials, the following U.S. assets were told to stand down and NOT respond to Americans pinned down by terrorists in Benghazi, according to interviews with federal law enforcement sources, documents, and public information:

- CIA/FBI/Special Ops FEST Unit
- FAST Company Europe in Italy
- FAST Company Central in Bahrain
- U.S. AFRICOM Special Forces

This largely secret bureaucratic mess cost Americans their lives. The Patriots killed in Benghazi include:

- J. Christopher Stevens, U.S. Ambassador to Libya
- Sean Smith, U.S. Foreign Service Officer
- Glen Doherty, Navy SEAL and CIA contractor
- Tyrone Woods, State Department Diplomatic Security Service officer and CIA Contractor.

Stevens was the first U.S. ambassador killed in the line of duty since 1979.

That doesn't include the wounded, the warriors on the ground who fought their way out of Benghazi while awaiting U.S. reinforcements like the FEST that never was permitted to deploy...

Mark "Oz" Geist was one of the six former elite military operatives who fought back that night along with former Army Ranger Kris "Tonto" Paronto and former Marine Sgt. John "Tieg" Tiegen. This trio -- fighting alongside Smith, Doherty, and Woods – were spared in Benghazi after fighting off heavily-armed hostile factions for nearly eight hours. The story of the three surviving Operators was adapted into the movie Thirteen Hours.

And just like a Hollywood movie script, FBI insiders may have been exposed to some creative, scripted Benghazi story plot as well.

The FBI agent present at McCabe's initial Benghazi briefing on September 11 said four days later the rhetoric at that meeting started to finally make sense. And it was somewhat shocking. The FBI insider said he watched in amazement on Sunday morning as U.S. Ambassador to the United Nations Susan Rice appeared on network television news shows and blamed the deadly Benghazi violence on a YouTube video that sparked civil unrest.

"It was the same exact bullshit McCabe was spouting in the meeting," the FBI agent said. "He was feeding us talking points about the YouTube video. It was all bullshit. I got on the phone and told other agents you're not going to believe what I just saw on TV."

How did McCabe have Rice's talking points four days before she unveiled them to the media on September 16th? And where was Mueller while McCabe was making sweeping unilateral decisions for the Bureau's response to Benghazi.

"When I look back on it, McCabe was listening to Susan Rice and the White House," Gritz said. "He was in with Rice. Now I understand what happened with everything that has come out about McCabe."

It was all seemingly quite coordinated. Mueller via McCabe and Petraeus folding the FEST contingency, an apparatus of the State Department run by Clinton via Kennedy.

Orchestrated like a well-oiled Op itself, capped off by Obama and Clinton meeting and 'consoling' the families of the Benghazi dead as their loved ones' caskets were carried off the military charter by U.S. Marine pallbearers. The perfect photo opportunity for two guilty bureaucrats who nobody in the United States government could even locate for several hours while the bloody terror in Benghazi unfolded.

From President Obama and John Brennan in the White House to Hillary Clinton's State Department, the CIA, the FBI, and the DOD. Even the Benghazi Report and the Benghazi Commission failed to address the FEST debacle.

Mueller and Petraeus were ordered to stand down but who gave the order, the President?

"Do you know what we call this in the FBI?" an FBI insider asked. "A Conspiracy. We used to investigate good cases like that."

Perhaps Sen. Chuck Grassley would agree.

And perhaps someone in power in Washington D.C. could do something about it.

Justice for the four dead Americans and their families. And the good folks who tried to save them. What a concept.

10 BRENNAN JIHAD

I simply had to take a deep breath and laugh in recent days, reading former CIA director John Brennan's comments about Saudi Arabia. He seems very bent out of shape by the death of Saudi 'journalist' Jamal Khashoggi who no doubt was a Brennan asset.

The headline caught my eye in Townhall.com: "John Brennan Accuses Trump of Conspiring With the Saudis."

Now that is about as fucking rich as it comes. You have to give it to Brennan, he has some set of balls. All balls, no brain though. And that pretty much is the prerequisite for a career as a government intelligence operative turned political hit man. If Trump were or is conspiring with the Saudis, he would merely be following in the footsteps of Brennan himself, who bent over for the Saudi regime time and time again like a tramp on prom night.

Per Townhall:

Former CIA Director John Brennan suggested Wednesday night that President Trump is conspiring with Saudi leaders to make up a story about journalist Jamal Khashoggi's disappearance. The Saudi journalist was last seen on October 2 walking into the Saudi consulate in Istanbul. Turkey says the Saudis killed him, but Crown Prince Mohammad bin Salman and Saudi King Salman bin Abdulaziz Al Saud deny the charge. Trump suggested that he had no reason not to believe him and cited our economic relationship.

That left Brennan with this theory.

"So they've been working to concoct a story that's going to stand up to the scrutiny that will be immediately put on it," Brennan said on MSNBC. "How can they claim then that Mohammed bin Salman had no responsibility whatsoever. Is he looking for the scapegoats inside of Saudi Arabia? Has he already taken action against them?"

Still, if U.S. intelligence has damning information about Salman's role in Khashoggi's disappearance, "his story is going to fall apart," Brennan said.

Immediate red flags triggered for me and I can smell complete bullshit right away – all the way from the Middle East.

Many times I contemplate whether these beltway players are stupid and inept or just removed so far from reality that they can't process comments and issues like normal, balanced Americans. You would think Brennan would keep his mouth shut about ALL things and count the millions he has raked in on the side, cutting security deals – and who knows what else. And people actually pay him big money in speaking fees as well. Liberals love to shell out the cash to listen to big names reaffirm their political ideologies. They need that pat on the back. Conservatives – at least the ones I know and associate with -- do not.

Note that in the above article, Brennan literally

states "his story is going to fall apart." He's right to be projecting, and Brennan is a classic projectionist. A first-year law student could pick him apart during cross-examination. The story that is falling apart belongs to Brennan. And his secret jockeying with the Saudis. And his knowledge of an exclusive deal between the Saudis and Iranians to not only house Osama bin Laden – but other members of al-Qaeda – including bin Laden's son who ran the terror faction after his father's reported death at the hands of America.

According to interviews with Intel insiders and documents, Brennan was well versed on the deal between the Saudis and Iranians to safeguard bin Laden. But now we are raising the stakes. The agreement to give bin Laden refuge in Iran was a package deal extended to the top personnel in al-Qaeda and their family members, per our earlier revelations in this work.

Intelligence experts believe that did include Ayman al-Zawahiri, al-Qaeda's leader who took the reins after bin Laden's reported demise and has been working with bin Laden's son in Iran to wage jihad on global targets, as well and launder money and traffick opioids in the name of Allah. But recent works on al-Zawahiri place him in Pakistan, possibly Afghanistan and if those reports by journalists are correct, then he blew out of Iran years ago – but not before the U.S. had a chance to botch Intel and fail to search for him.

Given the evidence detailed in this work about the Osama bin Laden in Iran cover up, it seems hardly an intellectual stretch to consider the likelihood al-Zawahiri too had been using Iran as a terror and home base. Any solid investigator or analyst would conclude, based on the bin Laden evidence, al-Zawahiri has not been captured because the U.S. doesn't want him caught. Or killed. Yet. If that is not true, can someone show me any evidence that the U.S. used its intelligence and diplomatic prowess to sweep Iran for this man? It simply was ignored.

There is a $25 million reward on al-Zawahiri just as there was for bin Laden. I hadn't indeed pondered the al-Zawahiri intelligence until I received a phone call, I believe it was very late at night from an intelligence source who stated the U.S. government might be setting al-Zawahiri up for a "trophy kill" similar to what many folks believe was done with bin Laden when he was moved from Iran to Pakistan, and mere months later, he was killed.

"I just heard on CNN that the U.S. thinks al-Zawahiri is in Pakistan," the source said. "That could be the kiss of death for al-Zawahiri. I wouldn't be surprised if they pull a raid on him. He may have outlived his usefulness now with Trump in office. It's not the same ballgame as it was under previous presidents.

"I am confident if it was leaked to CNN, it was done so for a reason."

CNN on its own rarely breaks any stories of significance on national security. Perhaps it was just coincidence, or maybe the story was placed.

This was an interesting point, especially since there were no current events in play at the time in the news media involving al-Zawahiri or al-Qaeda -- absent the anniversary of Sept. 11th. It was merely blurted out, for lack of better phrasing. And the liberal media usually does not come up with such content – especially high-level national security Intel linked to terrorism – if it wasn't planted by someone "in the know" and for a specific reason.

I wanted to put this out in case al-Zawahiri ends up on the wrong end of a U.S.-led raid shortly. It certainly would fit the pattern employed to bring his mentor, bin Laden down just months after he arrived in Pakistan after approximately eight years using Iran as a base, according to our Intel assessments.

Back to Brennan.

Brennan, after leaving the CIA for a stint to head a private intelligence shop, returned to Obama's White House to tackle counter-terrorism and national security. He reported directly to Obama, according to Intel insiders. Though he was not National Security Advisor, he performed as an NSA at large and wasn't afraid to step on other's toes when it came to providing analysis and new intelligence, intelligence insiders said. Brennan had his sights on the CIA director post and was running his own Intel Op from inside the White House, many times even usurping the U.S. intelligence apparatus.

When I was running security and anti-money laundering at Citi – this was often the exact behavior you would look for to pinpoint a fraudster. By Citi's standards, Brennan would be the poster boy for a potential fraudster. Inside the White House, he answered to only Obama. He did what he pleased, talking to foreign governments, informants and dignitaries – operating not only as an Intel analyst at times but also a diplomat. With no checks and balances, Brennan was a runaway ox cart. He could have been conducting his own negotiations with foreign governments, usurped Intel agencies, and worked to shroud previous deals he hatched when he was running point for the CIA – on the ground – in places like Saudi Arabia. Where were the checks and balances? There were none.

I previously ran Citi's anti-money laundering and anti-fraud Ops in Los Angeles, Chicago and Delaware. At Citi, we would put an executive like this – and his boss or bosses – under investigation because the behavior was outside the corporate structure. It was a rogue set up, and to honest people paying close attention, it stands out as highly suspect and likely problematic. Management is management – whether corporate of government -- and white collar banking crimes differ little from the foundations of political corruption.

Perhaps this is the very reason Brennan was put in this post by Obama, to operate like the president's private CIA. Of course, in top-secret cables at the time Brennan is tagged as "PRESIDENTIAL ASSISTANT" to Obama. Do we really think Brennan was in the White House to fetch the president his lattes?

Before his White House stint, Brennan's Intel pedigree included a resume of Middle Eastern Who's Who: Director, National Counterterrorism Center; director, Terrorist Threat Integration Center; deputy executive director, CIA; chief of staff to director of central intelligence, CIA; chief of station, Middle East, CIA; executive assistant to the deputy director of central intelligence, CIA; deputy director, office of Near Eastern and South Asian analysis, CIA; daily intelligence briefer at the White House, CIA; deputy division chief, Office of Near Eastern and South Asian analysis, CIA; chief of analysis, DCI's counterterrorism center, CIA; Middle East specialist and terrorism analyst, directorate of intelligence, CIA; political officer, U.S. Embassy in Jeddah, Saudi Arabia, Department of State; and career trainee, directorate of operations, CIA.

That resume puts Brennan in Saudi Arabia in the employment of the CIA during the Sept. 11, 2001 terror bombing and during the time frame Osama bin Laden "vanished."

And let's not leave out where Brennan worked when he vacated the CIA before Obama's election in return for big bucks to run the Analysis Corp., as president and chief executive. The company provides private analysis to the federal government's counterterrorism efforts. Another pesky government contractor like Fusion GPS that at least under Brennan seemed to always be embroiled in controversy like Fusion GPS. It's little wonder Brennan returned to the safe confines of federal government employment – where mistakes and homicides are suspicious deaths are brushed over and covered up without all these bothersome homicide detectives snooping around.

Case in point:

From True Pundit, with reporting from the Washington Times and The American Thinker:

A key witness in a federal probe into Barack Obama's passport information stolen and altered from the State Department was gunned down and killed in front of a District church in D.C.

Lt. Quarles Harris Jr., 24, who had been cooperating with federal investigators, was found late at night slumped dead inside a car. He was reportedly waiting to meet with FBI agents about his boss John Brennan.

Back in March 2008, the State Department launched an investigation of improper computer access to the passport records of Barack Hussein Obama, and days later those of Hillary Clinton and John McCain. The investigation centered on one employee: a contract worker for a company that was headed by Brennan, a key Obama campaign adviser who later became assistant to the president and deputy national security adviser for Homeland Security and Counterterrorism. Ultimately Brennan was appointed CIA director.

First, Obama's passport records were accessed and altered. Then days later -- likely to provide cover -- Brennan's private Intel company accessed Clinton's and McCain's records as the State Department had already flagged the Obama breach by that time.

Brennan's company accessed and altered Obama's passport BEFORE the 2008 presidential election, while Brennan was also working on Obama's campaign team. After the election, Brennan took a job inside the White House.

A month after the passport breach the key witness, in this case, was murdered. Harris was shot in the head in his car, in front of his church.

Lt. Harris told federal investigators before he was murdered that he received "passport information from a co-conspirator who works for the U.S. Department of State." What became of the "co-conspirator"? Why wasn't he/she brought to trial?

There is no way to tell what might have been done to Obama's passport records by those who accessed them. Key information could have been altered or destroyed. On April 8, 2008, after the breach became public, Obama confessed to having taken a trip to Pakistan in 1981. The then-candidate said: "I traveled to Pakistan when I was in college."

Journalist Jake Tapper was surprised and said:

"This last part -- a college trip to Pakistan -- was news to

many of us who have been following the race closely. And it was odd that we hadn't heard about it before, given all the talk of Pakistan during this campaign."

Did Obama confess to this trip, which he doesn't mention in either of his autobiographies, because of the passport breach?

Or did Brennan simply erase the trip from Obama's passport records through his role as CEO of Intel contractor Analysis Corp, where Brennan worked between his CIA career and Obama's White House on Brennan's journey to CIA head?

Only Brennan's employee Lt. Quarles Harris knows. And the FBI.

And dead men tell no tales. Especially in D.C. Just ask Seth Rich.

And the FBI cannot be trusted.

An unsolved murder in The Swamp.

Case closed.

Mystery, intrigue, and backstabbing always seem to surround the Intel workings of Brennan, along with the propensity to always come down on the wrong side of issues when weighed against the U.S. Constitution and the U.S. criminal code. And lies. Many lies. Internal cables and top secret White House memos, in fact, show Brennan to be a sympathizer with the Middle Eastern and Saudi plights and strong supporter of Islam.

"Brennan is never on the right side," one well-placed intelligence official said. "He only advanced to the top because his bosses weren't on the right side either and that includes Obama."

Brennan, in a series of top-secret communications and conversations, from his White House post as Homeland Security Advisor to Obama, received actionable Intel on al-Qaeda and bin Laden years before his death. Yet, he did nothing to follow up on the information, documents and testimonies show.

Saudi Arabia Crown Prince Nayef bin Abdul-Aziz Al Saud spoke directly to Brennan about the bin Laden, his son, and al-Qaeda operating in Iran, according to well-placed intelligence officials and documents.

"At one point Saudi Prince Nayef was complaining to Brennan that the al-Qaeda terrorists that had been put in Iran were lashing out against Saudi targets and he was agitated," a high-ranking intelligence official confessed. "He was not asking for help to try and get the Iranians to get better control of al-Qaeda, which was very strange because they would normally ask for help in that regard, especially since they lost control because al-Qaeda had grown so much in Iran."

(I wasn't aware "PRESIDENTAL ASSISTANTS" spoke directly to the Crown Prince of Saudi Arabia. I must have missed that in Mr. McGlynn's U.S. Government class senior year in prep school.)

Prince Nayef at the time was listed in top-secret U.S. communications as "SAUDI INTERIOR MINISTER." Nayef served in that role through Oct. 2011 when he was promoted to Crown Prince. During the conversations with Brennan, Nayef was also Saudi Arabia's Second Deputy Prime Mister in addition to spearheading the interior ministry. According to intelligence sources, the top secret memos involving Nayef and Brennan refer to the

Saudi as "Saudi Second Deputy Prime Minister and Minister of the Interior."

"These were conversations with Brennan and Nayef long before Osama bin Laden and members of his family were moved to Pakistan" before the U.S. raid in Abbottābad, Pakistan. "So bin Laden was still in Iran, and Nayef was angry that al-Qaeda was not following the ground rules of the arrangement they (Saudi Arabia and Iran) struck in 2001. There was a formal arrangement early in 2001 and an informal arrangement after 9/11."

In a top-secret document detailing a conversation between Brennan and Nayef before bin Laden's death, Nayef railed against the Iranians for violating an accord not to attack one another. The agreement was struck between the two nations in 2001 before the attacks on the World Trade Center and U.S. targets including the Pentagon by al-Qaeda, killing 3,000+ Americans.

Nayef complained to Brennan, per one White House cable in 2009:

"Over the past two years Iran has hosted Saudis – including Osama bin Laden's son who had contacts with terrorists and worked against the Kingdom of Saudi Arabia."

Nayef continued, during another 2009 exchange, talking about Osama bin Laden himself grooming his son in Iran, to help run terror networks for al-Qaeda, according to intelligence sources who said that part of the conversations between Brennan and Nayef were redacted and later altered from top-secret documents between 2009 and 2011.

In 2001, the two countries described as arch enemies entered into a security pact – in one of the first treaties between the country. On paper, it was a pledge to work together to curb terrorism and money laundering in the Middle East. But Intel officials said the tenets of the treaty-like deal was to ensure the Saudis would not be targets of terrorism while Iran could have potential access to commerce and possible banking with Saudi Arabia. Just weeks before the attacks on 9/11 in America, the two alleged sworn enemies were working together to improve relations, security and commerce, according to the tenets of the deal.

Saudi Arabia also loosened immigration controls, allowing a more accessible path for dissidents (like al-Qaeda who had been previously disavowed) to re-enter the Kingdom. In fact, records show, many bin Laden family members were allowed to return to Saudi Arabia from Iran years after 9/11. Per Osama bin Laden's own files, al-Qaeda operatives and soldiers were traveling and residing in Iran under new identities and passports bought in Tehran. It makes me wonder why U.S. officials like Brennan didn't press to capture the terrorists coming back into Saudi Arabia from Iran, but that would first require wanting to arrest them.

An analytical mind may surmise whether the U.S. played a role in moving people in and out of Iran and Saudi Arabia like pieces on the global-terrorism chess board. That is just me thinking out loud.

In one top-secret exchange between Brennan and Nayef, the Saudi Interior Minister and soon-to-be Crown Prince complains that Iran is not obeying the "security agreement" with Saudi Arabia. Because bin Laden's al-Qaeda network and his son were either waging or planning to wage jihad on Saudi targets.

Brennan expresses no dismay or offers little input or seeks the location on the bin Laden's from Nayef. And notice that Nayef is not complaining about al-Qaeda using Iran as a base to conduct jihad on global targets. He is only concerned when it involves Saudi targets. Yet, Brennan shows little concern either way, even though al-Qaeda rained holy war on American soil in 2001.

"The Saudis worry about the Saudis, and at the time under Obama, our State Department and White House were kissing their asses," one seasoned diplomat said. "It was a little over the top."

Brennan along with the State Dept.'s Richard Erdman even agreed to lobby against European allies on behalf of the Saudis, White House documents show. Erdman, a career diplomat, serving as Charge 'd' Affaires at the U.S. Embassy in Riyadh, Saudi Arabia, shared telephone conversations with Prince Nayef as well as with Brennan in the White House, top-secret documents show. Erdman, in White House documents, recalls one of the talks with Nayef:

According to White House documents, Erdman wrote: "The prince also complained that Iran had breached its 2001 security agreement with Saudi Arabia and was supporting aggression against the kingdom. He expressed frustration with European nations for allowing terrorists to operate against Saidi Arabia rather than handing them over and requested US intercession to change this to change this European policy."

Yet Prince Nayef did not ask the United States to intercede in Iran to squelch a resurging al-Qaeda led by the bin Laden bloodline. That speaks volumes. The Saudis only wanted Brennan and the State

Department to muscle and lobby its European allies on behalf of the Kingdom. Interceding in Iran was never on the table.

"Nayef was exploring diplomatic channels with his ambassador to Iran and the Saudi Ministry of Foreign Affairs," one well-placed intelligence veteran said. "They did not want the United States involved in those negotiations or talks with Hassan Rohani."

Rohani was the Iranian National Security General at the time.

Diplomatic channels? I thought Iran and Saudi Arabia, again, were arch enemies?

Moreover, was Nayef demanding the return of terrorists to the Kingdom from Europe so these scofflaws could renter Iran and be reunited with al-Qaeda? And using the United States' diplomatic juice to do so? Seems outlandish, but possible, especially if Brennan was steering the ship. It certainly would be an elaborate scheme to pluck high-value al-Qaeda brass from Europe and safely tuck them away in the Middle East – if one would be so inclined to do – all in the name of keeping ally Saudi Arabia happy.

And since when does the United States lobby against its European allies on behalf of Saudi Arabia for extraditing terrorists?

Yet Brennan just days ago in late Oct. 2018, accused Trump of colluding with the Saudi Crown Prince. That's rich. During Brennan's tenure as White House Homeland Security Advisor to Obama, we could question – based on his correspondences -- just which homeland he was protecting, America's or the Kingdom of Saudi Arabia's?

High-level intelligence sources said wording was often changed before top-secret correspondences were finalized, memorializing the exchanges between Brennan and Nayef and other officials in Middle Eastern countries. Often Brennan would speak Arabic, and when "Allah" was mentioned by either party during the conversations with Middle Eastern officials, including Saudi's Nayef, the word would be changed to "God" in U.S. reports.

Saudi royalty spoke fluent English and Brennan spoke Arabic, so conversations floated in and out of both languages and included Brennan offering Middle Eastern officials the customary Muslim greeting "As-salāmu ʿalaykum," which means "peace upon you;" and the response "wa ʿalaykumu s-salām," which translates to "and peace be upon you."

But those exchanges were edited out of transcripts, along with references to Osama bin Laden and references to high level al-Qaeda operatives, intelligence sources confirm.

"Nayef was concerned with a breach by Iran where Iran agreed to not attack Saudi Arabia or the United States," a high-level intelligence source said. "Nayef becomes the Crown Prince after his discussions with Brennan, this was the top man in Saudi Arabia venting that the Iranians were allowing bin Laden to groom his son to ramp up jihad on Saudi targets. He openly talked about this and Brennan agreed."

Yet Brennan did nothing to address the bin Laden's conducting al-Qaeda business in Iran or asking Nayef where they were in Iran so the United States could pursue them.

This was the Obama White House talking about bin Laden and al-Qaeda conducting terror operations in Iran after its deadly attacks on U.S. targets in 2001 and previously. And intelligence officials said it was not the only communication Brennan had with the Saudis from the White House that amounted to discussing the location of al-Qaeda personnel in Iran but failing to pursue these wanted criminals – or ask the Saudi for help to do so.

And these are merely a sampling of Brennan's cables from inside the White House. Obtaining his communications during his tenure as CIA director – and long before that time, including his role as CIA station chief in Saudi Arabia during 2001 would prove more than interesting.

But wait, I thought the Saudis and Iranians hated each other, according to the slew of experts who seem to remind me of that daily? The two countries are supposedly on the opposite side of all significant issues in the Middle East. Isn't that what critics and so-called scholars have preached how these two countries would never work together to shield al-Qaeda or its leaders? This is why scholars and experts can be easily manipulated into discounting reality – mistaking it for misinformation crafted by Deep State puppet masters.

Why until now had this gem of international terrorism Intel escaped all the experts for 17-plus years?

Just months ago, in March 2008, current Saudi Crown Prince Mohammed bin Salman attacked Iran, alleging that Iran was harboring Osama bin Laden's son and providing supporting as the new leader of al Qaeda.

Reuters News, another Deep-State controlled media arm, quickly tried to quell the story by citing the sheer impossibility of the Saudi Crown Prince's 'outrageous' allegations.

Reuters tried to spin the story:

"Decades-old animosity between Sunni Muslim kingdom of Saudi Arabia and revolutionary Shi'ite Iran has deepened in recent years as the two sides wage proxy wars in the Middle East and beyond, including in Iraq, Syria, and Yemen.

Shi'ite Muslim Iran and strict Sunni militant group al Qaeda are natural enemies on either side of the Muslim world's great sectarian divide. Yet intelligence veterans say that Iran, in pursuing its own ends, has in the past taken advantage of al Qaeda fighters' need to shelter or pass through its territory."

Really, Reuters?

Is that why Brennan's name is on top secret documents discussing bin Laden's son living in Iran and running al-Qaeda under the tutelage of his father and disciples? Reuters seemed to leave that part out.

Reuters failed to mention the accord between the two countries struck in 2001 either.

Saudi Crown Prince Mohammed bin Salman said during an interview with CBS' 60 Minutes accused Iran of indeed protecting al-Qaeda operatives, including numerous bin Laden relatives.

"This includes the son of Osama bin Laden, the new leader of al Qaeda. He lives in Iran and works out of Iran. He is supported by Iran," the Saudi Crown Prince said.

Iran's Foreign Ministry called the Crown Prince's allegations a "big lie."

Perhaps this helps shed needed light on why the new Saudi Prince jailed hundreds of the kingdom's wealthiest political players and powerbrokers while consolidating his own power quickly after becoming Crown Prince. That included hammering the bin Laden family construction conglomerate that earned billions in profits under the Saudi flag.

Per Reuters:

Three Bin Laden brothers, senior executives in the family firm, were among more than 200 businessmen, royals and officials detained in November 2017 in an anti-corruption drive ordered by the prince. Bakr and two of his brothers, Saleh and Saad, eventually transferred their combined 36.2 percent stake in the family firm to the state in April 2018. Bakr, in his late 60s, is still in custody, although no charges have been made public.

On the night of Nov. 4, 2017, Saudi authorities detained Bakr bin Laden in Jeddah along with more than 200 other members of the Saudi elite, in what officials said was a crackdown on corruption. Dozens of Bin Laden family members, including the brothers' children, had their bank accounts frozen and were banned from traveling abroad, said associates of the family. Brothers who were overseas at the time were recalled to the kingdom.

The purge affected royals, ministers and business leaders. The Bin Laden family's hometown of Jeddah, once the economic capital of Saudi Arabia, was particularly hard hit. Many of the city's merchant families had maintained close relationships with previous kings; few of them were spared in the crackdown.

The government publicly has not said precisely why the Bin Laden terror group - or any of the other individuals caught up in the anti-corruption campaign - were detained. King Salman said at the time the purge was in response to "exploitation by some of the weak souls who have put their own interests above the public interest, to illicitly accrue money."

(SIDE NOTE: Brennan had worked for the CIA as station chief in Jeddah in 2001, the hometown of the bin Laden clan).

"Prince bin Salman didn't like what he learned after becoming Crown Prince," a former U.S. intelligence official who worked in the Middle East with Brennan said. "Perhaps he tripped across these things you're asking about between the (Saudi) Kingdom and Iran and that set him off. It sure seems like he was shot out of a cannon."

In the same CBS interview, the Saudi Crown Prince doubled down on comparing Iran Supreme Leader Ayatollah Ali Khameini to Adolf Hitler.

"He wants to create his own project in the Middle East very much like Hitler, who wanted to expand at the time," Prince Mohammed said. "Many countries around the world and in Europe did not realize how dangerous Hitler was until what happened, happened. I don't want to see the same events happening in the Middle East."

Khameini, don't forget, presided (or still presides) over the Committee of Nine – Iran's unofficial board of directors that pinpoints targets and green lights terror strikes globally, per earlier intelligence revealed by Tom Orest in this work. Khameini was instrumental in striking the deal to house bin Laden and al-Qaeda in Iran, per Orest.

This is, quite possibly, more hard evidence to explain why Brennan has attacked Saudi Crown Prince Mohammed so viciously in recent weeks.

"Suddenly Brennan wants Saudi reforms," one intelligence source said. "Reforms in the form of getting him private contracts with his old Saudi contacts who have little power now or to cover his ass if these things blow up."

Or perhaps Brennan just wants to distract the Trump administration from investigating his role in the Bush and Obama CIA, as well as the Obama White House -- and what role he played in working to hammer out what would appear to be a very troubling treaty with the Saudis and Iranians to protect terrorists with the "hands-off" approval of the U.S. intelligence apparatus whose leaders boast and profess how tirelessly their plebes are working to capture the very radical Islamic terrorists they have cut deals behind the Middle Eastern curtain to protect.

If that deceit doesn't teeter on or constitute outright Treason, nothing does.

Keep in mind, well-placed intelligence officials and analysts point out, Brennan never did go out of his way to share the information about the bin Laden family – or any individual or entity -- running al-Qaeda inside Iran's borders. And still, no one in the federal government lifted a finger to not only try to extract bin Laden from Iran but even seek details on his location from Saudi officials, including Nayef.

However, fast forward a decade, and the documents recovered during the Navy SEAL raid of bin Laden's compound in Pakistan produced documents showing bin Laden's sons were living in Iran for years. And relatives confirmed this as well. The CIA is withholding hundreds of thousands of documents that will likely never be declassified, including details or evidence linking the boys' father to Iran. One report, a manifesto written by a bin-Laden al-Qaeda consigliere, details how Iran allowed bin Laden and his network safe harbor after 9/11. (See chapter 11)

"You'll never see these materials," one FBI agent said. "They wouldn't even let the FBI or the (FBI) lab examine that stuff (recovered from bin Laden's compound). Brennan locked it all away when he became CIA director."

Are we to believe bin Laden's sons – who were with him when his Pakistan compound was raided in 2011 – were not with their father before the terror chief was relocated from Iran in late 2010. Where were his sons then? Even Brennan and Nayef discussed the bin Laden father and son in Iran, per previous revelations in this chapter. U.S. officials said during the raid on bin Laden in Pakistan one son – 23-yr-old Khalid -- was gunned down and killed. The other – 20-yr-old Hamza -- reportedly escaped when the SEALs stormed the house, according to the U.S. reports of the military operation. Why would the sons be residing with their father in Pakistan, but not Iran? In the mid-2000s, Hamza was 14 and Khalid 17 yrs old. Where did they live, if not with their father? Osama bin Laden's brothers attest the sons were raised in Iran.

In a bizarre move, intelligence insiders who are familiar with Brennan's top secret communications, said specific mentions of bin Laden's son in Iran linked to al-Qaeda labeled the boy as Ibrahim bin Laden, instead of Hamza bin Laden.

"Big problem because Ibrahim would have been

about five years old at that time," one well-placed Intel insider said. "He wasn't running a major terrorist operation. Not yet."

But his older brother was just 20 years old. Was Hamza's name removed from U.S. cables to shield his identity and connection to al-Qaeda or was the mention of his 5-yr.-old brother Ibrahim in his place merely an error? And why and how did Hamza escape from his father's compound the night of the U.S. raid? There are mixed reports of course. U.S. officials maintain Hamza was at the house. Pakistani ISI confirms he was not at the residence during the strike.

Now Hamza dubbed the "Crown Prince of Terror," remains elusive like his father.

Think of the utter absurdity and sheer irony fueled by bureaucratic stupidity. The United States classified Hamza as a Specially Designated Global Terrorist in January 2017, effectively blacklisting him and branding him an international fugitive. Yet he was left in Iran alone – unfettered by the United States for a decade -- to help rebuild and lead al-Qaeda under the tutelage of his father, Osama bin Laden, and his radical inner circle.

Scholars and journalists have afforded too much weight on the U.S. government's bin Laden archives -- troves of documents that fail to mention even the possibility bin Laden was in Iran after 9/11. Experts and authors often cite bin Laden's letters to family members as proof of his travels. But these letters and writings were released by the CIA years after they were reportedly grabbed during the 2011 raid on his house in Pakistan. Thousands more were released in 2017, six years after his death, including a video of Hamza bin Laden's wedding.

As journalists and investigators – and even common-sense analysts – are we to believe 'evidence' released by the CIA in a slow-drip format over the years? I certainly don't. To shed some needed light here, I knew folks and worked with folks who can fabricate any document in the world, and they are in the employment of the federal government's Intel apparatus. And researchers and journalists et al. who believe bin Laden documents released by the Feds to be true and correct are beyond help. Do you think the CIA would release any material from its troves of unreleased materials on bin Laden indicating he was in Iran? If anything the Agency and the FBI – along with the State Dept. have gone to extreme lengths to quash any notion of it.

I read the books by scholars and journalists about bin Laden's travels after 9/11 in 2001 from writers versed much more than myself in the war on terrorism, and almost all use the data supplied by the U.S. government as a backbone for their research and Intel. That is undoubtedly flawed, from an insider's perspective. Why would the Deep State hand over evidence to incriminate itself? And there is little mention in previous literary works, if any, linking bin Laden to living in Iran. And no mention of the U.S. government burying Intel about it and targeting whistleblowers. That is the danger of journalists writing inside a government-sourced echo chamber and regurgitating the same data points while adding their own creative flair and insights. There are massive holes left in all the "official" narratives. Perhaps this work, while indeed not gospel or infallible, will help fill the gaps

Even the wedding video of Hamza bin Laden,

released last year by the CIA, contained little information about where and when it was filmed, and it is doubtful the entire video was released. Yt Intel folks I tapped to examine the video said it was clearly shot in Iran, even though the Agency failed to disclose that pertinent fact.

But the bin Laden patriarch wasn't in Iran, where all his sons were? According to who, the CIA and loyal jihadists trying to protect al-Qaeda's founder?

Meanwhile, Brennan and the U.S. never lifted a finger to hunt, find and extract either bin Laden. But now, the U.S. is suddenly interested in apprehending him? You could not make this stuff up if you tried. It is either wild ineptness or a nefarious plot to aid and abet terrorism.

Director of the Defense Intelligence Agency Lt. Gen. Robert P. Ashley told members of the Senate in March that al Qaeda "remains a serious and persistent threat to U.S. interests worldwide," and in South Asia, "retained the intent and limited capability to threaten coalition and Afghan forces and interests in the region."

Unless you have actionable intelligence against bin Laden – any bin Laden – in Iran.

Internal communications indeed show Brennan seemed much more interested in discussing the tenets of Islam with Saudi Arabia and Middle Eastern officials -- and how radical terrorists disparaged the religion's image, according to intelligence insiders directly involved with Brennan's White House cables and communications.

"What kind of presidential homeland security advisor ignores intelligence on high-value terrorist targets from the Middle East and Osama bin Laden?"

a former White House official asked. "Brennan is discussing and praising Islam with the Saudi Arabian government, with Jordan and many others."

Often Brennan would speak Arabic, and when "Allah" was mentioned by either party during the conversations with Middle Eastern officials, including Saudi's Nayef, the word would be changed to "God" in U.S. reports. And omitted from reports were Brennan's customary Muslim greeting "As-salāmu ʿalaykum," and the response "wa ʿalaykumu s-salām," with Middle Eastern dignitaries.

If these were merely cultural niceties, why delete them from the record, top-secret or not? Why conceal such exchanges?

Intelligence official said Brennan's cables from inside the White House were usually sent to the Secretary of State, CIA, National Security Council, and various embassies and consulates depending on the content.

"No one expects to see the word "Allah" coming from a U.S. official in a Secret—NOFORN (document)," one intelligence insider said. (Secret—NOFORN is a type of document classification which labels the document as secret, and the information cannot be shared with foreign nationals.)

One such direct example is extracted from confidential communications from Brennan's White House post in an exchange with Saudi leaders in 2009 – again – two years before the raid on bin Laden.

Saudi Official to Brennan: "We've achieved many things in protecting the country and Allah willing, we will achieve many more things with our friends."

"Allah" was swapped out for "God" in U.S. correspondences.

Brennan in the same exchange: "I wish other countries in the world were as willing and capable. Saudi Arabia is on the front line of terrorism and a model in preventing individuals from being corrupted by the propaganda of al-Qaeda and instrumental in demonstrating to the West and U.S. that al-Qaeda was a perversion of Islam and did not represent the true faith."

Brennan is more concerned with the portrayal of Islam in the United States that he is about pursuing bin Laden, his son, and al-Qaeda – and protecting Americans from their terror regime. Brennan is an ambassador of Islam's "true faith," and this is where his focus was while he was sitting next to Obama in the White House – and later as CIA chief.

For years there have been numerous rumors about Brennan's conversion to Islam among CIA hierarchy and in intelligence sources. Even dopey and feckless Snopes.com was deployed to help quell such rumors and without any proof – Snopes concluded Brennan is not a practicing Muslim. Wow, that was easy. But his cables, speeches, and communications with Middle Eastern envoys indicate the opposite.

Throughout the research for this book, I keep asking myself why the U.S. government would fail time and time again to follow credible leads on bin Laden. I keep arriving at sinister and troubling motivations. I picked the brain of one cleric versed in Islam. He ended formulated an astonishing hypothesis I had failed to ponder.

"Have you ever pondered that Brennan was obligated to help bin Laden, to aid bin Laden no matter what the cost was to the United States?" he asked. "It's the rule of Islam to go against and crush the kafir above anything else, except Mohammed. Brennan may have had little choice according to his beliefs."

The kafir. What in the hell is the kafir, I thought.
From Politicalislam.com, kafir is explained and defined:

We now come to a new subject—the unbeliever or non-Muslim. The word "non-Muslim" is used in the translation of Sharia law, but the actual Arabic word used is "Kafir." But the word Kafir means far more than non-Muslim. The original meaning of the word was "concealer," one who conceals the truth of Islam.

The Koran says that the Kafir may be deceived, plotted against, hated, enslaved, mocked, tortured and worse. The word is usually translated as "unbeliever," but this translation is wrong. The word "unbeliever" is logically and emotionally neutral, whereas, Kafir is the most abusive, prejudiced and hateful word in any language.

There are many religious names for Kafirs: polytheists, idolaters, People of the Book (Christians and Jews), Buddhists, atheists, agnostics, and pagans. Kafir covers them all because no matter what the religious name is, they can all be treated the same. What Mohammed said and did to polytheists can be done to any other category of Kafir.

Islam devotes a great amount of energy to the Kafir. The majority (64%) of the Koran is devoted to the Kafir, and nearly all of the Sira (81%) deals with Mohammed's struggle with them. The Hadith (Traditions) devotes 32% of the text to Kafirs1. Overall, the Trilogy devotes 60% of its content to the

Kafir.

Hadith 37%
Sira   81%
Koran 64%
Total 60%
Amount of Text Devoted to the Kafir

The Sharia does not devote nearly that much to the Kafir since Sharia law is primarily for Muslims. Besides, the Kafir has few rights, so there is little to expound on.

Religious Islam is what Muslims do to go to Paradise and avoid Hell. What Mohammed did to Kafirs was not religious, but political. Political Islam is what is of concern to Kafirs, not the religion. Who cares how a Muslim worships, but every one of us is concerned as to what they do to us and say about us. Political Islam should be of concern to every Kafir.

Translated: A devout Muslim is obligated to protect other practitioners of Islam at the expense of the kafir. Even if employed by a kafir-run government.

Is this why the Saudis helped protect bin Laden and al-Qaeda as well?

The cleric concluded:

"This might be the true motivation," he said while noting Brennan's boss at the time may have shared the same dogma.

Perhaps Brennan's own words tell a better story:

"Our enemy is not 'terrorism' because terrorism is but a tactic," Brennan said in a 2010 speech at the Center for Strategic and International Studies in Washington, D.C. *"Our enemy is not*

'terror' because terror is a state of mind, and as Americans, we refuse to live in fear.

Several months ago, I had the opportunity to speak at NYU (New York University) where I was hosted by the university's Islamic center and the Islamic Law Students Association. After I was finished speaking, person after person stood up to share their perspective and to ask their questions. Mothers and fathers, religious leaders and students, recent immigrants and American citizens by birth. One after another, they spoke of how they love this country and of all the opportunities it has afforded them and their families. But they also spoke of their concerns, that their fellow Americans, and at times, their own government, may see them as a threat to American security, rather than a part of the American family. One man, a father, explained that his 21-year-old son, an American born and raised, who was subjected to extra security every time he boards a plane, now feels disenfranchised in his own country.

Moreover, describing our enemy in religious terms would lend credence to the lie—propagated by al-Qaeda and its affiliates to justify terrorism—that the United States is somehow at war against Islam. The reality, of course, is that we never have been and will never be at war with Islam. After all, Islam, like so many faiths, is part of America.

Nor do we describe our enemy as 'jihadists' or 'Islamists' because jihad is a holy struggle, a legitimate tenet of Islam, meaning to purify oneself or one's community, and there is nothing holy or legitimate or Islamic about murdering innocent men, women, and children."

Yet Brennan did nothing to stop the murdering of innocent men, women, and children in the name of

Islam.

Islam first, at the expense of a nation of kafir.

11 SMOKING GUN FROM BIN LADEN

Of all the documents released by the CIA that were recovered from bin Laden, this is one of the best in my opinion – and in the opinion of experts we had examine it and translates it. That clearly was the point of the CIA releasing it in Arabic. If you translate it straight – without using the filters of jihad and terrorism, most of the content would slip through the cracks. And how many Americans are going to go through the hassle of hiring experts versed in the conflicts of the Middle East to translate the document? Very few. But we did. Keep in mind, this has been translated in the Middle East so grammar, usage and some spelling is off. We did not want to tamper with the content too much because swapping one word can alter the message.

To frame the bombshell we have here, this was a manifesto written by a high-ranking al-Qaeda general to its radical soldiers. Our experts pin this document down to about 1997, and it serves as a status report on al-Qaeda business and more importantly, the logistical and financial help the terror network is receiving from Iran. In fact, the author likely wrote portions of this document while in Iran, according to the experts who broke this down. And bin Laden indeed wrote or helped construct at least parts of this. The report does show al-Qaeda was using Iran as its base after Sept. 11, 2001 – while the Bush and Obama administrations were focused on Afghanistan.

The enemy of my enemy is my friend. That is the mantra and battle cry for al-Qaeda here after 9/11 … get to Iran and regroup. Iran hates America, We hate America. Iran is now our friend, per al-Qaeda's own admissions uncovered here. Most al-Qaeda had vacated Afghanistan. The U.S. military was chasing ghosts. How did the CIA miss this? It's amazing. Of course, they didn't miss anything. This is why they ignored Iran, who was helping al-Qaeda set up new identities with fake IDs in Tehran and Iranian radicals were renting houses for al-Qaeda as well. Safe houses. Others were given visas by Iran to enter the country.

This confirms what I said throughout this book and what others testified to as well here. So, al-Qaeda was safe to rebuild and hide, and the people running our government allowed them to do so. If they feign ignorance, they admit they were terrible at their posts, but we all know that wasn't the case. No one is this inept – even at the federal government level.

If you think al-Qaeda's rank-and-file fled Afghanistan in droves – why would bin Laden stay behind?

He didn't. Yet U.S. troops were in Afghanistan?

بسم الله الرحمن الرحيم

In The Name of Allah, Most Gracious, Most Merciful

محمد ورسوله الله عبد على و السلام والصلاة حمده، حق لله الحمد
وصحبه وآله.

Praise be to Allah, and prayers and peace be upon his servant and his Messenger, Muhammad, and his family and companions.

/وبعد

لمشايخنا والتبيين لإخواني النصح رقمها اقتضى صفحات فهذه
الإيراني، الرافضي النظام مع المجاهدون إخواننا كيفتعامل ومحببينا
الذب، ضمئا به يحصل بما والاستقبال، فيالحال إليه ينظرون وكيف
الله سددهم إخواننا عرض عن.

These pages include a number of brotherly recommendations from our elders and friends as to how our fellow Mujahideen brothers treated the regime of the Rafidis (Shiites) in Iran, and how they see it now and in future to defend the honor of our brothers, may Allah reward them.

محاور ثلاثة في الكلام أنظم أن وسأحاول:

I will try to organize the speech in three main parts:

- مقدمة ..

- Introduction

- ثم بعض السرد، التاريخي وأقتصر على المفيد..

- Then some historical narratives limited to useful ones

- ثم أذكر بعد ذلك ما أعرفه من مواقف وسياسة إخواننا وفقهم الله.

- Then I will mention what I know about the positions and policy of our brothers, may Allah reward them

المحور الأول: مقدمة لأبد منها:

First Part: Inevitable Introduction

الصدمة الكبيرة والارتباك والتشتت:

فلا شك أن مضاعفات واستتباعات وضربات الحادي عشر من الأكثرين،فحسب تصور فوق وربما جداً كانتكبيرة سبتمبر وما علمي أتذكره الآن، فإن الذيكنا نتوقعه ويتوقعه الأخوة أكثر من حولي في أفغانستان عندما حصلت ضرباتسبتمبر كان هو: ضربات أمريكية صاروخية وجوية، وأنهم محدودة) وأنهم سيقومون(الأمريكان المخالفين، أي الشماليين جماعة أحمد شاه.مسعود وبعض الأخوة كان يتوقع أن تهادن أمريكا وتركن للموادعة، وتطلب السلم.وقدتصور بعض الإخوة أيضا أنها تركن ويحصل فيها لكن انهيار، هذين الأخيرينالتصورين كانا عند بعض الإخوة ضعفاء التصور.

There is no doubt that the consequences and
reverberations of the September 11 attacks were very
big and beyond the imaginations of a majority of the
people, and as far as I know and what I currently
remember, which we and the majority of brothers
around me in Afghanistan expected when the
September 11 attacks happened was that the US
would carry limited missile and air strikes, and they
(the Americans) would support the northerners, i.e.
Ahmad Shah Massoud group. Some of the brothers
expected that the US would compromise and seek for
peace, and some of the brothers also thought that the
US would kneel down and collapse, but these two
thoughts were adopted by some of the brothers who
had a weak imagination.

أقف لم فهذا بالضبط، يتصور مثلا أسامة الشيخ كان كيف ندري لا
بهم التقيت سبتمبر،والذين من عشر الحادي بعد لمنره لأننا عليه،
الشيخ، وتصورات موقف بدقائق علم يكنعندهم لم بعدها، رأوه ممن
ترورا نهاية إلى رافقوه ممن أخصأصحابه من رجل سألت إني حتى
في يتحدث الشيخ لميكن :لي فقال بعد، فيما عنه انفصلوا حتى بورا
تقيم في أحدحديثا أي معه يفتح ولم ويصبّر، يبشر كان وإنما الأمر،
وقت هو الوقت لأن جدا، طبيعي وهذا ..ذلك نحو أو حصل ما

ولا ونحوها، وتدقيقات حسابات وقت وليس فعلا، وتصبير تبشير
!إدروس حتى.

We do not know how sheik Usama was thinking
exactly, I don't know this, because we did not see him
after the September 11 attacks, and the ones I met

who saw him afterwards didn't know the Intricacies
of the position and perceptions of the sheikh, I even I
asked a man of his close companions who
accompanied him to Tora Bora until they separated
later, he said to me: "The sheikh wasn't speaking in
this subject, but he was preaching and asked us to
have patience, and no one opened a conversation
with him to get his evaluation of what happened or
so".. This is very normal, because that time was the
time for preaching and patience and not the time of
calculations, evaluations or even lessons.!

نتصور نكن فلم تصورنا، فوق جدا كبيرا الأمريكي الرد كان بالجملة
إلى طبعا راجع والسبب السرعة، بهذه ستنهار إمارةطالبان أن أيضا
القصفوالتدمير وبشاعة الصدمة قوة.

In whole, the US response was very much over our
perception, we did not imagine that the Emirate of
Taliban would collapse so quickly, and the reason, of
course, is the strength of the shock and the horror of
the bombings and destruction.

فوضى حصلت بالانسحاب، الأوامر وصدور الإمارة انهيار مع
وكثير الإخوة، من جدا كبيرة أعداد وتشتت،فتدفقت وارتباك كبيرة
وبدأت كراتشي، باكستان،وخصوصا إلى عوائلهم، مع منهم
..!أموروأمور الأخوة،وحصلت على للقبض الباكستانية الحملات

With the collapse of the Emirate and orders to
withdraw being issued, there was a great chaos,
confusion and distraction, so very large numbers of
brothers, many of them with their families, fled to

Pakistan, especially to Karachi, and Pakistani campaigns began to arrest the brothers and things happened..!

في منه طرفا سنحكي مما أمور وحصلت إيران، على أعداد وتدفقت المحور الثاني.

And large numbers went to Iran, and I will explain in the second part how the situation developed.

أكثرنا، تصور فوق جدا شديدة كانت الصليبية الحملة أن المقصود عارمة، وفوضى وارتباك وتشتت انهيار سريع وحصل قبل من وللهالأمر. اوغيرها وأموال نفوس فيها ضاعت ومن بعد.

The crusade was very strong and over the perception of most us, and there was a quick collapse and a great chaos, confusion and distraction, where souls, money and other stuff were lost.! It's all in Allah's hands.

للمرحلة التأريخ عند بالحسبان يؤخذ أن لابد فهذا وتقييمها.

This must be taken into account when writing the history and evaluating this time.

القلوب فيها تبلغ التي الصعبة المواقف هذه مثل في من أشياء يُتصور باللهالظنون، الناس ويظن الحناجر حال في يُتصور لا ما وغيرها، ارتكاب الضرورات الاختيار والسعة.

مثالاً لكم سأذكر ولهذا:

In such difficult situations where the hearts reach the throats, we commit things for necessity that we can't imagine committing them if we have the choice. And I will give you an example:

وقعت التي الضرورية والمحاولات الأفكار بعض :

الواقع) رمضان من والعشرين الحادي ليلة في أنا أذكر وعشرين اثنتين سنة من وواحد، لعله ألفين سنة في محمدعمر الملا المؤمنين أمير من الأمر صدر (للهجرة سيسلمونها لأنهم قندهار من بالإنسحاب الله سدده فعلا تحقق قد العجز لأن غداصباحا، القبائل لمجلس معهجزاهم الثابتة الصابرة والثلة المؤمنين أمير واضطر بعد الأمروتسليمه، ترك إلى الله، وثبتهم خيرا الله سائر ومن البشتون، القبائلورجال من شديد ضغط العدوان بشاعة بسبب وممثليهم، الشعب الناس يطقه لم الأمريكيالذي.

Some necessary ideas and attempts that took place:

I recall that in the night of 21st of Ramadan (2001 or 1422 H) Emir Al-Mu'minin(Faithful), Mullah Mohammad Omar, issued the order to withdraw from Kandahar because they were going to hand it over to the Tribes Council in the next morning, because the deficit had already accrued and Emir Al-Mu'mininwith the few men standing with him, may Allah reward them, had to leave the matter and hand it over after heavy pressure from the tribes and Pashtun men, and the rest of the people and their representatives, because of the horror of the US aggression that the people couldn't withstand.

مع الأمريكان الجنود مقابلة في قندهار مطار في كنا الأوامر فجاءت.آغا جل مليشياتالزنديق الردة جنود المدينة إلى فرجعنا انسحبوا :مشفرة سريع بشكل هي الوجهة وكانت التفاصيل، فوجدنا(قندهار) يطولذكرها أمور وحصلت ..خوستوجرديز.

We were in Kandahar airport while the American soldiers were meeting with the soldiers of the apostasy soldiers, the militias of the infidel, Gel Agha. The orders quickly came encrypted ordering us to withdrew, so we returned to the city (Kandahar) to be updated with the details, and the destination is Khost and Gardez. Other things happened, but I won't mention them because they are long.

حيث خوست، إلى الليلة نفس في توجهنا المهم لقوا وقد هناك، المجاهدينالعرب من كبيرة مجموعة قدرهم، الله ورفع منهم، الله تقبل الوادي، في أهوالا خوستوجرديز مدينتي فتفرقنافي.

In the same night, we went to Khost province, where a large group of Arab jihadists was stationed there who saw horrors in the valley, my Allah accepts their sacrifices, and we were scattered in the cities of Khost and Gardez.

آراء هناك كانت :وتنسيقات اجتماعات وبدأت
المفضّل والاختيارات،بين الرأي في واختلافات
والثبات للبقاء المفضل وبين باكستان، إلى للانسحاب
الموت حتى علىالمواجهة.

Meetings and coordination began: there were
differences in opinions and choices, there were ones
who preferred to withdraw to Pakistan, and others
preferred to stay and confront the enemy to death.

على الكثرين رأي استقر أيام عدة مرور مع ثم
إلى متتالية فيدفعات انسحبوا وبالفعل الانسحاب،
إلا يبق ولم باكستان، سائر إلى ثم وزيرستان
ومن الأوزبك من ومجموعة العرب قليلةمن مجموعة
التركستانيين.

After several days, the opinion of most of the
brothers was to withdraw. They indeed withdrew in
successive waves of Waziristan and then to the rest of
Pakistan, and only a few number of the Arabs and a
group of Uzbeks and Turkistanis.

في مرة كنا الأيام تلك خوست في كنا لما أننا الشاهد
مصعب وأبو العدل فيهسيف كان للتشاور اجتماع
الليبيوأبو الليث وأبو السوري خالد أبو وصاحبه السوري
يتدارسون الأخوة كان وآخرون، الكندي الرحمن عبد
التي الاقتراحات ضمن فكانمن والمشاكل، الحلول
الله بحزب الاتصال محاولة الأخوة بعض طرحها
مندوبا أرسل الله فعل حزب أن بعضهم وذكر فيلبنان،
أو جاءوا أنهم بلغني منتكلم، ومع وصل أين أدري لا)

وعرض (الأفغانية القيادات بعض طريق عن أرسلوا
التي الأفكار ضمن من وكان ..الإخوة لإيواء أيمساعدة
اقترح حيث السوري أبيمصعب الأخ من فكرة طرحت
نظام) العراقي بالنظام الاتصال هو يتولى أن
الشخصيات بعض يعرف إنه :وقال (صدامحسين
أيام عرفهم صدام،ممن نظام في المرموقة القديمة
القرن من الثمانينيات أوائل سنوات العراق في إقامته
وتجربة سوريا في الإخوة جهاد أثناء الماضي الميلادي
وأنه بهم العلاقة بهموتجديد الاتصال يمكنه وأنه حماة،
الإخوة بإيواء يساعدون أنهم يتوقع.

When we were in Khost those days, there was a meeting for consultation attended by Saif al-Adl, Abu Musab al-Suri, Abu Khaled al-Suri, Abu Laith al-Libi, Abu Abdul Rahman al-Canadi and others and they were examining the issues and solutions. One of the proposals forward by some of the brothers were attempting to contact Hezbollah in Lebanon, and some stated that Hezbollah had sent a delegate (I don't know where he arrived and to whom he spoke, I have been advised that he came or was sent through some Afghan leaders) and offered any help to accommodate the brothers. One of the ideas was proposed by Abu Musab al-Suri in which he suggested that he contact with the Iraqi regime (Saddam Hussein) and said that he knew some of the prestigious old figures in Saddam regime, whom he had known during his stay in Iraq in the early 1980s, during the Jihad of the brothers in Syria and the experience of the Hama, and that he could contact them and renew their relationship and that he expected they would help accommodate the brothers.

..طرح مما أشياء هذه

These were among the proposed ideas..

نفعل كيف هي -تلحظون كما- الكبيرة المشكلة كانت شك ولا !نؤويهم؟ وأين الإخوة، الكبيرمن العدد هذا في ..!عقولالحلماء تطير جدا كبيرة مسؤولية أنها

The big problem - as you can see - was how could we do this for such large number of brothers, and where to accommodate them?! There is no doubt that this very great responsibility that make the patient people unrest!

والاتصال الله، بحزب الاتصال :الخيارين كلا طبعا، رفضوا الإخوة معظم يحصلا،لأن لم العراقي، بالنظام .يقبلوهما ولم الاقتراحين

Of course, both options, contacting with Hezbollah, and the Iraqi regime, did not happen, because most of the brothers rejected both of them.

شيئان وهما ذكرتهما، اللذان الخياران إلا يبق فلم :وهما ، مجتمعان

Leaving only the two mentioned options, and they are two combined things:

الأول: انسحاب الأكثر، إلى باكستان ثم الذي يبقى
حتى مناسبا ترتيبا ونرتبلهم فليبق، هناك مستترا
آخر، حال إلى الانتقال أو الحال بتغير الله يأذن
إليه الذهاب يستطيع آخر بلد أو بلده إلى والذييسافر
والتقلل تسفيرهم لابدمن العوائل سيما ولا فليفعل،
مؤونتهم من.!

First: the withdrawal of most of the brothers to
Pakistan, and who remains hidden there can stay, and
then we later arrange an appropriate arrangement for
them until Allah change things, and who can travel to
his country or another country can go, especially the
families of the brothers as they must travel and reduce
their supplies.!

الثاني: بقاء مجموعات قليلة من الإخوة للقتال وعدم
تفريغ ساحةبشكلأفغانستان، كامل يثبتون ويقاومون
ويؤسسون للحرب الطويلة، القادمة ثم ينضمبالتدريج
إليهم إخوانهم إن شاء الله.وهو ما حصل، بالفعل
والحمد لله رب العالمين.

Second: Few groups of brothers have to stay to fight
and not empty the battlefield of Afghanistan, and to
stand their grounds, resist and make a foundation for
the long war ahead, then gradually be joined by their
brothers, Allah willing. That is what has happened
already, thank Allah, the Lord of the Worlds.

كان ثمت من واقتراحات أفكار في تلك الشدة العظيمة
والشاهد من كل هذه الحكاية أن أعطيكم صورة لما

عرضالنبي جنس من لعلها وهذه الكبيرة، والمحنة
ثمار ثلث وهوازن غطفان على وسلم عليه الله صلى
هناك يكون أن يمكن كان الأحزاب،وإن يوم المدينة
فارق.

The moral of this story is to give you a view of the
ideas and suggestions in that great hardship and
tribulation, this is perhaps the same approach taken
by the Prophet (PBUH) with Ghatfan and Hawazen
tribes where he gave them one third of the fruits of
Al-Madina in the Battle of the Trench, although there
could be a difference.

العظيم، وفضله بلطفة تعالى الله سلم لله، والحمد
جيد، بشكل الأمور والصدمة،وانفرجت الشدة ومرت
الصعوباتبما يتخطوا لأن المجاهدين تعالى الله ووفق
البذل وحب والصبر، الثبات من عليهم ألقى
ولله مشرفة هوسيرة الغالب فكان والتضحيات،
ما ومع منه، لابد والقصور النقص بعض مع الحمد،
الله نسأل المستعان، والله أسر، وقتل منأهوال حصل
يسترنا وأن جميعا، أحوالنا يصلح أن

والآخرة الدنيا في.

Thanks to Allah, the distress and shock went away,
and things were going well. Allah helped he
Mujahideen to surpass the difficulties by giving them
persistence and patience, so the success was a great
story to tell with some inevitable shortcomings and
imperatives, and what happened from the horrors and

killings of families. We ask Allah to bless us all and cover us here and in the hereafter.

حقيقية وأمريكا إيران بين العداوة:

واقعة عداوة هي وأمريكا إيران بين العداوة نعم، ما كل إن ويقول خلافذلك، يتصور والذي وحقيقية، ونحو والشتم السب ومن بالعداوة تظاهر من بينهما لا جاهل فهذا "تمثيلية" و "مسرحية" هو ذلكإنما الحقائق يعرف!.

The enmity between Iran and America is real:

Yes, the enmity between Iran and America is between reality and truth, and whoever thinks differently and says that whatever hostility and war of words is going on between them is play-acting and a show, he is ignorant and does not know the facts!

هذا فإن أدلة، وسرد ذلك في التطويل إلى أحتاج ولا بين كما بينهما العداوة ومثل..!عندنا المسلمات من أن عن فضلا العداوة، من الكفار من كثير دعواهم، بحسب ولو- ينتسبون الرافضةالإيرانيين وإلى إلىالإسلام -لهم الصلبيين حسبان وبحسب المحمدية الملة.

I do not need to say more in this matter and list evidences, as this is a postulate..! Such enmity is like the enmity among many of the infidels, and the Iranian-Rafidis belong (even if, according to their claim, and Crusaders view for them) to Islam and to the Muhammadiyah denomination.

والآخر ، ناجز عدو أحدهما لكن ..لنا عدو كلاهما ثم
مؤجل عدو.!

Both are our enemies.. But one of them is an absolutecurrent enemy, and the other is a postponed enemy.!

مصالحه وله يقولون، كما "أجندته" له وكلاهما
والثقافة الدين والمبنيةعلى الحيوية، الاستراتيجية
الشخصية ومكونات عناصر وكافة والحضارة والتاريخ
القوميةالمليَة...

Each of them has his "Agenda" as they say, and has his vital strategic interests, based on religion, culture, history and civilization and all elements and components of national personality...

الإيرانية البراغماتية:

الاصطلاح في مستعمل لفظ "البراغماتية" لفظ
التقريب علىوجه ومعناه المعاصر، السياسي:
المؤقتة ولو تراعيمصالحها التي المفرطة العقلانية
والقيم المبادئ عن وتتخلى والعاجلةالسريعة،
أنهذا مع ذلك، سبيل في المعلنة، والشعارات
من قربا أكثر استعمال يستعمل أحيانا أيضا المصطلح
السياسية الإباحية هي والتي"الميكافيلية" معنى
الوسيلة تبرر الغاية ومبدأ.

Iranian pragmatism:

The term "pragmatism" is a term used in the contemporary political terminology, meaning approximately: excessive rationality that cares for it interests, even the temporary ones and the rapid urgent ones, and abandon its proclaimed slogans, principles and values in order to achieve that. This term is also sometimes used to accomplish a meaning closer to the "Machiavellianism", which is the political pornography and principle of "the end justifies the means".

أوضح من هو الإيراني النظام فإن تجربتي بحسب وأنا
السياسة في لبابالبراغماتية والأمثلة النماذج!.

Based on my experience, the Iranian regime is one of the clearest examples of pragmatism in politics.!

ومذهبهم إمامية، عشرية إثنا رافضة شيعة فالإيرانيون
فينا ومعتقدهم بكاملالوضوح، جميعا لنا معروف
فينا وخصوصا السنة أهل في معتقدهم معروف؛
للسيطره وطموحهم معروف، واضح نحالسلفيين،
القيادة زمام إلتولي وتوقانهم الإسلامي العالم على
دين أصحاب وكونهم كذلك، معروف الإسلامي، للعالم
كل بأهوائهم، مصنوع مخترع موضوع لهو طائفيقومي
وشعاراتهم لديناحميعا، المعرفة تمام معروف ذلك
معروفة يرفعونها التي...

The Iranians are Shiite Muslims, believe in 12 Imams, their religion and beliefs regarding Sunni Muslims and particularly regarding us, as Salafi Muslims, is known;

so is their aspiration to control the whole of Islamic world and to take over its leadership. Their belief in sectarianism which is based on their imaginations as well as their slogans are all very well known to us…

مع حتى للتعاون الاستعداد أتم على فإنهم ذلك ومع التعاون هذا أن رأوا حيثما"وهابية"و سلفية الناس أكثر ينبذونه ثم مؤقتة، ولو لهممصلحة يحقق والتعامل مثلا المناسب فيالوقت.

However, they are ready to cooperate even with most Salafists and Wahhabis where they believe that this cooperation would achieve something for them, though cooperation will be temporary and will end at a suitable time.

بعض الثاني المحور في التاريخي سردنا في وسيأتي لهذاالأمر الموضحة التفاصيل.

In the second part in which we will talk about history, there will be some details showing this.

بسيطة أمثلة إلى هنا سأشير ولكن:

But I will refer here to some simple examples:

أي شخص يريد أن يضرب أمريكا فإن إيران مستعدة - مما المطلوب وبكل بالمالوالسلاح ومساعدته لدعمه على يشتغلون فهم..!وواضح بشكلصريح يورطهم لا يد في دليل أي وقوع من يخافون ولكنهم بجد، أمريكا بصمات أي يتركوا ألا جدا يجتهدون أمريكا،ولهذا

العملهم!!.

- Any person who wants to hit America, Iran is ready to support him and help him with money, weapons, and whatever else, openly and clearly… They are working very hard on the United States, but they are afraid of leaving any evidence and therefore are very diligent to leave no clues of their work!!

- من إخواننا بعض على عرضوا أنهم ذلك أمثله من بالمال يدعموهم أن(سفّروهم الذين) السعوديين التدريب عليهم وعرضوا يحتاجونه، ما وبكل والسلاح مصالح ضرب مقابل لبنان، في الله حزب فيمعسكرات هذا إلى سنشير كما!!.السعوديةوالخليج في أمريكا فيما بعد.

-For example, they offered money, arms and everything they needed to some of our Saudi brothers who supported them, and offered them training in Hezbollah camps in Lebanon, in return for striking America's interests in Saudi Arabia and the Gulf!! And I will refer to this later.

- وهم أعرفها مجموعة على يعرضون، ومازالوا عرضوا يدعموهم أن الأوزبك منالأخوة معنا، تواصل على إيران في والمرور والإقامة والسلاح بالمال كذلك في أمريكية أهداف ضرب مقابل يحتاجونه وبكلما أزبكستان.

-They offered, and still offering support to a group of

Uzbeks, with money and weapons and safe passage to and from Iran and whatever else they need, in return for targeting United States' targets in Uzbekistan. I have other examples, but I am content with what I have said for now.

ذكرته الذي بهذا أكتفي ولكن أخرى، أمثلة وعندي - الآن.

- I have other examples, but this would suffice.

منهما واحد أيّ (وإيران أمريكا) العدوّان هذان وبالجملة أي لدعم مستعدة الآخر؛فأمريكا أعداء لدعم مستعد أنتضرب تريد كانت، مهما صغيرة ولو جماعة أو شخص مع هذا فعلوا وقد الإيراني، النظام على وتشتغل إيران محافظة في البلوش الإخوة من معروفةلدينا مجموعة عرضوا شرقإيران، جنوب في وبلوشستان سيستان على وعرضوا بالفعل، دعموهم بل الدعم عليهم هذا مثلنا، جهاديون سلفيون وهمإخوة كذلك، غيرهم الفرسوالأكراد، من للعلمانيين دعمهم إلى بالإضافة حسب ذلك وسيطوّرون..الهواز في العرب والقوميين مع بالتوازي الحالية المدة في بشكلمكثف معلوماتنا ..!قاصمةلإيران ضربات لتوجيه الاستعدادات

These two enemies(US and Iran) each of them is ready to support the enemies of the other one; the US is ready to support any person or a group or even a small group that wants to hit Iran and operate on the Iranian regime. They did this with a group known to us from the Baluchi people in Sistan and Baluchistan

Province in southeast Iran and offered them support and already supported them. They offered support to others as well, which were Salafi jihadists like us, this is in addition to their support of the Persians, Kurds, and Arab Nationalists in the Ahvaz. They're going, according to our information, to intensively expand this support in the current period in parallel with their preparations to direct deathblows against Iran..!

جماعة أو شخص أي لدعم مستعدة إيران وكذلك أن تريد الدين، أو منالمعتقد كانت ومهما صغرت مهما مكان أي في الأمريكية والمصالح الأمريكان تضرب فيالعالم.

Also, Iran is ready to support any person or a group or even a small group regardless of their belief or religion, that wants to hit the US and US interests anywhere in the world.

آنفا المثلة بعض لكم وسقتْ.

And I stated some examples above.

سلفية جماعة أو شخصا أن كيف تتعجبون قد فأنتم إيران تدعمها الايرانيين، نظرالرافضة بحسب "وهابيبة" أمريكا لضرب!!.

You may wonder how Shiite Iranians could have supported Salafists or Wahhabis to strike America!!

هذا، استبعد ربما يجرب ولم المور يعرف لا والذي

قلة من كله وهذا وظنالظنون، تفسيره في حار وربما
عرف لمن واضح فالأمر وإلا غير، لا المعرفة!!.

One who does not understand this situation, or
doubts it, is due to his lack of knowledge and nothing
else, otherwise the situation is clear for whoever
understands it!!

الأذهان في والتثبيت والفرض المبالغة سبيل وعلى
الإسلام شيخ لدعم إيرانمستعدة إن :لكم أقول أنا
وأنالظروف حي أنه قدر لو نفسه الوهاب عبد بن محمد
ظروفنا مثل في أمريكا ليضرب تدعمه لكي واتتها
الحالية!.

As an example, and in order to get it fixed in minds, I
can say that in current circumstances, Iran would be
ready to support and help Muhammad ibn Abd al-
Wahhab (i.e. the founder of Wahhabism) if he was
alive with whatever needed to target the United
States.

التقية هو -تعرفون كما- دينهم الرافضة والإيرانيون
يبطنون، ما خلف وإظهار التمثيلوالتلعب وهذا والكذب،
والخصوم،والاستعداد الأعداء وجوه في والضحك
أيسر من هو للود، إظهار وبكل بلطف معهم للتعامل
متوارث وهو عليه، ومربون هممعتادون عليهم، الأمور
طباعهم في عميق فيهم،!!.

The religion of the Iranians-Rafidis (as you may
know) is hypocrisy and lying; and acting,

manipulation, showing things other than what they intend, laughing in the faces of the enemies and opponents and dealing with them nicely are the easiest things to them, as they are accustomed and were raised on this; it's their a legacy, deep in their DNA.!!!!

م كل وننهى ذلك، قبول عدم هو إخواننا عند والمبدأ فنحن المداخل، هذه الدخولفي عن به صلة لنا من الغالب في منهم يأتي ولا عنهم، غنى في الله بحمد تفاهم محاولة من حصل الذي الشيء وإنما الشر، إلا أو إخواننا بعض إقامة مخصوصلأجل وقت في إيران مع بمنزلة وكان الخاص ظرفه له كان عبورهم، إن الثاني المحور في فيه سأتكلم كما الضرورةفقط، الله شاء.

The principle of our brothers is not to accept this, and to forbid anyone related to us from entering these hallways. Thanks to Allah, we can do without them, and nothing can come from them but evil, but the thing that happened from the attempt of understanding with Iran to give accommodations to some of our brothers or help them cross the borders to Iran, had its own circumstances and was out of necessity, and I will talk about this in the second part.

ضرورية أراها التي المقدمات من القدر بهذا وأكتفي الموضوع لفهم.

I deem the mentioned introduction sufficient to understand the subject.

المحور الثاني: بعض السرد التاريخي للأحداث:

بعد سقوط المارة الإسلامية، في أفغانستان، من المجاهدينالمهاجرين والإخوة الطلبة وانسحاب معظم توجه وغيرهم، العرب إلى المهاجرين الإخوة الذين ثم رأساً، إيران إلى منهم قسم باكستان،وتوجه باكستان، مكثفي من منهم باكستان إلى توجهوا إلى رجعوا الذين ومنهم إيران، إلى توجه من ومنهم كانت الذين وهم المطارات، عبر منباكستان بلدهم ظروفهم تسمح بذلك.

The second part: some historical narrative of events:

After the fall of Islamic government in Afghanistan, and the withdrawal of our Mujahideen brothers, both Arab and others, most of them went to Pakistan and some to Iran. Among those who went to Pakistan, some stayed in Pakistan, and some went to Iran, and some, who could afford it, returned to their home country from Pakistan through airports.

هو الإخوة جمهور عزائم عليه تنعقد الذي الشيء كان وسيعاودون فيه مأذون انسحابمشروع حالة في أنهم جديد،والحمد من وأعوانه الصليبي العدو لجهاد الكرة أمير بأمر أفغانستان أرض من أكثرهم خرج وإنما لله، من فائدة لا ولأنه أنفسهم، محافظةعلى المؤمنين القصفومتابعة تحت الداخل في كبيرة أعداد بقاء

قاتلهم الجواسيس توجيهات تسيره الذي الطيران
الله.

The thing all the brothers agreed on is that they were
in a legitimate withdrawal, and that they would try
again to fight the crusader enemy and his aides again,
and thank Allah, most of them went out of
Afghanistan by order of Emir Al-Mu'minin to save
themselves, because the stay of large numbers in
Afghanistan under bombardment and follow-up of
fighter aircrafts, which was guided by the directives of
the spies, was not useful.

إلى ثم وزيرستان إلى خرج ممن شخصيا أنا كنت
أوامر جاءتنا ثم أشهر حواليالثلاثة فيها وبقينا كراتشي
من الكثير وكان إيران، إلى بالتوجه الإخوة من
هكذا، القيادات أوامر كانت ولكن لذلك، الإخوةكارهين
غيرهم أو المقاتلة أوالجماعة القاعدة، قيادات سواء
إلى، الإخوة من كبيرة جمهرة فدخل ..كثير
من التأشيرة أخذوا حيث رسمية بفيزا إيران،بعضهم
تأشيرة بدون كراتشي،وبعضهم في الإيرانية القنصلية
بطريق دخلوا المعظم أو ذلك بعد الكل ثم أصلا،
وهو الحدود، تسلل وعبر بالتهريب أي "قانوني"غير
من الغرض سهل،وإنما هو بل بالصعب ليس أمر
أراد إذا حتى تأشيرة الأخ جواز في تكون أن التأشيرة
ذلك يمكنه ذلك بعد آخر بلد إلى إيران يسافرمن أن
إلى هاجر فعلا،ممن الكثيرون فعله ما وهو بسهولة،
إلى أو أوروبا، إلى أو الأصلية، بلدهم إلى أو العراق،
"ختم" يبقى وغيرها، الإفريقية، الدول أوبعض ماليزيا،

تكون بسيطعندما أمره وهذا ، الإيراني الدخول
الإخوة لأن جوازك، في موجودة الإيرانية التأشيرة
ربط ولا كبير تدقيق عندالإيرانيين وليس يصنعونه،
والخروج الدخول بأختام يتعلق كمبيوتري.

I personally went to Waziristan and from there to Karachi and stayed there for about 3 months, and then we got the orders from our brothers to go to Iran. Many of our brothers did not like the idea but this was the order from our leadership, both al-Qaeda and other fighters. A large number of our brothers went to Iran, some with official visas, which we got from the Iranian consulate in Karachi, and some without visas. Then everyone after that or the most entered by an "illegal" way, i.e. through smuggling and border infiltration, which was an easy thing. The purpose of the visa was to enable who wanted to travel from Iran to another country to travel to that country easily, which many had done already, some traveled to Iraq, their home country, Europe, Malaysia, some African States, and other states. The only thing remaining is the Iranian entry stamp, and this is a simple matter when you have the Iranian visa in your passport, because the brothers are able to fake it, and the Iranians don't have great scrutiny and have no linked computerized system that checks the stamps of the entry and exit.

متعددة دفعات عبر إيران إلى دخلوا الإخوة.

The brothers entered Iran in various waves.

أبو الأخ القيادات من إيران إلى دخل من أول من وكان
تلك في القيادات بتفويضنمجن الموريتاني حفص
بعيدين كانا والدكتور الشيخ لأن (الأزمة قيادة) المرحلة
أبو دخل أقول .. بورا تورا بعد بهما اتصالات ثمت ولميكن
بعضهم الإخوة من ومعهمجموعة الموريتاني حفص
والصغرى المتوسطة القيادات من أيضا، قيادات
الأخرى الجماعات من إخوة إلى بالإضافة فيالقاعدة،
الإسلامية المقاتلةبقياداتهاوكالجماعة كالجماعة
المصرية، الجهاد جماعة وبقايا المصرية
وغيرهم الزرقاوي، جماعة مثل والجماعاتالشامية.

The first person who went to Iran from the leadership was Abu Hafs al-Mauritani through a mandate from of leaders at that time (Crisis Leadership) because the Sheikh and the Doctor were far away and there were no contacts with them after Tora Bora. Abu Hafs al-Mauritani entered with a group of brothers and some medium and junior leaders in al-Qaeda, as well as brothers from other groups such as Egyptian Islamic Group and remnants of the Egyptian Jihad Group, and Shamian groups such as al-Zarqawi group, and others.

يتولى أن هو حفص أبي عند الذي التفويض كان
بالعبور ليسمحوالإخواننا الإيرانيين مع التفاهم
وبالإقامة في البلد (إيران.)

The mandate of Abu Hafs was to establish an

understanding with the Iranians to allow our brothers
to cross the border and to stay in the country.

أبي من قريبين كانوا إخوة من ذلك بعد علمته الذي
في الإيرانيين أن إيران، دخلوا إلى من أوائل ومن حفص
مع وشروطاً نقاطاً حددوا وبالفعل رحبوا، البداية
كمسؤول حفص أبي مع يتكلمون وصاروا أبيحفص،
اشترطها التي ضمنا لشروط ومن جميعا، الإخوة على
أي نهائيا، الهاتف الإخوة يستعمل ألا الإيرانيون
تراقب أمريكا لأن الهاتفية الاتصالات يمتنعونعن
لا لكن بيوتيؤجرونها في يسكنوا وأن الاتصالات،
النظار، تلفت وتجمعات تحركات ولا نشاط أي يعملون
أمنية شروطا كانت كلها أنها والحاصل ..ونحوذلك.

What I learned later from brothers who were close to
Abu Hafs in the early days of their stay in Iran was
that they were very welcomed, and in practice, they
agreed on some issues with him, and they were
dealing with him as the person in charge of the group.
One of the Iranians' conditions was that since the
Americans monitor all their communications they
must refrain from use of telephone completely and
stay in the houses they rent, and they should not have
any kind of activities or gatherings which may draw
attention… These were all security conditions.

.ذلك على والإخوة حفص أبو وافق

Abu Hafs and other brothers agreed with them.

(وغيرهم الاستخبارات) الإيرانيين معاملة وكانت في يبشون الغالب كانوافي بل طيبة، معاملة للإخوة ويعتبرونهم محبة، عن لهم ويعبرون الإخوة وجوه تقية هو أو منهم، صادق هذا هل نعرف لا أبطالا،طبعا أعلم ذلك؟الله غير أو ومسايسة؟؟..

The treatment of the Iranians (intelligence and others) to the brothers was good, but even they were mostly smiling in the faces of the brothers and show them love and looked at them as heroes, of course, we do not know if this was true, or just acting?? Or other? Allah only knows..

في العاديين للأفراد بالنسبة أنه لي يظهر الذي لكن صادقين كانوا فهؤلاء البسيجوغيرهم، أو الاستخبارات كأبطال إليهم ينظرون وكانوا الخوة، محبة في فعلا ضربواأمريكا..!

But what appears to me that the ordinary people in the intelligence services or Basij and others, were truthful in their love of the brothers, and they looked at them as heroes that hit the US already..!

منهم ذلك يفعل من يكون قد أعلم، فالله القيادات وأما ومكرومسايسة تقية عن يفعله..!

As for the leaders, Allah only knows as they might have been doing this out of hypocrisy!

يعرفون لا منهم كثيرون منهم، العاديين الناس لأن ذلك بمذاهبهموغير حتى وجهلاء شيئا،..!

Most of the ordinary people know nothing about their doctrines and other stuff..!

دلائل عندنا ذلك من وتحصّل فيه، شك لا معروف وهذا كثيرة.

This is known, no doubt, and have many evidences.

جدا ويحترمنا يحبنا من الرافضة الشيعة في ووجدنا.

We found ones in theRafidi-Shiites who loved and respected us very much.

مدينة في معظمهم وكان إيران، في الإخوة جلس سيستانوبلوشستان ولاية عاصمة زاهدان.

The brothers stayed in Iran, mostly in the city of Zahedan, capital of Sistan and Baluchestan Province.

ولم بالاتفاقات يلتزموا لم إخواننا أن حصل الذي لكن كانوا فقد عليهم، السيطرة على قادرا حفص أبو يكن البشر، من وأنواع وأشكال مختلفة جنسيات من فلم ذلك، وغير والفوضويون المستعجلون وكانفيهم وخاصة استخدامالهواتف عدم بشرط يلتزموا والتجمعات اللافت التحرك بشروط ولا.!الموبايلات..!

But what happened that our brothers did not abide by the agreements and Abu Hafs was not able to control them, as they were of different nationalities, forms and types of people, they included ones that are in a hurry of their matters and anarchists ones and others, so they did not adhere to the condition of not using phones, especially mobile phones, and also did not adhere to the condition of not moving gatherings and avoid any moves attracting attention..!

يحبون كما يتحركون وأخذوا السيارات فاشتروا مضافات شبه مدةوجيزة في لهم وصارت ويتجمعون بأهل وعلاقات المدينة، في جدا لافتة وحركة ونحوها، ذلك وغير المدينة السنةفي.

They bought cars and moved as they wanted and gathered in groups and, in a very short period they set up guest-houses, and very noticeable moves in the city, and relations with the Sunni people in the city and others.

أفراد بعض يتحمله حطأ وهذا) بإخواننا الأمر وصل بل أكثر أو مرة خرجوا أنهم (القياداتالصغرى من القاعدة ونصبوا (صحراء) زاهدان ضواحي بعض إلى نشر تتطلب التي المدى طويلة الكبيرة أجهزةالمخابرة والأعمدةالكهربائية فوقالأشجار بها الخاصة الأنتينات، الشيشان في الإخوة مع وتحدثوا وغيرها، عليه تصنت قد ذلك أن المتوقع من طبعا بشكلمباشر، الأمريكان.

And even the brothers (this mistake is shouldered by some junior leaders in al-Qaeda) went once or more to some of the outskirts of Zahedan (the desert) and set up the large long-range communication equipment that required the deployment of its antennas above the trees, Utility poles and others, and spoke with the brothers in Chechnya directly, of course, it is expected that this was eavesdropped by the Americans.

يرتب أن حفض أبو أخونا استطاع المرحلة هذه في أن (وغيرها السعودية)الجزيرة شباب من لكثير بلدان إلى يمشوا أو بلدانهم إلى ويرجعوا يسافروا الإيرانية المخابرات وكان وغيرها، سوريا أخرمثل يريد أخ أي تسفير في ويساعدون جدا، متعاونين السفر.

At this stage could our brother Abu Hafs managed to process the safe passage of many of the brothers from the Arabian Peninsula (Saudi Arabia and other), managing to send them off to their home countries or to other countries like Syria. That was with the support of Iranian intelligence who was very helpful and helped in sending off any brother who wanted to travel.

على وقبضوا مداهمة حملة الإيرانيون عمل فجأة ثم جدا، الكثيرين على إنذاروقبضوا سابق بدون الإخوة عاديون شباب منهم كثير وغيرها، القاعدة من ومن وغيرها والكويت الجزيرة شباب من منالمجاهدين القدامى من القاعدة من العربي،وقليل المغرب بلدان المعروفين.

Then suddenly the Iranians launched a campaign and arrested the brothers without warning and arrested so many people, from al-Qaeda and other groups, many of them were ordinary young Jihadist from the Arabian Peninsula, Kuwait and other countries in the Arab Maghreb, and a few of the well-known al-Qaeda veterans.

غير بيوت في كانوا ممن الحملة من الإخوة بعض ونجا والكتمان السرية أنيلتزموا واستطاعوا معروفة البيوت خارج الحملة ساعة كانوا أو والاحتياط،.

Some of the brothers survived the campaigns they were staying in unknown houses and were able to hide and take precautions, or they were outside the house at the time of the raid.

الإخوة على الإيرانيون يشنها حملة أول هذه كانت ..!شيء كل تغير وبعدها..!ازاهدان في

This was the first campaign launched by the Iranians on the brothers in Zahedan..! Then everything changed..!

في كأنهم زاهدان في يتصرفون البداية في الإخوة كان ..!!وتسعين وثمانية تسعة أيام بيشاور

In the beginning, the brothers were acting in Zahedan as if they were in Peshawar in 1998 and 1999..!!!!

أنهم الإخوة وعرف شيء، كل تغير الحملة هذه وبعد والاختفاء إلاسرية يجدي لا وأنه القبضة في إلخ....تماما.

After this campaign, everything changed, and the

brothers knew they were right in the middle of the Iranian fist and that complete secrecy and disappearance was that only useful thing....etc..

فوضويون الإخوة بأن ذلك بعد الحملة برروا الإيرانيون يلتزموا لم وأنهم (الحقللأسف من شـيء فيه وهذا) ربما أو شـيء فيه هذا وأيضا .!والعهود بالشـروط اللأسـف الحق من حتىالكثير ...!!!

The Iranians justified the campaign by that the brothers are anarchic (and this, unfortunately, was partially right) and they did not abide by the conditions and covenants.! Also this, unfortunately, was partially or even fully right..!

من الكثير سـجلوا قد الأمريكان إن (:الإيرانيون) وقالوا بها واحتجوا إلينا بها وأتوا (اتصالاتالأخوة) اتصالاتكم أخباركمطلعت والآن إلخ...الإرهابيين نؤوي وأننا علينا، عليكم شـرطنا ونحن علينا، خطر وهذا وفشـت، إلخ...تلتزموا وأنتملم البداية، من شـروطنا

.السجن في للإخوة هذا قالوا

They (the Iranians) said: "the Americans have recorded many of your calls (brothers calls) and brought them to us and used it as proof that we provide houses for terrorists...etc. Now, your news are spread and this is dangerous to us, we told you our terms from the beginning, and you did not now abide by them...etc." They said that the brothers in prison.

هذه بعد أي الوقت، هذا في هنا، إيران إلى دخلت إلى أنا
لا والأخبار زاهدان، إلى إليها، وجئت المشار الحملة
تغيرتماما قد الأمور ولكن الحملة، عن طازجة تزال
أو زاهدان في سواء إيران، في يوجد من كل وصار
فشيئا شيئا الإخوة نفسه، وتفرق يكتم مختفيا غيرها
قصدها طهران العاصمة: الإيرانية المدن في
وشيراز وأصفهان دفعتي، من وكثير أنا كثيرونمنهم
وغيرها عباس وبندر ومشهد.

I entered Iran at that time, after this mentioned campaign, and I went to Zahedan, and the news was still fresh about the campaign, but things have changed completely and every one remaining in Iran, both in Zahedan or other places, was hiding himself, and the brothers slowly scattered in the Iranian cities; many went to the capital, Tehran, and I along with my batch was among them, Isfahan, Shiraz and Mashhad, Bandar Abbas and others.

الموثوقين إخواننا طريق عن بيوتا يؤجرون الجميع وصار
خيرا الله جزاهم منهم كثير ممنهب السنة أهل من
على وحثهم المجاهدين، إخوانهم لخدمة
من الخير أهل ومشايخهم الصالحون ذلكعلماؤهم
كل فكان لهم، وللقاعدةالمناصرين لطالبان المحببين
السنة أهل البلوش الإخوة بعض لها تدبر مجموعة
للعوائل البيوت تأجير في معهم ويشتغلون أوالأكراد،
من كثير في الوثائق يزوّرون الإخوة وكان.وللعزابوهكذا

أوالأكراد، البلوش الأنصار الإخوة لهؤلاء الحالات
والأمر مزورة، هوية وأوراق ببطاقات البيوت ويؤجرون
أهل من الشخص يكون أن إيران،المهم في جدا بسيط
سهل أمرها (الأوراق) والباقي البلد،.

Everyone began to rent houses through trusted al-
Sunna brothers. Many of them, may God reward
them, rushed to help their jihadi brothers, urged by
the righteous scholars and Sheikhs who are loyal to
and supporters of the Taliban and al-Qaeda. So each
group [of jihadis] was assisted by a few Kurdish or
Sunni Baluchi brothers who worked with them to
rent houses for families and bachelors alike. In many
instances, the brothers forged documents and used
fake IDs to rent houses. This is a simple matter in
Iran, the only thing important was that the person
should be a resident of the city and the rest (papers)
was easy.

الأخ يعرف فلا نحن، نعبر كما البيت "انحرق" لو فحتى
بتأجيره قام الذي..

Even if the house got discovered, they wouldn't know
the brother who rented it..

تقريبا هكذا تفعل المجموعات كل الناس، كل وهكذا،.

Thus, all the people, all the groups were doing so.

الإخوة من جدا كثيرون وهم سافروا، سافروا والذين
وغيرهم السعوديين.

Those who traveled were a lot of our Saudi brothers and others.

إليها المشار الحملة في الإيرانيون عليهم قبض والذين
جميعا بدوناستثناء، سفروهم، كلهم.

And these arrested by the Iranians in the campaign were deported without exception, all of them.

بسرعة هيا تسافر، أن تريد أين :الأخ يخيّرون وكانوا
عنده يكن لم وإذا نفسك، إليه،وجهز تسافر مكانا اختر
(الاستخباراتالإيرانية) هم كانوا (سفر جواز) أوراق
جوازا لنفسك دبر له يقولون أو سفر، جواز له يدبرون
جوازا واشتر طهران في الزنقةالفلانية إلى اذهب
معروفةبأنها طهران العاصمة وسط في مشهورة زنقة]
وكل والبطاقات للجوازات والمزورين التزوير مأوى
الأوراق.[...

They gave the brothers a choice and asked them; "Where do you want to travel? Hurry up and pick a place to travel to, and prepare yourself". And if the brother did not have papers (Passport), they (Iranians) arranged for a passport for him, or told him to arrange a passport by himself and guided him to go to an alley in Tehran and buy a passport [An infamous alley in the center of the capital Tehran, known as a haven of forgery of passports, IDs, and all forged papers].

من شفاه من صحيح، ثابت لكم أقوله الذي كله وهذا

كما عادوا، ثم خرجوا الكثيرمنهم لأن ذلك، لهم قيل
شاءالله إن سأوضح.

All I'm telling you is true, as I heard it from the lips of ones that the above was told to them, as many of deported brothers returned, as I'll explain, Allah willing.

أو بلدك، إما :هو الإيرانيين خيارات أحسـن كان
لا خيارا أيضا تركيا وكانت.ماليزيا أو العراق، أو باكسـتان،
به بأس.

The best options for the Iranians were either your country, Pakistan, Iraq, or Malaysia. Turkey was also an acceptable option.

إلا أوروبا إلى الذهاب يسـتطع لم الأصعب، كانت وأوروبا
من اثنين شخصيا أنا منهم قليلين،أعرف إخوة بضعة
المطاربمساعدة من خروجوا الليبيين، أصحابي
الإيرانيين المعارف وبعض الاسـتخبارات.

Europe was the most difficult, and only a few brothers were able to go there, and I personally know two of them who are my Libyans friends, they came out of the airport with the help of Iranian intelligence and some Iranian contacts.

واضحة الاسـتخبارات.

Theintelligence is clear.

معارف للإخوة يكون وكيف هم ما هؤلاء المعارف طيب،
عادية نحن عندنا الأشياء رافضة؟هذه إيرانيون
وقائع يعيش عندما الإنسان لأن وبسيطة
عجيبة، تناقضات به تمر وغيرها، السياسةوالحروب
من شبكةمعقدة داخل أحيانا نفسه يجد وقد
يخض لم الذي البعيد الأخ لكن والعداوات، الصداقات
قديستغربها الأمور هذه.

Okay, who were those contacts and how could the
brothers have Iranian contacts? These things are
ordinary and simple to people like us because when
the person lives in politics and wars and others, he
sees bizarre contradictions, and sometimes he finds
himself within a complex network of friendships and
enmities, but the brother that didn't live this live can
see these things strange.

أشبه فهذا قليلا، الصورة تقريب هنا سأحاول
السيرة إلإكمال سنرجع بعده ثم بالاستطراد،.

I will try here to make thing clearer, this is like a
digression, and then that we'll be back to complete
our subject.

التي السنين وهي نسميها، كما العجاف السنين في
في الجهادية حصلتللحركة التي الانتكاسة تلت
مجموعة سيطرة من تعرفون ما بسبب الجزائر،
الإسلامية الجماعة" قيادة على فاسدةمنحرفة
هناك، الأكبرللمجاهدين التنظيم وهي "المسلحة
الجماعة تفكك عنه نشأ مما وضللهم وانحرافهم

مآس من ذلك غضون في كان وما وانهيارهاوتفتتها،
إلخ...الله قاتلهم"التكفيريون" الخوارج ارتكبها ومجازر
انكسار أيضا والاحباط الانكسار هذا إلى وانضاف
في المقاتلة الجماعة قادتها الجهاديةالتي الحركة
أواسطسنة بين القذافي، الطاغوت نظام ضد ليبيا
وتسعين سبعة سنة أواسط إلى وتسعين، خمسة
وزاد الاحباط زاد مما ،(تقريبا سنتين مدار على)
كل في الجهادية الإسلامية الحركة على أيضا الضغوط
مكان..

During the lean years as we call them, which are the years that followed the setback that happenedto the jihadi movement in Algeria, because of what you know from the control of a corrupt perverted group of the leadership of the "Armed Islamic Group", which was the largest organization of Jihadists there, and due to their malfeasance and misguidance the group collapsed and fragmented, and what happened during that time of tragedies and massacres committed by the Kharijites "Takfirites", may Allah fight them...etc. This refraction and frustration was supplemented by the collapse of the jihadist movement led by theFighting Group in Libya against the regime of the tyrant Gaddafi, between mid-year ninety five, to mid-year ninety seven (nearly two years), which increased the frustration and also pressures on the Islamic Jihad movement in every place..

عدة مع تقريبا ترافقت أو زمنيا الاحباطات هذه تقاربت

للأخوة السودان حكومة طرد : أخرىمنها كبيرة أحداث
أسامة الشيخ رأسهم على بلدها، من
: ومنها وغيرهم، المقاتلة الليبية وجماعتهووالجماعة
خطاب الشيشانبدخول في الثانية الحرب بدء
أفغانستان، في طالبان ظهور بدء : ومنها لداغستان،
بسبب تأييدهم في مترددين البداية الأخوةفي وكان
كبيرة أمنية بدءحملات :ومنها بعد، عليهم التعرف عدم
غير أمنية وتنسيقات المرتدة الدول من عدد في
سبعة حوالي بتسليم السعودية قامت مسبوقة،حيث
الزنديق الليبيين،إلى العلم طلاب من أخا عشرة
مصريين إخوة سلمت الإمارات وكذلك القذافي،
وغيرها، الأردن، مثل منالدول، وغيرها وغيرهم،
انتقال بعد ثم جدا، شديدة حملات ووقعت
أفعانستان إلى السودان س وأصحابه الشيخأسامة
بعدما قندهار انتقلإلى ثم آباد، جلال في أولا استقر)
فيهم ووثق إليهم واطمأن جيدا طالبان على تعرف
ودار نيروبي ضربات بعدها جاءت ثم ،(بهوأحبوه ورحبوا
ملاحقة في ذلكبدأت قبل أمريكا وكانت السلام،
يتعاون من وكل (القاعدة) وجماعته أسامة الشيخ
حيث الأولى المرة في الصومال بعدأحداث معها
الخلفيةفي قواعدهم من انطلاقا الإخوة ساهم
القوات ضرب في وأوجادين، كينيا وفي السودان
(الأمل إعادة الأمريكانبحملة سماه ما) الأمريكية
خاسئين، الصومال من الهروب إلى الأمريكان واضطر
النقطة هي هذه كانت كلنتون، عهد في وكانذلك
لملاحقةالأمريكان الرسمية والبداية الأساسية
وعلى عليهم الضغط وزيادة وجماعته أسامة للشيخ

الجماعات من يقاربهم أو يتعاونمعهم من كل
الذي الشديد الضغط ونتيجة والأشخاص،
المرتدة الدول في عملاؤهم ومعهم مارسهاالأمريكان
الشيخ طرد من إلىبعضه أشرت مما حصل ما حصل
كل في للأخوة والتتبع القبض عمليات ثم والقاعدة،
ثمرة كان الذي الأمني والتعاون مكانوالتسليم
في الردة دول أمنيةبين واتفاقات ومؤتمرات اجتماعات
ومتابعة أمريكي بإشراف ذلك كل وغيرها، تونس
وضغوط.

Such frustrations happened or coincided in parallel
with several other major events, including the expel of
brothers by the government of Sudan, headed by
Sheikh Osama and his group and the Libyan fighting
group and others; the start of the second war in
Chechnya by the entryof Khattabto Dagestan; the
start of the emergence of the Taliban in Afghanistan,
and the brothers initially were hesitating in supporting
them because they hadn't known them; the start of
security campaigns in a number of apostateStates and
unprecedented security coordination, where Saudi
Arabia had handed over about seventeen brothers of
Libyan students to the infidel Gaddafi, as well as the
UAE had handed over Egyptian brothers and others,
and other countries, such as Jordan, and others, and
very strong campaigns had taken place, and then after
Sheikh Osama and his companions moved from
Sudan to Afghanistan (first he settled in Jalalabad,
then moved to Kandahar after getting to know

Taliban welland felt safe and trust towards them and
they welcomed and loved him), and then followed by
the Nairobi and Dar es Salaam strikes and the US had
already started chasing Sheikh Osama and his group
(al-Qaeda) and who ever cooperated with them after
the events of Somalia in the first time, where the
brothers helped from their rear bases in Sudan, Kenya
and Ogadenin hittingUS forces (What the Americans
called "Operation Restoring Hope"), and Americans
were forced to flee from Somalia after losing and this
was in the era of Clinton, this was the key point and
the official start of the Americans chasing Sheikh
Osama and his group and increasing the pressure on
them and all whoever cooperated or had ties with
them, and as a result of the strong pressure exerted by
the Americans and their puppets in the apostate
States, the sheikh and al-Qaeda was expelled from
Sudan, then followed by the arrests, tracings, handing-
oversof the brothers in every place and security
cooperation, which was the result of the conferences,
meetings and security agreements among the apostate
States in Tunisia and other places, all under US
supervision and pressure.

التقريب وجه على وهي الفترة، هذه أن المقصود:
سنوات: سبعة وثمانية، وتسعين، وتسعة وتسعة
وتسعين، إلى سنة ألفين أيضا، كانت شديدة
الأخوة علىالجدا من كل الجماعات الجهادية العربية
خصوصا قبل التعرف علىالطالبان ولجوء الكثرين إليها.

287

The point is thatthis period (Approx.; 1997, 1998 ,1999 and 2000) was very hard on the brothers of all Arab jihadist groups, especially before knowing Taliban well and many brothers reaching out to it.

ملاذات في تفكر أن الجماعات هذه من الكثير اضطرت الجميع طرد الذي بعدالسودان وملاجئ، لأفرادها تتبعتهم الخليج ودول والسعودية تقريبا، ليبيا إلى الكثيرين سلمت كذلك وسلمتهم،وتركيا ليبيا إلى بأسبها لا مجموعة سلمت والأردن وغيرها، البلدين هذين في عشت شخصيا وأنا وغيرها، ومصر الجزائر، من خروجي بعد منهما فيكل شهور عدة حياةتخفي الحياة وكانت والأردن، تركيا في أعني قبضوا وقد الاستخبارات، ملاحقة تحت جدا، وصعبة رب لله والحمد البلدين، الأخوةفي من عدد على والسلمة واللطف العافية دوام الله نسأل العالمين،.

Many of these groups were forced to think ofsanctuaries and shelters after Sudan which expelled almost everyone related to Arab jihadist groups then Saudi Arabia and Gulf countries which followed in its footsteps, and also Turkey whichhanded over many to Libya and others, and Jordan which handed overa significant group to Libya, Egypt and other countries, and I personally lived in each of these countries for several months after my departure from Algeria, I mean in Turkey and Jordan, and it was a very difficult hiding life, under the pursuit of intelligence, and they had already arrested a number of the brothers in the two countries, thanks to Allah, the Lord of the

Worlds, we ask Allahfor wellness and peace.

أقول: حاولت الكثير من الجماعات إيجاد ملاذات
فكان معهم، التي ولأفرادهاوالعوائل لقياداتها وملاجئ
سبق وقد إيران، منها دول، عدة في التفكير
فذهبوا الإسلامية، الجماعة من المصريون إليهاالأخوة
قادرين ويكونوا ولكييرتاحوا واستوطنوها، إيران إلى
بعض ويمارسوا ما نوعا هانئ بشكل العيش على
مع تكلموا وقومهم، لبلدهم العمل من مايمكنهم
عندهم علمالإقامة معها وتفاهموا الإيرانية الدولة
بين والتنافر التناقض مستغلين رسمي، بشكل
قالوا ذلك، في تجربة لهم ومصر،وكانت إيران دولتي
الإسلاميةمثل الجماعة إخوة أعني) بعد فيما عنها
حازم وأبي الاسلامبولي، شوقي محمد الشيخ
إنها: عنها قالوا (ياسروغيرهم وأبي حمزة، مصفى
والمرارة الفشل وسبب ..!!ومريرة فاشلة تجربة
ناس مع تتعامل أن والصعوبات الظروف أنكاضطرتك
مقدساتك، رافضةيسبون بل فقط، مرتدين ليسوا
على ورد ...!!وصحابته وأزواجه نبيك عرض في ويطعنون
يحاولون أو) منك يأخذون إلا شيئا يعطونك لا ذلكأنهم
يعرفون يحاولون منه،فكانوا أكثر (يأخذوا أن ويضغطون
الجماعة في الإخوة عمل عن التفاصيل أدق
كثيرا منهم يتضايقون الإخوة كان الإسلامية،حتى
مفاصلة إلىشبه المرات بعض في معهم وصلوا وحتى
طالبان عند ملاذا الإخوة وجد إن ما وبالفعل .!تامة
منهم يبق ولم إيران، وتركوا إليها كثيرمنهم هرب حتى
ضغطعليهم ثم جدا، قليلون أنفار إلا إيران في
أبو آخرهم من وكان وسفروهم ذلك بعد الإيرانيون

ثم سفروهم إنهم وقيل (رفاعيطه) ياسر وأبو حازم
عليهم، ليقبضوا المستقبل الطرف لدى بهم وشوا
طبعا أعلم والله الأخوة، يظن هكذا الأقل أوعلى
بالحقيقة.

Many of the groups tried to find sanctuaries and
shelters for its leadership, members and their families,
so they considered several states, including Iran,
which has already been the destination of the
Egyptian brothers of the Islamic Group, as they went
to Iran and settled there, in order to relax and be able
to live a fairly good life and do what they can for their
country. They spoke with Iranian state and agreed
with it on settling in Iran officially, exploiting the
contradictions and inconsistencies between Iran and
Egypt, and had an experiment regarding this, about
which they said later (I mean the brothers in the
Islamic group such as Sheikh Mohammad Shawqi al-
Islamboli, AbuHazemMostafa Hamza, Abu Yasser
and others): "It is a failed and bitter experiment.!!!!
The reason for the failure and bitterness that
circumstances and difficulties forced you to deal with
people who are not only apostate but Rafidis who
insult your sacred beliefs and stabbing in the honor of
the Prophet, his wives and his companions..!!!!
Moreover, they do not give anything unless they take
(or try and push to take) more from you, they were
trying to know the details of the work of the brothers
in the Islamic group and the brothers were very angry
of them, and in some cases it escalated to full

boycott.!"When the brothers found a shelter with the Taliban, many of them fled to it and left Iran, and only few individuals stayed in Iran, then the Iranians pressured on them and deported them, the last of deported ones was Abu Hazem and Abu Yasser (RifaiTaha), and it was said they had deported them and then snitched on them to the country of their arrival to arrest them, or at least this is how the brothers think, of course, Allah knows the truth.

النظام مع "تعامل" و أيضا علاقة إقامة في فكروا ممن الليبية، المقاتلة الجماعةالإسلامية الإيراني الرافضي وجماعة الصادق الله عبد أبي الخ رأي وكان الشديدة، للحاجة ذلك على الإقدام هو منالقيادات القذافي بنظام علاقاتهمسيئة الإيراني النظام ولأن رأي كان لكن المصري، بالنظام سيئة هي كما ومعه المنذر أبو الشيخ رأسها وعلى اللجنةالشرعية حال في إلا جوازذلك عدم وغيرهما يحيى أبو الشيخ عبد أبا أن مع بعد، الضرورة حال إلى نصل ولم الضرورة من تقترب أو ضرورة إنها يقولون وغيره اللهالصادق افعلناها لو الضرورة!.

Among those who thought of making a relationship and "deal" with the Iranian-Rafidi regime was the Libyan Islamic Fighting Group, and the opinion ofAbu Abdullah al-Sadiqa some leaders was to make that happen because of extreme need and that the Iranian regime had a bad relationship with the Gaddafi regime as the Egyptian regime, but the opinion of the Sharia Committee, headed by Sheikh

Abu Al-Mundhir and Sheikh Abu Yahya and others, was that it wasn't permissible except in the case of necessity, and they hadn't reached the necessary state yet, although Abu Abd Allah al-Sadiq and others said that it was a necessity or close to necessity if we do it!

النظام وبين المقاتلة الجماعة بين علقات تقم لم الشرعية معارضةاللجنة بسبب الإيراني.

There were no relationships between the fighting group and the Iranian regime because of the opposition of the Sharia Committee.

تركيا في متمركزة قيادتها كانت أيام الجماعة ولكن بعض بعثت (وتسعةوتسعين وتسعين ثمانية سنة) إيران، لاستطلاع القيادات من أحدهم إيران إلى الإخوة الكوادر من الأخ وهذا أحبابي، من جيدا أعرفه وهوأخ مكان إلي بعثته ودبلوماسيا،لو اجتماعيا الموهوبة الصحابي قول المرء ليتذكر حتى الأعاجيب، فيه لفعل بعد لربح، التراب في تاجر لو عوف بن الرحمن فيعبد له عليهوسلم الله صلى النبي دعاء.

But the group, whose leadership was based in Turkey (in 1989), sent some brothers to Iran, one of them was a leader, to explore Iran. That leader was a brother I know very well and he is amongst my loved ones, and this brother is one of the socially and diplomatically talented cadres and if I sent to a place, he does wonders. I recall the words of the companions of the Prophet in Abdul Rahman bin

Auf;"if he deals in dust, he willmake money", after calling the Prophet (PBUH).

إيران، في العلاقات بعض يكون أن استطاع الأخ هذا أوراقه تقديم يريد أنه قم،بدعوى مدينة دخل إنه حتى ما على الفارسي الأدب دراسة) هناك للدراسة هناك العرب بعض على وتعرف ،(العنوان أظن،بهذا هناك يدرس وغيرهمممن وتونسيون جزائريون منهم وكون زمن، من إيران في ويعيشون تشيّعوا وممن يناقشهم وكان حوارات، معهم له صداقاتوكان معهم كل معينة،فمع ميزات له الأخ هذا لكن ويناظرهم، ويستفيد الأصدقاء يكسب كان والمناظرات المناقشات الدراسة إمكانية له ووفروا فعلا خدماتهم،فخدموه من تعرف إلى الكبراء،بالإضافة بعض على وعرفوه والسكن من أيضا، إيران دخلوا ممن آخرين وإخوة هذا، أخينا ناس على تعرفهم :أقول وغيرهم، الليبيينوالمصريين ممن الإسلاميالفلسطينيين، والجهاد حماس من يجربعضها والعلقات والمعارف إيران، في يقيمون إلبعض.

This brother was able to make some relations in Iran. He entered the city of Qom, claiming that he wanted to submit his papers to study there (study Persian literature, I think, by this title), and made relations with some Arabs there, including Algerians, Tunisians and others who were studying there and those who were living in Iran for a while and got accustomed to it. He befriended them and had conversations with them. He discussed things and made debates with them, but this brother had certain advantages as with all the discussions and debates he made friends and benefited from their services. They actually served him and provided him with the possibility of studying and housing and introduced him to some of the elders. Also, this brother and other Libyan and Egyptian brothers who entered Iran made relations with Palestinians people from Hamas and Islamic Jihad who was residing in Iran. Contacts and relationships drag themselves closer.

يوجد كان لما كالمثال وهي مختصرة لمحة كانت فهذه في إخواننا بعض من المعارفوالعلاقات بعض من الإيرانيين بعض مع المختلفة الجماعات.

This was a brief overview and it is an example of the existence of some of the contacts and relations of some of our brothers in different groups with some Iranians.

ولا قيادة أي منها دخل أنه أعلم فلا القاعدة وأما أفغانستان إمارة قبلسقوط لإيران أبدا مرموقة شخصية حكيته كما إليها للدخول واضطرارهم الإسلامية.

As for al-Qaeda, I do not know that any leadership or A prestigious figure ever entered Iran before the fall of the Islamic Emirate of Afghanistan and that they had to enter it as I mentioned earlier.

المواقف، هذه مثل في إخواننا حال لسان وكأن هذا،
يرى أن الحر على الدنيا نكد ومن" :القائل قال كما **
بد صداقته من ما له عدوا

Our brothers in such situations were like, as the poet
said: "The worst thing that can make the free man live
bad ** An enemy that he must befriended with"

الزنديق، الرافضي الإيراني النظام فإن لكم، قلت وكما
مرونة وعندهم أبعدالحدود، إلى أيضا براغماتي هو
فيه أن يظنون ما لتحقيق والتعاون التعامل في
أن بد فلا الحدود، أبعد إلى مؤقتة، ولو مصلحةلهم،
جيدا هذا تستحضروا.

As I have told you, the Iranian-Rafidi regime, is too
pragmatic, and they have the flexibility to deal and
cooperate with anyone in order to achieve what they
think is in their best interest, even temporarily ones,
you must remember this.

تلك بعد الإيرانيين مع الإخوة سيرة إكمال إلى نرجع
الكبيرةالأولى الزاهدانية الحملة.

We return to complete of the story of the brothers
with the Iranians after that first big Zahedan
campaign.

نقاط في سأتكلم الآن:

I will speak now in points:

عليهم؟ قبضوا الذين الأخوة الإيرانيون عامل كيف -
وكيف سفروهم؟

إيران؟ خارج سافروا ممن ذلك بعد الإخوة فعل ماذا -

نجوا ممن إيران في بقوا الذين الإخوة بقية فعل ماذا -
من تلك الحملة أو ممندخلوا بعدها؟

- How did the Iranians treat the arrested brothers? How did they deport them?

- What did the brothers do after they traveled outside Iran?

- What did the rest of the brothers who stayed in Iran who survived the campaign or those who entered after the campaign?

عليهم؟ قبضوا الذين الأخوة الإيرانيون عامل كيف أما
وكيف سفروهم؟

As for how did the Iranians treat the arrested brothers? And how did they deported them?

الاحترام، غاية وفي جدا حسنة كانت منهم فالمعاملة
فكانوا يقبضون علىالأخوة يعاملونهم كإخوة
محترمين لدرجة أنهميعتذرون للأخوة ويقولون لهم
دائما: نحن مضطرون للقبض عليكم لمصلحتنا
ولمصلحتكم، ونحن نعاني من كبيرة ضغوطكبيرة جدا، كما
تعرفون ونحن نحبكم"، وغير اذلك!!.

The treatment of the Iranians was very well and very

respectful. When they arrested the brothers, they treated them as respectable brothers, so much so that they apologize to the brothers and always say to them, "We are forced to arrest you for our benefit and for your benefit, and we are under a very great pressure, as you know, and we love you." And other things!!

ولا إهانة ولا ضرب لا :جدا محترمة المعاملة وكانت شيئانادرا إلا ذلك،اللهم غير ولا توجع، كلمة.

The treatment was very respectable: no beating, no insulting, no hurting words, and nothing else, except for rare incidents.

شيء أي (معظمهم مع أو) الإخوة مع يحققوا ولم جلسة أخ كل مع فقطيجلسون كانوا تحقيقا، يسمى وبلده اسمه عن ويسألونه ملفا له يعملون الأخ لهم يقوله ما وكل العامة، وعمرهوالمعلومات ومعظم شيء، تكذبولا أنت له يقولون ولا يسجلونه غير بشكل المعلومات أكثر يعطي كان طبعا الإخوة حقيقي.

Upon arrest, the brothers (or most of them) were interrogated respectfully and it was far to be called an investigation. They only sat with each brother and made a file for him and asked him about his name, country, age, and the general information. And everything that the brother tells them was recorded without validating the authenticity of the information, and most of the brothers, of course, was giving wrong information.

في بل ما، حد إلى محترمة سجون في ووضعوهم يعني فنادق، في وضعواالأخوة الأولى الدفعات بعض هذا وقع يسفروهم، حتى فقط، جبرية إقامة شبه بها، أمسكوا التي الأولى الدفعات بعض مع فيالبداية معارفي من وغيرهم،وبعضهم ليبيون إخوة منهم الشخصيين.

They put then in relatively respectful prisons, in fact, they even housed the first waves of brothers in hotels, some kind of house arrest, until the Iranians managed to send them off. This happened at first with the first waves of arrested brothers, including Libyan brothers and others, some of them are of my personal acquaintances..

ولا أحد، على، يعتدوا ولم جيدا، أكلا لهم ويقدمون مخزنة يجدونها الأموالالتي إلا أحد، من أموال أخذوا يأخذونها، كانوا البيوت، يقتحمون عندما البيوت في نصرف هذه: لهم يقولون كانوا الإخوة بها وعندماطالب ولا !أنفسكم؟ منهاعلى تصرفون ألستم منها، عليكم الموال أما أخذها، في معتدون ظالمون أنهم شك شيئا أحد من يأخذوا فلم الأخ جيب توجدفي التي من أكثر أخمن من أكثر أخبرني كما علمي حسب سفروا ثم سجنوا ممن دفعة.

They gave them decent food, didn't offend anyone, didn't take money from anyone, except for the money they find stored in houses when breaking into houses and when the brothers asked to return them, they said to them: "We are spending on you with this money, didn't you use it to spend on yourselves?!" This is injustice with no doubt. As for the money in the pocket of the brothers, they did not take anything of it as far as I know as I learned from more than a brother from different waves of those who were imprisoned and then deported.

معاملة ويعاملونهم جدا، الإخوة يحترمون كانوا بالجملة عن وإبعادهم سجنهم ويعتذرونعن للغاية، حسنة البلد.

In general, they were very respectful to the brothers, they treated them very well, and apologized for their imprisonment and their deportation from the country.

الإخوة تسفير تفاصيل في الآن وسأدخل:

مرحلتين عبر :لنقل أو مرحلة، من أكثر عبر مر وذلك رئيسيتين :

I will now go into the details of the brothers' deportation:

This was through more than one stage or, let's say, through two main stages:

زاهدان دفعة) الأولى الدفعات في كانوا قلت، كما وبعدها قاربها وما (الحملةالأولى :إليها أشرت التي وحتى واثنتين، ألفين سنة امتداد على بقليل

299

وثلاثة ألفين سنة من الأولى الثلاث أو تقريباالشهرين عندما كانوا (..للعراق الغزوالأمريكي حصول قرابة إلى) السجنويعاملونهم في يضعونهم الإخوة على يقبضون كالآتي يسفرونهم ثم ، ذكرت كما الحسنة المعاملة:

As I've said, in the first waves (the Zahedan group to which I've referred: the first campaign) and what followed it during the rest of 2002, and until almost the first two or three months of 2003 (almost near the American invasion of Iraq),the brothers were put in prison and treatedwell as I've mentioned, and then deport them as follows:

عدة من يناسبه ما إنسان كل الإخوة على يعرضون ما بحسب الأقل أوعلى لهم بالنسبة متاحة خيارات الآتية الخيارات وهي هم، يدّعون:

They offeredeach brotherto choose what suited him from several options available to them or at least according to what they claim, which were the following options:

ممن ونحوهم السعوديين من كان إن الشخص بلد - السعوديين ومعظم إلبلدهم، السفر على يقدرون سفروهم البداية من عموما الخليج وأهل والكويتيين بدون أو طهران، في السعودية سفارة مع إمابالتعاون بعد أحد يبق تقريبا،ولم جميعهم وسافروا ذلك، سافروا إما كانوا الجزيرة أهل بالجملة ..الأولى الدفعات إلى والرجوع بلدهم بسفارة بأنفسهمبالاتصال الإيرانيونوسفروهم، عليهم قبض أو وغيرها، السعودية

البداية من سافروا طويلة، لمدة أحد منهم يبق ولم كلهم.

- The home country of the person if he was a Saudi person or others who can travel to their country, most Saudis and Kuwaitis and those from the Gulf generally were allowed to leave Iran either with the assistance of the Saudi embassy in Tehran or without it.Almost all of them travelled and no one was left of them after the first waves.In whole, all people belonging to the Arabian Peninsula either traveled by themselves by contacting their country's embassy and returned to Saudi Arabia and elsewhere, or was arrested bythe Iranians and was deported.None of them remained for a long period, they all travelled from the beginning.

فقد خاص بشكل السعوديين للأخوة بالنسبة وهنا فيه رأوا ممن (منهم قليلجدا نفر) بعضهم على عرضوا ما جدد، شباب أنهم ولاحظوا وليونة معهم مرونة إذا وتدريبهم لدعمهم استعدادهم من ذكرتهلكم ومساعدتهم فيلبنان الله حزب معسكرات في شاءوا الأهداف ضرب في يشتغلوا أن أرادوا إذا وغيره بالمال صح الذي هذا فقط، والخليج، السعودية الأمريكيةفي ولم الأخوةالسعوديين، بعض عرضوهعلى أنه عندنا الحكومات ضرب مثل أحد على عرضوا أنهم يبلغني لا كما غيرها، ولا مثلا، سعود آل المحليةكحكومة تلك شيئامن منهم قبل الإخوة من أحدا أن أعلم الإخوة مع إلا والإغراء العرض هذا يحصل ولم العروض،

301

يقبل قد أنه الإيرانيون فيه ظن والجددوممن العاديين
فلم المعروفونوالقدامى الإخوة وأما مثل، عرضهم
حدعلمي على هذا، من شيئا أحد على يعرضوا.

With respect to the Saudi brothers specifically, the Iranians proposed to a few of them (very few)— among those who had recently become jihadis and whom they judged to be ideologically malleable—that they would be prepared to support them and train them in Hezbollah training camps in Lebanon if they wished; that they would support them with money and other kinds of assistance if they wanted to hit American targets only in Saudi Arabia and the rest of the Gulf … it did not reach me that they proposed to anyone to attack the local governments, like the Saudi regime for example, or others. I am also not aware that any of the brothers accepted any of these proposals. These kinds of propositions were only made to ordinary/low-ranking newly enlisted brothers whom the Iranians believed they would accept. As far as I know, they did not make such proposals to known jihadi veterans.

- الإخوة من كبير عدد إليها وذهب اختارها وقد العراق،
رحمه الزرقاوي الشيخ ومنآخرهم الدفعات، سائر من
أمير "الصادق الله عبد أبو" وقبله الله،
كثير، وغيرهم الليبية، المقاتلة الجماعةالإسلامية
منها ثمسافر أشهرا فيها بقي الصادق الله عبد لكن
عنه يفرج أن الله نسأل أسر، ثم آسيوي بلد إلى.

- Iraq, and it was chosen by a large number of brothers from all waves, and the latest one was Sheikh Zarqawi, Allah bless his soul, and proceeded by Abu Abdullah al-Sadiq, leader of the Libyan Islamic Fighting Group, and many others, but Abdullah al-Sadiq had stayed for months there and then traveled to an Asian country then got arrested, ask Allah to be released.

داخل) الحدود على الأخ يضعوا بأن وذلك باكستان، - اختارها وقد...!اذهب :له ويقولون(الباكستانية الأراضي قيادات ومنهم الأولى، الدفعات من وخاصة الإخوة أكثر نحبه، قضى الذي ومنهم الآن، الحي القاعدةمنهم من عبد والشيخأبو المهاجر، الرحمن عبد أبو منهم وبعض ..كثير وغيرهم إم، بي بال المعروف الرحمن وسفروهم الأولى الدفعات مسكوافي ممن الإخوة في الحدود على وضعوهم)باكستان إلى ثم دخلوا (باكستان إلى يدخلوا حتى منطقةتفتان، من هؤلاء إيران،ومن إلى أخرى مرة متسللين رجعوا بعد أخرى مداهمات في عليهم القبض الإيرانيون أعاد ذلك.

- Pakistan, where they put the brother on the border (inside Pakistani territory) and say to him: "Go ..."! And it was chosen by the most brothers, especially from the first waves, including leaders of al-Qaeda who are alive right now and who are dead, including Abu Abdul Rahman al-Muhajir, Sheikh Abu Abdul Rahman, known as BM, and many others. Some of

the brothers who were arrested in the first waves and
was deported to Pakistan (They put them on the
border in the area of Taftan, to enter Pakistan)
entered then returned by crossing the borders back to
Iran, and among those who returned, a number of
them were arrested again by the Iranian in other raids
later.

- ومتاحة جيدة إليها السفر ظروف كانت ماليزيا،
غلاء بسبب يجتنبها كانأكثرهم الإخوة لكن للكثرين،
وذهب اختارها وإنما ذلك، وغير هناك المعيشة
غيرها إلى منها ليعبر الإخوة إليهابعض.

- Malaysia, the conditions of travel to it were good
and available to many, but the most of the brothers
avoided it because of the high cost of living there and
so, but some chose it and went to it to go to other
countries through it.

- التسفير الإخوة بعض على عرضوا البداية في تركيا،
بعد ويمشي الحدود، يضعوهفي بأن أيضا تركيا إلى
تهريب :يعني بنفسه، ذلك.

- Turkey, initially, they proposed to some brothers
also to travel to Turkey by putting them on the
borders, and then walk by himself, in other words;
smuggling.

إليها الإخوة يسفرون كانوا التي الجهات أهم هذه..

These are the most important destination that the

brothers were deported to..

الإيرانيين تعامل في الأولى المرحلة هي كانت وهذه
إلبإيران الداخلين إخواننا مع.

This was the first stage in the Iranians treatment with
our brothers entering Iran.

فيها تغيرت التي وهي: أخرى مرحلة ذلك بعد أتت ثم
على قبضوا إذا فصاروا الإيرانيينوسياستهم، فكرة
كالليبيينمن) وغيرها القاعدة من العرب الإخوة
الجهاد جماعة من والمصريين المقاتلة، الجماعة
السجن، في بهم يحتفظون(الإسلامية والجماعة
الآن إلى المستمرة المرحلة وهي.

Then there was another stage in which the Iranians
minds and policies were changed. If they arrested the
Arab brothers from al-Qaeda and other groups (such
as Libyans of the Fighting Group, and the Egyptians
from the Jihad Group and the Islamic Group), they
would keep them in prison, and this stage in
continuing until now.

الأمريكي الغزو بدء مع تقريبا بدأت المرحلة وهذه
كبيرة دفعة آخر صدام،فكانت نظام وسقوط للعراق
طهران في الإخوةمجموعتان من مسكوهم
مجموعات، ثلاث: يعني مشهد، في كبيرتانومجموعة
منهم عوائلهم مع منالأخوة به بأس لا كبير عدد فيها
الجماعات من غيرها وفي القاعدة في القيادات بعض.

This stage began almost with the start of the US invasion of Iraq and the fall of Saddam's regime. The last big wave of brothers who were arrested consisted of two groups in Tehran and one group in Mashhad, i.e. three groups in total, containing a large number of brothers and their families, including some leaders in al-Qaeda and other groups.

هذه يتابعون وهم فترة أخذوا الإيرانيون طبعا الإخوة ويتتبعون عنها المعلومات ويجمعون المجموعات أوبيوت العوائل بيوت سواء البيوت معظم إلى فوصلوا يوم في (اعتقال حملة) كبسة عليهم وعملوا العزاب، متوالية ثلاثة أو يومين أو ، (العدد الأكبر) تقريبا واحد (.التكميلات)

Of course, the Iranians took a while watching these groups, collecting information and following the brothers. They reached most of the houses, whether they were the families' or bachelors' houses, and they made a raid on them in about one day (the largest number) and two or three consecutive days (the remaining).

نتابع ونحن وثلاثة، ألفين سنة مطلع مع هذا كان الغزو العراق الأمريكية الاستعدادات...!

This was with the beginning of 2003, while we were following the American preparations for the invasion of Iraq ...!

عليهم يعرضون المسجونين من دفعة أخر هذه

..التسفير

This was the last wave of prisoners that deportation was proposed to them.

التسفير عملية منتصف في ثم أعدادا، منهم فسفروا رأيهم وغيروا توقفوا تقريبا.

They deported a number of them, and then in almost the middle of the process of deportation, they stopped and changed their minds.

المنذر أبو الشيخ الدفعة هذه أهل من سفر ممن من وجماعة ومنهمالزرقاوي عنه، الله فرج الساعدي وغيرهم أصحابه.

Amongst the people deported from this wave was Sheikh Abu MundhirSaadi, may Allah release him, al-Zarqawi and a group of his companions, and others.

إنهم حتى الجميع، سفير -كالعادة- يريدون وكانوا إلى التسفير مثل الإخوةالليبيين بعض على عرضوا لأنه)تركيا إلى التسفير وطلب فرفض الآن، حالا ماليزيا بخلف حاله، ويدبر يذهب وأين معارف تركيا في عنده وكان تركيا، إلى تسفيره في بأنيسعوا فوعدوه (ماليزيا على الخارجكانت في وزوجته عندهم السجن في هو (الإيرانية المخابرات أعني :بواسطتهم) به اتصال كل بالتفاصيل وتأتينا سري بشكل اتصالنا على وهي رأيهموسياستهم الإيرانيون غير وفجأة يوما، كذا كل يوقفوا بأن لهم العليا القيادة من تعليمات وجاءتهم

‏.‏عملياتالتسفير!

They wanted - as usual - to deport everyone, so they proposed to a Libyan brother to be deported to Malaysia right then, but he refused and asked to be deported to Turkey (because he has contacts in Turkey and know where to go and how to manage his matters, unlike Malaysia) and they promised him to seek to send him to Turkey, He was in prison with them and his wife was outside and she was in touch with him (through them: I mean the Iranian intelligence), but also she was in touch with us in secret and brought us details every few days. Suddenly, the Iranians changed their minds and policies and were instructed by the High Command to stop all the deportations!

‏أمر لعله وقلنا رأيهم، تغير في نأمل ظللنا ذلك ومع أنهم أيضا، سياسةجديدة أنها توقعنا مع مؤقت، للتسفير هذاالتوقيف يعللون كانوا الله قاتلهم وبأن الأمريكان، من بخوفهم والاحتفاظبالإخوة، وغير إلاالأمريكان، تسربت الإخوة هؤلاء عن معلومات أو المعارف، بعض بواسطة يأتينا كان هذا وكل ذلك، وكنا السجن في أزواجهن كان اللاتي بواسطةالنساء بهن، ونتصل أمورهم(الخارج في الذين) نحن نتابع على ويلحجن مسكينات يضغطن كن وهن أزواجهن مع بتسفيرهن الايرانية مكاتبالاستخبارات اللاتي) النساء قدجمعوا وكانوا أزواجهن، شأن ويتابعن بلا وتركوهم خاصين بيتين في (السجن في أزواجهن‏

لطلباتهم يوميا عليهم يمرون إنما شيء، ولا حراسة
وبعضهن معهن، بنساءللتعامل يأتون وكانوا ذلك، ونحو
العربية يتكلمن.

However, we hoped that their opinion would change, and we said that it may be temporary, and we expected it to be a new policy as well, because their argument for the arrests was deportation and keeping the brothers, for their fear of the Americans, and information about these brothers was leaked to the Americans. All these information came to us through some contacts, or through women whose husbands were in prison and we (the ones outside the prison) were checking up on them and getting in touch with them. They pressured and begged the Iranian intelligence offices to allow them to travel with their husbands and take care of their husbands. The Iranians gathered the women (whose husbands were in prison) in two private houses and left them unguarded, and they were passing on them every day for their requests and so on. They brought women to deal with them, and some of these women were speaking Arabic.

وبعضهم أطفال لهم كان طبعا الإخوة نساء وأغلب
عنده الذي صغار، لهمأطفال والكثيرون البلوغ، قاربوا
خمس وحتى وأربع ثلاث عنده والذي اثنان أو واحد.

Most of the brothers' wifes had children and some of them came of age and many had young children of 1,

2, 3, 4 and even 5 years old.

يغير ولم وثلاث، وسـنتان سـنة ثم الشـهور مرت
بهؤلاء الاحتفاظ اسـتمروافي بل سـياسـتهم الإيرانيون
في عوائلهم مع الإخوة وجمعوا السـجون، في الإخوة
في سكنية مباني الجبرية، كالقامات سجونهي
الأمر ومازال الأمنيةالمحصنة، مجمعاتهم من مجمع
سـنوات ثلث منذ الشـكل بهذا.

Months passed, then a year, two and three and the
Iranians did not change their policy, but continued to
keep these brothers in prison. The brothers were
reunited with their families in prisons such as house
arrest, residential buildings in a compound of their
fortified security compounds, and this has been the
case for three years.

الإخوة من اثنان عامين حوالي قبل السـجن من هرب
من السعيد الله الشيخعبد وهو ليبي أحدهم
مغربي آخر أخ ومعه المقاتلة، الإسـلامية الجماعة.

About two years ago, two brothers, one of them a
Libyan, Sheikh Abdullah al-Saeed of the Islamic
Fighting Group, and another Moroccan brother
escaped from prison.

فيها اسـتغلوا وبسـيطة ظريفة عملية في هروبهما كان
قبل وذلك المجمع، لأزواجهنفي النسـاء زيارة ربكة
شرعوا كانوا بل عوائلهم،بقليل، مع الإخوة جمع
ومازال البعض وجمعوا عوائلهم مع الإخوة فيجمع

الإنشاءات يجهزونلهم وكانوا دوره، ينتظر البعض
النساء معظم كان المرحلة تلك في السكنية،
(المذكورين البيتين في) فيالخارج مازالوا والعوائل
معينة، مدة كل أزواجهم يزيرونهن وكانوا
الذي) المجمع إلى وتأخذهم تأتيهم بواسطةحافلة
ثميرجعونهن زمان من ساعة (الإخوة فيه.

Their escape was simple and funny. They took
advantage of the confusion that was happening when
women visited their husbands in the compound,
before the brothers and their families were reunited,
or when they began to reunite some of the brothers
with their families and some were still awaiting their
turn while they were preparing residential
constructions for them. At that stage, most of the
women and the families were still outside (in the
aforementioned two houses) and they were visiting
their husbands in certain periods by a bus that was
bringing them and taking them to the compound
(where the brothers were) for an hour and then
returning them.

استغلوا وصاحبه السعيد الله عبد الأخ أن المقصود
حركة في الحافلة النساءفي مع وخرجوا الربكة هذه
الخارج إلى وصلوا حتى بهم، يشعروا ولم جدا، لطيفة
الهروبات وهكذا معهم، أزواجهم وأخذوا ونزلواوهربوا
أكثرها وما وقصصها، السجون من.!

311

The point is that brother, Abdullah Al-Saeed and his companion took advantage of this confusion and went out with the women on the bus in a very nice move, and the Iranians did not notice their absence until they were outside and fled and took their wives with them. This is an example of prison breaks and their stories, and they are many stories!!

غزو مع الإيرانيين أن فيه نشك ولا تيقناه الذي الجهاد وبدء نظامصدام وسقوط للعراق الأمريكان بسرعة القاعدة واسم الزرقاوي وبروز هناك والمقاومة كورقة بإخواننا الاحتفاظ قرروا وتسارعالأحداث، عندهم!..

We've come to ascertain, without any doubt, that with the American invasion of Iraq—the fall of Saddam, the beginning of jihad and resistance there, the salient and rapid rise of al-Zarqawi, the emergence of the name of al-Qaeda, and the rapid unfolding of events, Iranian authorities decided to keep our brothers as a bargaining chip.

أعلم والله بوضوح، لنا يظهر كما الأمر هو هذا.

This is the matter as we see clearly, and Allah knows best.

لأنهم) بعدهم من ولا الدفعات تلك كل من يطلقوا ولم إلا (قليلة دفعات في عدةأشخاص على بعدهم قبضوا وسافروالآن أطلقوهم شباب صغار ليبيين إخوة ثلاثة دخلوا وكانوا جيدة كانت جوازاتهم أعني أوراقهم

جوازات يحملن واثنانمنهم لإيران، قانونية بطريقة
بغرض جاءوا أوروبا، في مقيمون أهلهم أوروبية،
عليهم القبض فألقي وزيرستان، في الالتحاقبالأخوة
من يطلقوا وسافروا،ولم فأطلقوهم، متأخرة، دفعة في
الإخوة من البيت نفس وفي الدفعة نفس في معهم
عندهم ليس ممن باكستان من القداميالداخلين
.شيء ولا تأشيرة ولا أوراق

They released from all these waves and ones followed
by them (because they later arrested several people in
a few waves) only three young Libyan brothers and
deported them because their papers, i.e. their
passports, were good and they had entered Iran
legally, and two of them hold European passports, as
their parents reside in Europe, and they had come to
join the brothers in Waziristan, and were arrested in a
late wave, then they were released and deported. They
didn't release anyone else that was in the same wave
and in the same house of the older brothers entering
from Pakistan who did not have papers, visa or
anything.

كما إنسانية لحالة المصريين الإخوة أحد أطلقوا وكذلك
ولحد الهلاك، على توشك مريضةجدا زوجته لأن قالوا،
.المستشفيات بعض في تتعالج هي آلآن

They also released one of the Egyptian brothers for a
humanitarian situation as they said, because his wife

was seriously ill, nearing her death, and until now she is being treated in some hospitals.

تعامل لمراحل واضح أنه أرجو موجز عرض فهذا
إخواننا مع الإيرانيين.

This is a brief narrative, which I hope it shows clearly the Iranians treatment with our brothers.

المستعان والله.

May Allah help.

إيران؟ خارج سافروا ممن ذلك بعد الإخوة فعل ماذا وأما

As for what did the brothers do after they traveled outside Iran?

أن: وخلاصته السابق، كلامي من تبين أنه فأظن
على وضعوا فالذين بلدانأخرى، إلى ذهبوا الكثرين
باكستان دخلوا معظمهم باكستان حدود
من ومنهم وزيرستان، في بإخوانهم بالفعلوالتحقوا
سافر وبعضهم كماقلت، ينتظر من ومنهم نحبه قضى
بلدان إلى انتقل ومنها كماليزيا أخرى بلدان إلى
فيها وبقي ماليزيا إلى سافر أحدا أعرف ولا أخرى،
غلاء من الأخوةجميعا شكوى بسبب تقريبا، مقيما
والله فساد، من فيها ما مع وصعوبتها، فيها المعيشة
المستعان.

I believe the answer to this question is clear from my

previous words, and its conclusion that most brothers went to other countries. Those who had been placed on the border of Pakistan, most of them entered Pakistan and joined their brothers in Waziristan. Some of them died and some still waiting for his time to come, as I have said. Some have traveled to other countries, such as Malaysia, and moved to other countries from it. I do not know anyone who traveled to Malaysia and remained in it because of the complaint of all brothers of the high cost of living and the difficult life there along with the corruption there, and may Allah help.

فيها، بقوا كذلك أكثرهم العراق إلى ذهبوا والذين
شأن، له وصار بالجهادهناك عليهم الله مَن من ومنهم
الله رحمه الزرقاوي الشيخ هؤلاء رأس وعلى.

And those who went to Iraq, most of them also remained there, and some of them joined Jihad there and became an important figure, and at the head of these people is Sheikh al-Zarqawi, May Allah have mercy on him.

الحرب قبل خرج ثم أشهرا فيها بقي من ومنهم.

Some of them had stayed there for months and then left before the war.

وهكذا.

And so on.

315

وأما: ممن إيران في بقوا الذي الإخوة بقية فعل ماذا
نجوا من تلك الحملة أوممن دخلوا بعدها؟

As for what did the rest of the brothers who stayed in
Iran who survived the campaign or those who entered
after the campaign?

فقد اعتمد الإخوة الذي بقوا بعد ذلك خططا أخرى أكثر
صرامة، في الاختفاءوالأمنيات وصاوروا متفرقين
متباعدين ممتنعين عن زيارة بعضهم بعضا إلا ما
ندر،وحتى في بعض حالات الحاجة إلى اللقاء يلتقون
في الخارج لا يعرف بعضهممبيوت بعض، وقللوا العلاقات
أهل إخواننا من أهل الإيرانيين(السنة) البلد أهل مع جدا
لأن كثيرا النقص الأمني يدخل منهم، لأنهم إما
بسبب علاقاتهميتكلمون فيخرج خبرك، وسرك أو
يكونون متابعين من قبل الاستخبارات الإيرانية
فيرصدونهم شهورا حتى يجمعوا أكبر قدر من
المعلومات ثم يقومون بالحملة.

The brothers who have stayed behind have adopted
other stricter plans for disappearances and security
and became scattered and far away from each other
and didn't visit each other except for rare incidents.
Even in some cases, when they had to meet for
necessity, the met outside and didn't know each
other's homes. They reduced the relations very much
with the residents of the country (our brothers from
the Sunnis of Iran) because their side had the most

lack of security, as due to their relations they were talking here and there and then your secret becomes known, or they had been followed by the Iranian intelligence for months to gather as much information as they can and then launch the campaign.

في إلا الموبايلات، استعمال عن أكثرهم امتنع وكذلك الكثيرة الاحتياطات ومعاتخاذ جدا، ضيقة حالات أسباب من مباشر سبب أنها من عرفنا لما الأمنية، استعمال من وقللوا عليهم، والقبض الإخوة تتبع ذلك وغير الانترنت،.

And most of them refrained from using mobile phones, except in very few cases, and took many security precautions when we knew that it was a direct method of tracking and arresting brothers, and we also reduced the use of the Internet, and so on.

جدا قليل نفر إلا إخواننا من إيران في يبق لم فالآن من ضروري بعضهم ووجود.وصفت الذي الشكل بهذا جهة في للأخوة والترتيبات الطريق أجل أفغانستانووزيرستان.

Now there is none left of our brothers in Iran except fora very little number as I've described. Their presence is necessary for the passageways and arrangements for brothers in Afghanistan and Waziristan.

من المجاهدين إخواننا بين جرى ما ملخص وهذا

فلا ذلك سوى الإيرانيين،وما وبين وغيرها القاعدة
الرافضة مع إخواننا من تعامل اي حصل أنه أبدا أعرف
.بعد من ولا قبل من غيرها، في ولا فيإيران

This is a summary of what happened between our
Mujahideen brothers from al-Qaeda and other groups
and the Iranians. And other than that, I never learned
that there was any kind of dealing or relations from
our brothers with the Shiites in Iran or in other
places, before or after they went there.

..المحور هذا في المهم معظم فهذا

What I've written is the most important in this part.

.نافعا يجعله أن الله وأسأل

I ask Allah to make it useful.

كما السرية غاية في وهو للضرورة، وكتبناه قلناه وإنما
.!!يخفى لا

I only mentioned and wrote it out of necessity, and
should be treated with utmost secrecy..!!

:الثالث المحور

حول إخواننا فكرة من شخصيا أعرفه ما بيان في
.ذلك معها،وغير والتعامل وإيران الرافضة

Third Part:

In a statement of what I personally know about the

opinion of our brothers about the Shiites and Iran and dealing with them, and so on.

أستعين وحده وبه التوفيق وبالله فأقول:

I say the following and may Allah help me:

إخواننا معرفة بيان في المقام أطول أن إلى أحتاج لا من ومروقهم بالرافضة وضلالهم الله شاء إن التامة فيهم علمائنا وكلام الدين،.

Our brothers are certain of the misguidance of the Shiites and their hatred of religion and the words of our sharia scientists in them, and I do not need to say a lot about this.

مسألة في يختارون -أعرف ما بحسب- والأخوة الإسلام شيخ علمائنا، وعن عن المشهور تكفيرهم فيهم التفصيل من الخصوص وجه على القيم وابن عليهم ونحكم زنادقة، أنهم الغالب فأئمتهموكبراؤهم ردة، كفر هو أنكفرهم إخواننا عند والمختار كفار، بأنهم احتمال ويظهر ذلك، في يبحث من الإخوة من وهناك عوامهم وأما ..أصلي كفر هو كفرناهم كفرهمإذا أن ضلال فيهممن ما على القبلة أهل من مسلمون فهم المذهب هذا على نشوئهم بسبب لكن وكفر، والتلبيس الجهل وبسبب يعرفونغيره، لا والضلال منتبين إلا بالإسلام وجهلتهم عوامهم على فنحكم بعينه كفره.

The brothers (as far as I know), in the matter of

319

whether the Shiites are infidels or not, follow the common opinion for our sharia scientists, especially the opinion of Sheikh al-Islam and Ibn al-Qayyim in them which states; "Their Imams and leaders are mostly heretics, and we judge them as infidels, and the chosen opinion by our brothers that their infidelity is an apostasy infidelity, and there are some brothers looking unto this, and there a possibility that their infidelity is an original infidelity. As for the public ordinary Shiites, they are Muslims that follow the Qiblah, in spite of their misguidance and disbelief, but due to the fact that they were born and raised on this doctrine and misguidance and they do not know anything else. Because of misguidance and confusion, we judge that the public ordinary Shiites are Muslims, except those who show their disbelief.

سـواء عموماً، الرافضة في إخواننا رأي مجمل هو هذا غيرها أو أوإيران باكستان أو أفغانستان في.

This is the overall opinion of our brothers in the Shiites in general, whether in Afghanistan or Pakistan or Iran or other places.

كل في علمائنا مذهب على إخواننا فإن وبالجملة والشـريعة، الدين سـائلمسـائل في كما المسـائل هذه فيالرأي اختلف من بينهم وما العالمين، رب لله والحمد وتسعها الاجتهاد يسعها مما فهي والاختيارات تعالى الله علمائنارحمهم واختيارات مذاهب.

In general, our brothers follow our sharia scientists in

all these matters as in the entire matters of religion and sharia and thank Allah the Lord of the worlds. And those who have different opinions and choices are driven their own interpretations and are acceptable in the doctrines and choices of our scientists, may Allah have mercy on them.

للرافضة إخواننا لرؤية النظري التأصيل حيث من هذا.

This is in terms of the theoretical rooting of our brothers' view of the Shiites.

الدول كسائر إخواننا فيراها الإيرانية للدولة بالنسبة الروافض دولة وبهتانا، وأنها زورا للإسلام المنتسبة الدولة هي وأنها الرفض، زنادقة دولة المارقين، عدو وأنها أمتنا، في المدمر الرافضة الداعمةلمشروع وصار الآن، صاريتغير هذا لعل) البعيد المدى على لنا (.أعلم والله رويدا، يقترب العدو هذا

As for the Iranian state, our brothers see it, as they see all the other countries affiliated with Islam falsely, a heretic state supporting the project of the Shiites that has a destructive effect in our nation and it is our enemy in the long run. (Perhaps this is changing now, and this enemy is approaching slowly, and Allah knows best).

على مستمرة تزال لا والتي الحالية إخواننا ورؤية ليس وأنه مؤجلاً، إيرانعدوا يرون أنهم علمي حسب وأنه سالمونا، ما نسالمهم وأننا الآن، حرب وبيننا وعلى مصالحهم، بعض مع مصالحنا بعض قدتتقاطع

أمريكاومعاداتها ضرب ذلك رأس.

The current vision of our brothers, as far as I know, is that they see Iran as a postponed enemy, and that we are not currently at war with it, and that we shall treat them with peace as long as they are treating us with peace, and that some of our interests may intersect with some of their interests, and on top of that interests is hitting America and make it our enemy.

أيضا علمي بحسب الآن إلى المستمرة الإخوة وفكرة أي إحداث وعدم إيران، الهدوءفي على المحافظة هو لإخواننا إلى ومعبر ممر من إيران تمثله لما فيها، حدث كان وإن ولوجستيك، وحركة دعم وساحة أفغانستان، هذا أيضا كان وإن مستترومتخفي، بشكل ذلك كل نتوقعأن وصرنا الخيرة، المدة في اعتباره يتناقص صار سياستهم الإيرانيون غير كما سياستهم الإخوة يغير وغيرها القاعدة من قبضواعليهم الذين الإخوة تجاه.

The opinion of the brothers continuing to this day, as far as I know, is to remain operationally quiet in Iran, not causing any incidents, given that it serves as a passageway for our brothers into Afghanistan, an arena of support for movement and logistics, notwithstanding that this is all being conducted in a clandestine fashion, and that its value has recently diminished and we expect that the brothers will change their policy as the Iranians changed their policy towards the brothers who were arrested from al-Qaeda and other groups.

بالطرق إيران مع يحاولون أنهم الإخوة ويرى
إخوانناالمأسورين سراح تطلق أن الدبلوماسية
نهائي بشكل أحسوا إذا ذلك يفعلون ولعلهم عندها،
ضربهم في أمريكا بدأت إذا أو أمريكاستضربهم، أن
سيكون الجميع أمريكا،وأن في النكاية باب من بالفعل،
بحسب هذا الأقل على لأمريكا، ضدا واحد خندق في
شيء فيه إخواننا عند مقام وهو ويطمعون، مايتوقعون
التفصيل من ..!ال

The brothers are trying diplomatic means with Iran
towards releasing our brothers detained there. The
Iranians may release them if America began to bomb
Iran, and if they were to do so it would be out of
spite, wishfully assuming that everyone would be
fighting on the same side against America. At least
this is according to what they expect and hope for.!

أنهم شك لا إيران، لدى القاعدة من المأسورون الأخوة
فمثل لهم، وإعاقة لقدراتالأخوة وتقييدا عبئا شكلوا
وعن إيران عن أسامة الشيخ سكوت تلحظون
وجود مراعاة ذلك أسباب من أن ظني الرافضة،وفي
وهكذا إيران، في المأسورين الإخوة.

The captive al-Qaeda brothers in Iran are
undoubtedly a burden, limiting and preventing Al-
Qaeda's operational abilities. Notice, for example,
Sheikh Usama's silence about Iran and the Shiites. In
my view, this is in part out of consideration for the
captive al-Qaeda brothers in Iran.

المجاهدين أن يرون فالأخوة مثلا العراق في أما
لما مؤيدون وهم بلاشك، الرافضة يضربوا أن عليهم
بين تفصيل على هناك، المجاهدون إخوانهم به يقوم
كجيش) قواتهم وبين حربنا عن العوامالمبتعدين
أبي تصرف ويقولونعن (..ونحوها بدر ومنظمة الدجال
في هناك إخوانه وسائر الله رحمه الزرقاوي مصعب
كل أن ويعرفون الغائب، يرى مالا يرى الشاهد:العراق
أحكاما التيتستوجب ومعطياتهم ظروفها لها ساحة
السياسة في يندرج مما مناسبة وسياسات
العالمين رب والحمدلله الشرعية،.

In Iraq, for example, the brothers see that the
Mujahideen are bound to hit the Shiites with no
doubt, and they support the of their fellow
Mujahideen there, separating between the ordinary
people who are away from our war and their forces
(such as al-Dajjal Army and Badr Organization, etc.).
They say about the actions of Abu Musab al-
Zarqawi,may Allah have mercy on him, and all his
brothers there in Iraq;"The witness sees what the
absent does not see", and know that each
battleground has its conditions and inputs that require
appropriate provisions and policies, which falls within
the sharia policy, and thank Allah the Lord of the
Worlds.

تجاه الإخوة لفكرة الملخصة النقاط أهم تقريبا فهذه
والرافضة إيران.

These are almost the most important points summarizing the view of brothers towards Iran and the Shiites.

لعدم فيها، الكلام تركت أخرى مسائل وهناك من فيهم إيرانوما في السنة أهل عن مناسبته، أي بمستقبل يتعلق وما وغيرها، وصفات جماعات إيران في عمل...

There are other matters about the Sunnis in Iran and their groups and their manners and others, and the future of any actions in Iran, and I haven't written about because it would be inappropriate...

حاولت ولكن لهم، رسمي ممثل أنني أدعي ولا تقريب أجل من أفكارهمورؤاهم، من عرفته عما التعبير لكم الموضوع هذا فهم.

I'm not claiming to be an official representative of them, but I tried to express what I knew from their ideas and visions, in order to bring the subject closer to you.

أعلم والله واطلاعي، فهمي بحسب كلامي كله فهذا وأحكم.

All this is my words, according to my understanding and knowledge, and Allah knows best.

العظيم العلي بالله إل قوة ولا حول ولا.

There is no power but from Allah Almighty.

أنت إلا إله ألا أشـهد وبحمدك اللهم وسـبحانك
إليك وأتوب أسـتغفرك.

Glory and praise be to Allah and I bear witness there is no God except you and I beg your forgiveness and repent to you.

محمد ورسوله عبده على وبارك وسلم الله وصلى
وصحبه وآله.

May Allah bless and bless His slave and His Messenger, Muhammad, and his family and companions.

وبركاته الله ورحمة عليكم والسلام

Peace, mercy, and blessings of Allah be upon you

للهجرة وعشـرين وثمان وأربعمائة ألف سـنة من محرم.

Muharram of 1428 H.

I MISS YOU, MOM.

Made in the USA
Lexington, KY
27 October 2018